BREWSTER GOLD

BREWSTER GOLD

The Story of
a Brewster Family in America,
1825-1996

By
LOIS ANNE BREWSTER

About the cover: The three gold artifacts shown were owned by William John Brewster and were pictured on the cover of a prospectus for his gold mining company in 1903. One of those artifacts remains in the Brewster family today.

With gratitude to Patricia Heady-Winholtz and L. Wayne Updike for their vital proofreading skills and advice in the preparation of this manuscript.

ISBN: 1-58597-187-1

Library of Congress Control Number: 2003105308

LEATHERS
PUBLISHING

A division of Squire Publishers, Inc.
4500 College Blvd.
Leawood, KS 66211
1/888/888-7696
www.leatherspublishing.com

Dedicated to the future generations of Brewster descendants, beginning with my wonderful grandchildren:

James

Haley

Christopher

Kelsey

Jeffrey

Brinks

Molly

Sean

Trevor

Lesley

Adam

Abby

TABLE OF CONTENTS

Chapter		Page

INTRODUCTION

In his generation, William DeForest (Bill) Brewster, my late husband, was the only descendant of his immigrant grandfather to have offspring bearing the Brewster surname. I have written this book primarily to preserve for our grandchildren a history of their Brewster lineage in America. However, I hope it is composed in a way that will be interesting to anyone who reads it. Its preparation has been a seven-year journey for me. I met a variety of characters along the way — ordinary and extraordinary, colorful and admirable — and I even encountered a crook or two. I tried not to be judgmental nor to whitewash or embellish the facts, but to communicate faithfully what my research turned up. The story often had color of its own.

Primary sources for this story of the Brewster family were hundreds of letters and documents dating back to 1888 that were contained in a large packing crate among my mother-in-law's belongings. I began the work of sorting and organizing those items in 1995. Some of the relationships and events that came to light in Bill's family background were previously unknown to him. After Bill's death in 1996 and that of his sister Marguerite in 1997, there was no family member left with first-hand knowledge to provide input for the book or to identify unlabeled pictures. To verify names, dates and locations, I searched census records and the early city directories of Kansas City. For background material, I used information from encyclopedias, history books, and newspaper articles. I also made use of the oral history I heard from my husband and his relatives over the 45 years of our marriage. I drew upon my personal experience after the story reached my entry into the family.

No biography, however complete, can tell the whole story of life that is lived moment by moment. With a realization that much history is lost with each person who dies, I have tried to preserve some of the Brewster history that would otherwise vanish. My hope is that succeeding generations may benefit from an awareness of the ancestral footprints in which they walk. If they look, they will find here lessons learned in the past, attributes to be emulated, mistakes to be avoided, traits handed down. I hope these pages will foster an appreciation of intangible blessings that have come through the Brewster forebears.

Lois Anne Norris Brewster

THE BREWSTERS OF FORT MADISON **1**

To HIS DAUGHTER-IN-LAW, WHO never met him, William John Brewster is a colorful, legendary figure. Born to greater privilege than most near the end of the Civil War, Will roamed the West as pioneers spread out across the land and prospectors probed the western landscape for precious metals. A friend said Will could "charm the socks off anyone." Apparently, he was as comfortable negotiating business deals with men of means as he was rubbing shoulders with cowboys or slogging through South American jungles and outwitting revolutionaries. When Will found occasion to swear, according to his son, his expletives were spiced with Shakespearean phrases and bits of Latin. Through most of his adult life, Will called Kansas City home, but he was born and grew up in Fort Madison, Iowa.

Will's father, Charles Brewster, was of Scottish descent, but he was born in Ireland. The following is quoted from a column by Ted Sloat, entitled "Madisonia," published in *The Evening Democrat,* the Fort Madison newspaper, in 1970:

Born in Ireland in 1813 Charles Brewster was 12 when he came with his grandfather to this country to live with an uncle in Philadelphia. Philadelphia was then a city of 75,000 and faced a bright future. Young Charles Brewster looked forward to the day when his uncle would set him up in business.

He was 24 when the Panic of 1837 shattered his dream. His uncle's business failed and throughout the East men walked the streets looking for work to feed their families. Young Brewster decided that his best opportunity was in the frontier country to the west and went to Indiana where he landed a job in the government land office at Vincennes on the Illinois bor-

Charles Brewster — born in Ireland in 1813. Died in Fort Madison, Iowa, in 1893.

der. He saved enough money to open a store there and was fairly successful, but he still believed that he would do better in pioneer country, for Indiana was already pretty well settled.

So he came to Fort Madison in the new Iowa country in 1844 and opened a dry goods store in the 600 block of Avenue H east of what is now an abandoned used car lot.

The store was a success and 32 years later Brewster was able to boast that he was one of the very few merchants in Fort Madison who had remained continuously in business that long.

Meantime he invested in real estate. The building in the 600 block of Avenue H where he opened his dry goods store in 1844 turned out to be exceptionally profitable. He sold the store to a man who failed to make a go of it and Brewster was forced to take as collateral real estate in Chicago which he didn't want. But the Chicago property boomed and he sold it at such a profit he was able to join Dr. Joseph Smith in 1876 and purchase the Bank of Fort Madison.

Brewster was with the bank when it merged with the First National Bank of Fort Madison and later when it became Fort Madison Savings Bank of which he was president. The Fort Madison Savings Bank is now the Fort Madison Bank and Trust.

Among other business activities, Brewster was one of the founders of the Fort Madison Chair Co. He was active in civic affairs, a member of the Presbyterian Church, and was one of the early members of the Republican Party.

According to a family "grapevine" story, Charles came west in a horse-drawn wagon that was equipped with a false bottom containing $50,000 in gold bullion. With that asset, the story goes, he bought the bank at Fort Madison. Could it be that he returned from the sale of the Chicago property, mentioned above, in that manner? This does seem a possibility, given the modes of transportation available in the mid-1870s and the mistrust of currency that was a legacy of the banking panic of 1837.

Life was often tenuous in the mid-nineteenth century before the advances of modern medicine. Charles Brewster was well acquainted with death. His first wife, Margaret Badolet, whom he wed July 12, 1848, in Lawrenceville, Illinois, died two years later, just four days after the birth of their daughter Margaret. Margaret, the daughter, lived only four years. On October 21, 1852, Charles married Eliza Jane DeForest in Sharon, Pennsylvania. Eliza Jane gave birth to eight children in the years between 1853 and 1866 but the first four and the seventh child died young. Charles V. lived 10 months; Mary — 8 years; Ann — 20 days; Emma — 6½ months and Charles DeForest — 18 months. Only three — Martha, James, and William — survived to adulthood.

Eliza Jane's lineage is interesting. Her maternal grandfather received a large grant of land in the vicinity of Brooklyn, New York, from King George III. Her mother, Nancy Quimby, was the daughter of a general. Her paternal grandfather, Abraham De La Forest, was of French Huguenot descent. Abraham enlisted in the Revolutionary War as a drummer boy. He had a run-in with a Hessian soldier who was fighting for the British. The Hessian cut Abraham's drum straps and told him, "Run, my little man. The Hessians show no quarter!" Abraham later served in the War of 1812 and in the French and Indian War, a total of seventeen years. One of the DeForests provided an endowment to Yale University with a stipulation that anyone bearing the name DeForest could receive a scholarship at Yale. With that in mind, several of the Brewster descendants were given DeForest as a middle name, only to learn later that

Daughter and mother, Martha Jane and Eliza Jane Brewster

Brothers: James (left) and William John Brewster

one's surname had to be DeForest to claim the scholarship.

Charles and Eliza Jane made their home in Fort Madison, Iowa. They were Presbyterians. Before breakfast on Sunday mornings, they gathered their children about them for Bible reading. After breakfast, they went to church for more Bible study. No one in the household was allowed to do anything but read the Bible and attend church on the Sabbath.

Several siblings of Charles Brewster also immigrated to this country and settled for a time in or near Fort Madison. A sister, Jane, married John Mitchel Farmer and lived on a farm six miles north of Fort Madison. Another sister, Ann, and her husband, Hugh Creelman, had two daughters, Eliza Jane and Martha. Ann died at age 29 and was buried in Fort Madison. The 1860 census lists 45-year-old Mary and 32-year-old James as members of the Charles Brewster household. Ireland is given as the birthplace of both. James' occupation is listed as merchant. Probably he was associated with his brother Charles in the dry goods store in Fort Madison.

One of Eliza Jane Brewster's sisters, Sarah DeForest, married Perry Buchanan, who was related to President James Buchanan. Perry and Sarah had three or four children among whom were a daughter, Eugenia, and a son, Lawrence. Perry journeyed around Cape Horn to California during the gold rush. Eventually, he wrote that he had struck it rich and would be home on the next boat, but he was never heard from again. Finally, the family assumed that Perry had been murdered for his gold.

About 1865, another merging of the Brewster and DeForest families occurred. James Brewster, brother of Charles, was in his late thirties when he courted and married sixteen-year-old Eugenia, daughter of Perry and Sarah DeForest Buchanan. With her marriage to James, Eugenia became the sister-in-law of her Aunt Eliza Jane and an aunt to her Brewster cousins. James and Eugenia eventually settled in Oxford, Kansas, where James established, or bought, a bank. Oxford is located in Sumner County, about 30 miles south of Wichita. Sumner County was often traversed by cattle drives on the trek from Texas to railheads in Kansas. James undoubtedly expected Oxford to grow, but it remains a small town today.

James and Eugenia Buchanan Brewster had a daughter, Anna Julia, and they adopted an older girl named Lillian. They also raised to adulthood an orphan boy who was fourteen years old when they found him in Council Bluffs, Iowa. The boy's name was Portice Cephus Kirkland, though he was called "Porter" or simply "Port."

The families of Charles Brewster and his brother James remained close despite the distance between their homes and the slow means of transportation and communication in the latter half of the nineteenth century. When they traveled, relatives stayed longer in those days than they do today. Lengthy visits were apparently enjoyed both in Fort Madison, Iowa, and in Oxford, Kansas.

SECOND GENERATION — Martha, Jim and Will 2

THE COMMON PRACTICE OF naming children for relatives of a prior generation was prevalent among the Brewsters. Charles, James and William are some of those repeated names. James, the son of Charles, was often called "Jim," which helped avoid confusing him with his Uncle James. In late years William John was sometimes called "Bill," but he was most often referred to as "Will." The nicknames, Jim and Will, are used in this narrative in reference to the two sons of Charles and Eliza Jane Brewster.

According to a family story, sometime in their youth, Jim and Will wanted to be older than they actually were. Since the large, leather-bound Brewster family Bible, dated MDCCCXLIV (1844), carried the only record of their birth, they simply altered their dates in that trusted register. Their Bible record shows them to have been ten and six years of age in 1870; but the 1870 census gives the age of James as eight and that of William as four, so the story is probably true. Martha was older than her brothers. The actual birthdates of the three siblings are believed to have been the following: Martha—July 26, 1859; Jim—November 19, 1862; Will—January 8, 1866.

In the late 1870s, Port Kirkland courted Martha Jane, the niece of his foster parents, James and Eugenia Brewster. A letter that was saved says that Aunt Gene, as Port called his foster mother, encouraged the match between Port and Martha. Two significant, emotionally charged events in the lives of the two families occurred on January 19, 1880. Martha and Port were married that day, and Martha's mother, Eliza Jane, died that day at age 57. She and Charles were married 27 years.

Several questions come to mind as one ponders how and

why the two events coincided. Was Eliza Jane on her deathbed and wanting to see her daughter married before she died? Was preparation for the wedding so strenuous that it caused her death? Was the emotion of the wedding too much a strain? Was the death the result of an accident? No explanation has been found.

Martha Brewster Kirkland

Port returned with his bride to Oxford, Kansas, where he was associated in the bank with his foster father and benefactor, James Brewster. About a year later, a son was born to Martha and Port. The baby was named Charles, undoubtedly the namesake of his maternal grandfather.

Port speculated in commodities (probably Kansas wheat) and suffered losses. One Saturday afternoon he was left alone to close the bank. When Port failed to return home that evening, a search was mounted for him. The vault at the bank was found empty. It seemed apparent that Port had taken its contents, but he was never apprehended. Whether Port's disappearance occurred before or after the birth of his son is not known, but Martha stayed on in Oxford for some time.

Charles Brewster dispatched his sons, Jim and Will, from Fort Madison with funds to help cover the Oxford Bank's obligations to its depositors. The nephews stayed on to help their Uncle James run his bank for a while. Ted Jefferson, grandson of James and Eugenia Brewster, recalled hearing that the Port Kirkland episode eventually resulted in the failure of the bank. James used his personal fortune to cover his business debts.

After James Brewster died in 1894, his widow Eugenia and daughter Anna (who became Ted Jefferson's mother) moved to Kansas City where Eugenia ran a boarding house and opened a bakery. Many years after the robbery, Port's foster mother, Eugenia, received a letter from the widow of a Charles K. Porter (an alias used by Port Kirkland). The widow wrote that her husband had spoken of his Aunt Gene. The letter reported that Port died in Miami, Florida, in 1903. It was learned later that Port had married two or three times under assumed names. So far as anyone knew he had no more children.

Meanwhile Charles Brewster provided for his deserted daughter and her son. In 1889, after Port had been gone for several years, Charles helped Martha file for divorce. Martha's son, Charles Kirkland, suffered a disease during childhood that left him impaired both physically and mentally the remainder of his life.

Jim Brewster, Charles' older son, was seventeen years old when his mother, Eliza Jane, died. Jim was slight of build. Though he was usually quiet and reserved, he had a subtle sense of humor. Jim attended the Bryant and Stratton Business College in Chicago. He was groomed for the world of business. In 1881 Jim mar-

Jim (left) and Will Brewster as young adults.

ried Eliza A. Merrill. They had two children, Eugenia Starr, born in 1882, and Charles Merrill, born in 1884. Young Charles Merrill Brewster was mentally impaired from birth and was usually referred to as "Charley." There were whisperings in the family that Charley's disability may have resulted from a failed abortion attempt.

Jim's wife Eliza died in 1887. The family Bible notes that she died in Oxford, Kansas. It is unclear whether she was visiting Jim's uncle and aunt or if she and Jim were residing in Oxford while Jim continued working at the Oxford bank. Jim and Eliza must have felt close to Uncle James and Aunt Gene to name their daughter after the aunt. However, the daughter used her middle name, Starr.

Young Will Brewster was fourteen years old when his mother died. As he matured, he became larger in stature than his older brother Jim and more robust and outgoing. Charles planned for Will to become a minister. When it was time for the younger son's professional training, he was enrolled in a Presbyterian seminary. If Charles had read Will's aptitudes and inclinations accurately, he probably would not have chosen that path for him.

Will was possessed of a spirit of exploration and adventure that left him bored and restless when his life became routine or repetitive. He was a marksman, having won shooting tournaments in Iowa. The excitement of the westward expansion of this nation in the 1880s beckoned him. When Will became convinced the ministry was not for him, he left the seminary as soon as he could.

Cowboys driving their herds across Sumner County likely piqued Will's interest during visits with his uncle and aunt in Oxford, Kansas. Joining a cattle drive was one of Will's early adventures. Only the young and strong could withstand the rigors of the long trek from Texas to the railheads in Kansas. Coping with life out in the open and managing a large herd of livestock was only the beginning of the challenge. There were sometimes prairie fires, storms, rustlers, a scarcity of water, and brushes with Indians and wild animals, including rattle-

snakes. After the animals were loaded on boxcars at the rail-
head, cowboys often accompanied the herd on the final leg of
the journey to the stockyards in Kansas City. Perhaps such a
scenario gave Will his first exposure to the city he would eventually call home.

Oklahoma in the 1880s was still set aside as Indian Territory. The richest Indian grazing land was the Cherokee Outlet, covering more than 6,000,000 acres in north central Oklahoma. It was largely unsettled. Cattle drives had traversed it
on their way from Texas to Kansas. There was pressure on the
federal government to allow whites to come in. In 1883 the
Cherokee Strip Livestock Association leased the Cherokee
Outlet for grazing land but the government declared the leases
invalid and ordered the cattle removed. Finally, the government yielded to demands for settlement. They bought 2,000,000
acres from the Seminole and Creek Indians.

The official opening of the newly purchased Oklahoma
Cherokee Strip was noon on April 22, 1889. Surveyors marked
out townships and some of the main streets prior to the opening. Pioneers by the thousands were held back by troops until
the starting shot was fired. Crowds of contestants joined the
wild race to stake claims. Many drove horse-drawn wagons or
buggies, some hauling their household goods.

Will Brewster, then in his mid-twenties, was on hand for
that event. Mounted on his trusty saddle horse, he was traveling light. When the starting shot was fired, he galloped ahead
and was among the first to reach the layout of a main street.
He quickly dismounted and planted the stake that was tied to
one end of his cord. Then he sprinted along the street with his
unwinding spool of cord until he met another man who had
raced toward him doing the same thing. Where the two met,
each drove another stake into the ground to which they tied
the other end of their cords. The cord that stretched between
Will's stakes defined the size of the block of land that he was
able to claim.

Fights broke out in some parts of the Cherokee Strip that
day as would-be settlers competed for the best locations. There

were scalawags who moved some of the stakes of others. In the space of one day, that previously unoccupied area gained about 50,000 settlers. Will was able to sell his claim immediately, and he rode away with a handsome profit.

Will continued to roam the West. In his travels, he came upon an opportunity to buy the Cave of the Winds in Colorado. Thinking of its potential as a tourist attraction, he wrote home to enlist his dad's capital to buy the property. Charles responded, banker fashion, with a hardheaded question, "How many acres tillable are there?" Will was disgusted and did not bother to reply.

Charles was forced to accept the fact that his younger son would not become a minister. However, the value of hard work was among the lessons Charles thought Will needed to learn to prepare him for whatever life path he chose. Through connections with a lumber company, Charles arranged to send Will out to sell a whole trainload of "skunk" lumber. Will turned out to be quite a salesman. He quickly sold the entire load to one customer. The intended lesson about hard work remained untaught but Charles did not give up.

THE KANSAS CITY CONNECTION **3**

CHARLES BREWSTER ACQUIRED REAL estate holdings
in several midwestern states. He and both of his sons maintained business and social ties to Chicago over the years. However, by 1888 Will had chosen Kansas City, Missouri, as his
home base. The business and social climate of Kansas City at
that time, as well as its location, made it a natural choice for
an adventurous, entrepreneurial young man like Will
Brewster.

The geographic location of Kansas City, in the heart of the
nation at the confluence of two major rivers, greatly influenced how the city developed. Settlement by the white man
began with a trading post on the banks of the Missouri River.
Before railroads spanned the continent, major trade and mi-
gration trails leading to Santa Fe, California, and Oregon traversed the area. Trade in supplies and services for wagon
trains encouraged further settlement. In the mid-nineteenth
century, due to its border location, Kansas City and vicinity
became a focus of clashes between the pro-northern abolition-
ists of Kansas and the pro-southern slavery forces of Missouri.
Civil War battles were fought in the area and border ruffians
roamed about causing havoc. Within the community, strong
feelings on both sides of the slavery issue festered and grew.
When the Civil War ended in 1865 Kansas City was a very
divided small town.

A turning point in the history of the city came in 1869,
with the completion of the first permanent span over the Missouri River. The Hamilton Railroad Bridge opened with great
fanfare. The heyday of steamboats on the Missouri River and
horse or ox-drawn conveyances for overland travel soon gave

way to freighting and travel by rail. The bridge quickly became a double funnel for meat and grain products through Kansas City from the West and capital and culture into Kansas City from the East. In the two decades following

Main Street in Kansas City, looking south from Ninth Street, 1874.
Jackson County (Mo.) Historical Society Archives.

the bridge opening, the city's population grew from less than 10,000 to almost 200,000.

The old Union Depot was completed in the west bottoms in 1878. Ten years later, when Will Brewster came to town, there were a dozen railroads using the station. Kansas City had become a leader in marketing hard winter wheat. Huge harvests of Turkey Red Wheat in Kansas boosted the Kansas City Board of Trade to national prominence. Stockyards in the west bottoms were supplying livestock to the nine major meat packing companies located nearby. Industrial districts were developing in the Blue River Valley and below the northeast bluffs. Banks were sprouting up to keep pace with the increasing trade and to join in the profits.

The introduction to the 1887 Kansas City Directory boasted that eastern capitalists would finally have to admit that Kansas City "is destined to be one of the most potent cities of the country." It touted, as "evidence of lasting prosperity," buildings that were either completed or being built:

• The Nelson Building at Missouri Avenue and Main costing $425,000

- The Board of Trade at Wyandotte and Eighth costing $550,000
- American Bank (ten stories) at Eighth and Delaware, $600,000
- New York Life Insurance at Wall and Ninth, $1,000,000
- A hotel at Seventh and Walnut, $1,000,000
- New England Life Insurance at Wyandotte and Ninth $600,000

The directory noted, "The day has passed when the capitalist will consent to put up second-rate buildings on the central streets of the city. He cannot afford to do it." It pointed out that "every leading thoroughfare in the city" would be paved by the end of the year. The 1889 directory reported that sixty miles of cable track had replaced the mule-car transportation system within the city in less than four years. It declared, " ... the system of cable railroads in Kansas City is the marvel of the outside world."

Burgeoning business enterprises were making millionaires of several Kansas Citians. Grand homes were being built along Independence Avenue and on Troost. The city boasted theaters, including two opera houses. It had a professional baseball team, the Blues. Horseracing was popular. There were bicycle clubs featuring bicycles with very large front wheels.

Kansas City had a tawdry side as well. There were cheap hotels, saloons, brothels, gambling halls, penny arcades, pawnshops, and billiard parlors. Many of these were located in the vicinity of the train depot and were designed to entice travelers, especially the cowboys who were paid after delivering livestock to the stockyards.

Kansas City was expanding. When Will Brewster arrived in 1887 or 1888, the city had spread from the banks of the Missouri River south to Thirty-first Street. Many of the business and cultural interests that were being pursued in eastern cities were being assimilated in Kansas City. Homes still had no indoor plumbing, electric lights, telephones, or central heating. Most citizens owned horses for their private transportation as automobiles had yet to be introduced. Cable cars were operating in a limited area, but much of the movement about the city was on foot, on horseback, or by horse and buggy. Depending on the weather, many streets were either dusty or muddy, as only the main thoroughfares were in the process of receiving paving.

Lawrence Buchanan, Will's cousin, was already in Kansas City when Will arrived. Lawrence was older than Will by fourteen years. After his father failed to return from the Gold Rush, Lawrence spent parts of his formative years with his DeForest grandparents in Pennsylvania, with his Aunt Eliza Jane Brewster and her family in Fort Madison, and with his sister Eugenia Brewster and her family in Oxford, Kansas. By 1886, Lawrence operated a fledgling home furnishings business at 504 East Twelfth Street in Kansas City.

The Bank of Fort Madison, of which Charles Brewster was president and his son Jim an employee, was bought in 1888 by the newly organized First National Bank of Fort Madison. The bank was turned over to the "new organization" in February, 1889. Charles was in his mid seventies, and he may have retired at that time.

In those days before telephones, radios, and television, news of the outside world came mostly by word of mouth, letters, and newspapers. The slow-moving postal service was a vital link between distant family members, friends, and businesses. A series of letters that Charles wrote in Fort Madison to his son Will in Kansas City between August, 1888, and April, 1889, reveal the father's efforts to teach Will basic business principles. The sums of money mentioned are very substantial in terms of values in 1888. Will turned twenty-three that year. Excerpts from Charles' letters follow:

August 18, 1888: Dear William, James told me when he returned from Kansas City that you wanted me to send you a draft for $1200. I now enclose with this a draft for that amount and hope you will make good use of it. Be prudent and careful of your loans. You will do well to watch con-

*stantly all parties you make loans to as no one in a healthy
state financially can afford to pay excessive rates of interest.
Let me hear from you often. I will be pleased to hear how
you are doing ... Yours Truly, Charles Brewster*

The Midland Investment Company was started on August
22, 1888. Will was one of four directors who each owned a
one-fourth interest in the company. Its business purpose was
to do things pertaining to the business of real estate and loaning money. They expected to make and receive notes, endorse-
ments, securities, deeds of warranty, quit claim, release, mortgages, etc.

*January 31, 1889:   Dear William, I have about $4000 on
hand that I would loan on good real estate security on say
about 1/3 present value. Have you any such loans now that
you would like to place for 3 or 5 years. The security must be
undoubtedly good and semi-annual coupon note given payable at one of your best banks ... Yours Truly, Charles
Brewster*

*February 4, 1889: Dear Will, I wrote you last week saying I
had $4000 to loan on 3 or 5 years. I have thought since then
that it might not be good policy to loan it on long time until
James and you come to some understanding about what you
are going to do when James leaves the bank. This will only
require a few days more. I suppose he will go to Kansas City
when Lawrence [Buchanan] and you can compare notes and
see what is best to be done ... I hope you will get your money
back with a good margin of profit ... Yours truly, Charles
Brewster.*

*February 6, 1889: Dear Will, I received yours of 5th. In it
you say that you had made arrangements for the $4000 loan.
I had concluded that you and Jim might need the money if
you went into business but as it may be some time before
you decide on doing anything I suppose it will be best to*

loan it for 2 years. I do not like to go back on your word as it might injure you. Be sure that the title is all right. You ought to get an abstract up to date. Examine into the title closely. If you can get coupon note with interest payable semi-annually at First Natl Bank of Ft. Madison I would prefer it ... We are turning over the bank today. Yours truly, C. Brewster

February 10, 1889: I received yours with letter of __?__ & Robinson in which they state they have placed the loan of $4000 at 7 percent. This leaves us out in the cold. It may be a lucky thing for us as something better may turn up than loaning it at 8 percent. As James intends going to K City this week I think it will be just as well for you to not loan it until he goes over. I do not know what he intends to do but he may get into something that will require money. I think you and James might get into some kind of business where you would be constantly employed. It is not improving your habits to be acting the loafer and I do not want James to remain out of business long enough to acquire lazy and foolish habits. I could loan that money here at 8 percent on good real estate security for three times the value of the loan but it might be a long time before I could get the money back. Do not loan it until James goes over without consulting me by letter. Your aff Father, Chas.

February 21, 1889: Dear William, ... I thought you sent the $600 note as part of the $4000 I had sent you to loan. I cannot see the profit in keeping $4000 without interest since I sent that to you. That I think is poor financiering. If you cannot use the money it could be loaned at 6 percent on Chicago Lumber Co., Harvey and other good firms. Your large interest does not pay as well as a smaller rate if you cannot keep it out ... Yours respectfully, Charles Brewster

February 26, 1889: Dear Will, I received yours of 22nd yesterday. I am very much afraid I am getting rusty in somethings. I cannot understand your policy of keeping $4000 on

*hand for a month without interest waiting for some party
who wants just that amount. Do you think such a party will
show up in the next 6 months. Now I think you would show
some business capacity in loaning it in sums of $500 or $1000
for the time you think you should loan it. Yes I told James I
thought of dividing it between you and Jas. But I fear you
will have no opportunity of loaning it to a <u>safe</u> party. I am
sorry now I sent it to you and I could loan it or rather could
have bought Chicago Lumber Co, T.W. Harvey and other good
paper at 6 percent but I supposed you could get a higher rate
of interest there and sent it. I hope James and Lawrence
[Buchanan] may find some good point to locate at soon as it
is not good for either of you to be acting the part of a loafer
much longer. The mind and body should be kept busy if you
expect to enjoy good health or expect to be prosperous in business. If the party who made the notes I got from Lawrence
will pay compound interest I do not want it until the notes
are due ... Yours, C. Brewster.*

If Jim did get to Kansas City, he must have soon returned
to Fort Madison. Charles' letter of April 26, 1889 reads:

*Dear William, I have just returned from the farm, James
and little Chas. [James' five-year-old son] were down with
me and found yours of 24 with two notes enclosed which I
herewith return to you with draft on Metropolitan Natl. Bank
Chicago for ten hundred fifty. I have sold bonds and will
divide the greater part between you and James. Will charge
you with the above draft as part of your share. Your aff Father, Charles Brewster*

The following letter carries no date, but it shows Charles'
fatherly concern and compassion for his son. The stationery is
identical to that used for the foregoing letters so it must have
been written near the same time. There is no way of knowing if
the "loss" referred to has anything to do with the loans discussed
in the foregoing letters, but it seems very possible it could.

Dear Will, Mr. Cashland is here and says you are feeling a little better and think your low spirits has a good deal to do with your sickness. You must cheer up and try to forget your loss. It will do no good now to mourn over it. I hope the lesson will be a cheap one in the end. It is certainly a pretty dear one. You need not feel disheartened about it or that I will lose confidence in your success hereafter. I hope and believe you will be more cautious in the future. Will write you more full soon. Your aff Father, C. Brewster.

On Thanksgiving Day, November 28, 1889, Will's brother Jim, who had been a widower for two years, married again. His bride was Daisy McClurg of Frankfort, Indiana. The couple made their home in Fort Madison where Jim was again (or still) associated with the bank that was under the management of the new owners. Daisy took over the role of mother to James' seven-year-old daughter Starr and five-year-old mentally handicapped son Charley. They had no more children. Domestic servants were on hand to help Daisy manage the family and the household.

Charles Brewster died on his birthday, November 12, 1893, at the age of 80. His will established a trust of properties in Chicago and in Fort Madison to be managed for the support of his daughter Martha and her son Charles Kirkland. Charles appointed his son Jim as trustee and son Will as successor trustee for their sister's trust.

The legacy that Jim and Will received is not spelled out in the trust arrangement. The letters quoted on the foregoing pages seem to suggest that Charles may have divided some of his estate between his sons before his death. Their inherited estate must have been quite substantial for the time. There is evidence that the two brothers jointly held both stocks and real estate properties for several years. Jim's and Will's management styles contrasted widely. One was able to build upon his legacy and to accumulate still more wealth while the other spent and lost his, ending up struggling to provide even life's necessities.

GOLD FEVER

4

DURING WILL BREWSTER'S BOYHOOD, he had visited his DeForest relatives in Pennsylvania with his mother. No doubt he heard the stories of his Uncle Perry Buchanan's fateful foray into gold country during the Gold Rush. The potential for adventure and wealth in the discovery and unearthing of rich natural resources drew Will like a magnet. His interest in mining started early and became a lifelong pursuit.

First, it was the mining boomtowns of Colorado that he explored. One evening Will invited himself into a poker game in a saloon called Queen Ann's Rest in Leadville. The man across the table from him was drinking heavily and was losing. Suddenly, the drunk drew his pistol and accused Will of stealing his poker chips. Will's knowledge of firearms came to his aid when he found himself looking down the barrel of the loaded gun. That weapon was designed to break open for loading. Will grabbed the gun barrel and jerked downward. The pistol broke open just as the trigger was pulled. Will jumped to his feet, whipped out his own six-gun, and struck the man on the head with it. According to Will, the drunken poker player was "out cold" when employees of the bar (called swampers) tossed the drunk into the street.

Will was returning late one day from a climb up Pike's Peak. Aware of the dangers of riding down a mountain trail in the dark, he got off his horse as daylight faded. Darkness closed in as he hiked along. Soon his feet slipped on loose gravel. Before he could stop himself, he slid into a pit with very steep sides. After several futile attempts to climb out, he decided to give up and wait for daylight.

Will built a fire of wood that he found in the pit. When he

had the flames blazing steadily, he sat down and looked up. There in the darkness surrounding the pit were several sets of eyes glowing in the dark. He was not sure what sort of beasts were looking at him. He had heard that there were wolves about, so he was glad his gun was still in his holster. He said he did not sleep much that night, and he was careful to keep the fire going. At dawn the owners of the eyes had vanished. Daylight revealed an escape route from the pit. Will found his faithful saddle mount grazing nearby and he rode off down the mountain.

Many would-be gold miners went prospecting with a pickaxe, a gold pan, and a burro, but that was not Will's style. He was interested in production on a larger scale. He became a mining engineer, perhaps aided by correspondence courses, but he was mostly self-taught.

In the spring of 1887 Will accompanied a Mr. Webber Sr., of the Webber Gas Engine Company in Kansas City, to the Clarks Fork River in northwestern Wyoming. The company had installed a steam-driven dredge on that river. The dredge was designed to work a sandy site using a long suction pipe with an agitator on the digging, or suction, end. Shareholders were disgruntled because the expensive machine had been abandoned as a failure. Mr. Webber's (and Will's) mission was to investigate the cause of the failure. The two discovered the site was unsuited to the extraction of gold by that machinery due to the boulders present. However, Will was impressed with the gold mining potential of the area. As late as 1941, he was still intrigued and hoped to promote a mine on the Clarks Fork.

Most of Will's mining ventures involved placer mining rather than lode mining. Placer deposits are usually found in or around streambeds and on or near the surface. They occur as a result of erosion or glacial action. Lode mining involves digging for veins of ore. The following comment on the two forms of mining appeared in a prospectus that Will wrote:

Placer gold deposits are always the first to be exploited in new or isolated districts, where these deposits exist, because it is by far the quickest, cheapest and surest way of recovering gold ... Almost everything needed in hydraulic mining may be usually found on the ground, except the pipe and fittings necessary to harness the water power used to wash the gravel, concentrate and save the gold in the riffles and flumes. The money cost of equipping Placer Mine mounting is inconsiderable compared with lode, or quartz mining, which require expensive mills and machinery for the reduction and milling of the ores mined.

William T. Urie was manufacturing mining machinery in Kansas City about the turn of the twentieth century. The 1898 Kansas City Directory lists Will as secretary and treasurer of the Urie Mining Machinery Company. He is also listed as a financial and mining broker. The following year Will is listed simply as manufacturer. The 1900 directory lists him as manager of the Brewster Dredge Company. The latter company does not appear in the listings in succeeding years.

John T. O'Brian was an associate or employee of Will. O'Brian was a mining consultant and, apparently, a Jack-of-all-trades related to mining. He evaluated mining sites, set up mining operations, and sometimes represented Will in negotiations connected with mining enterprises. O'Brian seemed constantly at work on projects far from Kearney, Nebraska, where his wife Mary and young son Brian lived.

Will expanded his exploration of gold mining to California and several other western states. He supplied dredges to mining operations in several locations. One of his letters stated that he was "all over Death Valley in 1889." Later that same year Will was in Portland, Oregon. He sent O'Brian to Canyon Creek in east central Oregon to check on a dredge he had supplied to a gold mining operation there. The buyer of the dredge at Canyon Creek must have been in default on his purchase agreement. O'Brian wrote that he was consulting an attorney in John Day, Oregon, about whether to file a lien on the property.

O'Brian's survey of the Canyon Creek site convinced him

that it had good potential. He felt it was more suited to being worked by hydraulic elevator than by dredging. There was a bidding competition for lands surrounding Canyon Creek. Negotiations with a private landowner, and others, including The Humbolt Company, were still in progress ten years later.

In 1898 and 1899 Will was successfully applying a gold-saving device on the Snake River in Idaho. Early in 1899 O'Brian was back in John Day trying to resolve Canyon Creek questions. O'Brian was eager to wrap up matters in Oregon because he planned to go to Skagway, Alaska. He asked Will for at least $500 to take along in case he found a "good bargain in a small rich claim that would require immediate action." It is doubtful whether O'Brian ever undertook the Alaska trip because Will's attention was already turning to Colombia.

THE GOLD FIELDS OF THE INCAS 5

WILL WAS IN TOUCH with Luis G. Johnson, a Colombian. In a ten-page letter written mostly in Spanish and dated June 20, 1898, Johnson described three groups of placer mines along the mountain streams between the cities of Remedios and Medellin in the state of Antioquia, Colombia, South America. He quoted production amounts from the mines as 1,000 to 1,200 pounds of gold weight monthly and indicated that "great riches" were still to be realized.

Johnson's letter outlined practical matters necessary to make a proper exploration of the mining properties. Travel by steamboat, railroad, and pack mule would be required to reach the sites. Drilling machinery, ropes, tents, and camping outfits would be needed for on-site inspections. He wrote that the transfer of property titles should be no problem because all of the properties were owned by one Jesus M. Perez. There would be a need for sufficient capital to set up a mining operation. And last of all, negotiations with various foreign groups were already in progress for some of the sites.

Back in Kansas City, Will put together the Colombia Gold Dredging Company. He was the company president with B.H. Chapman as treasurer and R.B. Taylor as secretary. The Board of Directors included R.B. Taylor, John S. Johnston, J.J. Lanergan, J.P. Mathes, Benton Flood, L. Flood, and S.T. Kemper. Will put capital into the venture and, presumably, the other officers and board members were also prepared to invest.

Joined to Central America by the Isthmus of Panama, Colombia has coastlines on both the Caribbean Sea and the Pacific Ocean. Altitude is a determining factor in the nation's climate. While temperatures are generally hot in the coastal lowlands, they moderate in the foothills and interior plains and they become quite cold where mountain peaks range up near 18,000 feet. Most of the mountain watersheds drain into one large river, the Magdalena, which might be compared to the Mississippi River in the United States. At the turn of the twentieth century, the Rio Magdalena, winding over its 950-mile course, was the main artery for the transport of goods and communication to and from the interior. The mine sites were located in a low range of mountains in Colombia's interior.

Will's "man Friday," John T. O'Brian, was still in Oregon when Will recruited him to go to Colombia. About May 1, 1899, after visiting briefly with his family in Kearney, Nebraska, O'Brian was on his way to South America. His first destination was Barranquilla, a port on Colombia's Caribbean coast at the mouth of the Rio Magdalena.

Aboard ship off San Salvador on May 10, 1899, O'Brian wrote to Will giving an account of his expenses and the state of his finances. Will had given him $250 to start the trip. Expenses had nearly exhausted that amount, and O'Brian was afraid of being "broke in a strange land." He wrote that he "never would have started on so light a margin but for your [Will's] imperative order to go." He petitioned Will to cable funds to Barranquilla to await his arrival there.

Of interest were O'Brian's transportation costs. A berth to Chicago from Kearney, Nebraska, was $2.50, to New York $26.50, and steamship to Barranquilla (including a cable to his contact person there) $84.50. Among his expense items were a rubber suit for $1.75, a steamer trunk $9.50, and a revolver with ammunition $8.50.

Three days later O'Brian wrote from Kingston, Jamaica. The tone of this letter was more upbeat. He reported being "thoroughly surprised" at the superior quality of an electric plant he visited there. O'Brian used his time in Kingston to talk to men who might enlighten him about mining in Colombia or who might provide the kind of labor he foresaw being needed on the mining operation he hoped to set up. He talked with one man who had done gold mining at a Colombian site with a crew of 50 men. They had used a diving bell with some success. O'Brian was becoming convinced there would be a lot of mining activity in Colombia in the next few years.

John Johnston, one of the board members of the Colombia Gold Dredging Company, was in Barranquilla to meet O'Brian when his ship docked. Other principals of the Company, including Mathes and one or both of the Floods, apparently visited mining sites on the Porce and the Guadaloupe rivers with O'Brian. Back in Barranquilla on July 23, 1899, O'Brian was very optimistic about the prospects at both locations. A decision was made to start their operations on the Porce River at a site called La Clara. It was located about 40 miles north of Medellin, Colombia's second largest city.

The political situation in Colombia was unstable. After the Spanish governments in South America were overthrown in 1819, Colombia was part of a single nation that included present-day Venezuela, Ecuador, and Panama. In 1830, Venezuela and Ecuador established separate governments; but confusion and civil war continued within Colombia until the constitution of 1886 took most of the power from the states and gave it to the central government. Even after that, revolutionaries continued threatening to topple the government from time to time. The political scene was apparently quiet as Will's group began their explorations in 1899, but things boiled up again before the year was out.

An important attribute of the La Clara site, where O'Brian and company chose to initiate mining operations in Colombia, was the abundant water supply in the Rio Porce on which it was located. Upon examination of the site, O'Brian believed that it could be worked more effectively with an hydraulic elevator than with a dredge. However, Will had already shipped a dredge to Colombia so they decided to store it in Barranquilla to await a possible buyer rather than to ship it on to the mine.

On August 21, 1899, O'Brian was in Medellin, a city of about 70,000, arranging for thirty cargo mules to transport three tons of supplies over the 40 miles of back roads and trails to La Clara. A week later he was on site surveying for the ditch they would need for their mining operation. He wrote, "I never saw such a rank growth of vegetation in my life." The area was tangled with vines, brush, and grass twenty feet high. Barefoot natives cut a path for him with machete. The ditch, or canal, he planned to dig was to be four and a quarter miles long, two feet deep, three and a half feet wide at the top, and two and a half feet wide at the bottom. It would fall to the water level of the Rio Porce from a beginning height of 330 feet.

There were many problems to overcome. Legal matters had to comply with Colombian law which was foreign to the company principals. It was difficult to find and keep workers for the operation. Estimating the amount of funding needed and transferring funds across international boundaries in time to meet commitments were complicated from the beginning. O'Brian felt the need for Will's assistance. He wrote urging Will to come to Colombia as soon as possible.

On October 11, 1899, with anticipation of early success, the company mortgaged much of the operation with a Kansas Citian named John Doggett. The mortgage of $10,000 was to be repaid in two installments. Two thousand dollars was due September 1, 1900, and the remaining $8,000 was to be paid October 1, 1901. The contract provided that, in case of default, certain properties would be sold, including equipment at the mine, the dredge that was stored in Barranquilla and equipment stored in New York. The proceeds, after expenses of sale, would first go to satisfy the debt owed to Mr. Doggett.

Nine days after the signing of the mortgage contract, war broke out again in Colombia. Work on the canal came to a standstill and O'Brian returned to Medellin until things quieted down. The Rio Magdelena was blockaded. O'Brian wrote, "We are completely cut off from all outside communication . . .Press Gangs infest every section and the peons have all dis-

appeared into the hills." Letters written weeks apart sometimes arrived together. There were no telephones but tele-
graph messages sometimes got through. Mail delivery often
took three or four months. Since mail could no longer come up
the Rio Magdelena, O'Brian hoped that it might be routed
from Colombia's Pacific coast.

O'Brian had another serious concern. He instructed Will
to sell a share of his stock and send the proceeds to his wife
Mary so she would not be in need. Will's arrangement with
O'Brian evidently included stock in the company but not a
regular salary. Will also received letters from Mary O'Brian
about her financial needs. She reported that the stenographic
work she usually depended on was no longer available because Kearney was a "boomed out town" and businessmen
were writing their own letters. She wrote that, if necessary,
she could run her household on twenty-five dollars per month,
though she would prefer a little margin to meet unexpected
expenses. She hoped the sale of one share of her husband's
stock would bring at least $150.00 to supply her needs for six
months.

On December 20, 1899, O'Brian wrote that he was still
very enthusiastic about the potential of both La Clara and
another mine for which he thought they should negotiate. He
thought Colombian government forces had the upper hand,
and he expected the conflict to quiet down in a few days so
work could resume on the canal. The revolution continued,
however, with skirmishes here and there. Though work on
the mine did resume, it took much longer and was much more
costly than expected. After the plant was constructed and
ready to start, several breaks in the ditch caused much delay.

Counting from O'Brian's first site evaluation, it took a frustrating eighteen months to get the first "cleanup" of the
mine. That came in November of 1900, and it was very dis-
appointing. The amount of gold recovered was small. The location of the hydraulic elevator proved unsatisfactory. An unexpected layer of boulders above the bedrock hindered the
operation. Surface mining in that area had been done for cen-

turies by the natives and later by the Spanish. Some stock-holders believed the operation was placed on ground that had been mined out. They wanted it moved to virgin soil. Moving the elevator would be time consuming and expensive. With income lacking and expenses still mounting, they were already late for their first mortgage payment to John Doggett.

Various Colombia Gold Dredging Company officers, board members, and shareholders (except Will) continued to spend extended periods of time in Colombia. By January of 1901, B.H. Chapman, the treasurer, was in Medellin on company business. Chapman went out to La Clara several times. He wrote that the trip took "a day and a half riding [presumably on muleback] over a mean trail and in the blazing sun." Both Chapman and O'Brian were having symptoms of malaria.

Doggett was pressuring Chapman by mail and cable from Kansas City to sell some of the company assets according to the mortgage contract. Chapman wrote to Will to do every-thing possible to head off court action by Doggett and to stall for time. Chapman was optimistic the mine would pay off before long but was unwilling to make predictions to Doggett which again might fail.

Rifts were developing among the shareholders. Chapman wanted to promote a reorganization of the company. Before doing so, he wanted to drop as many shareholders as possible to assure his, and possibly Will's, control of the company after the reorganization. Taylor disliked Chapman so much that he referred to him as I.E.A, which stood for "Ignorant, Egotistical Ass." He was ready to sell his stock and get out. Doggett also appeared to have little use for Chapman.

Letters from Taylor and Doggett indicate that they both trusted Will and were anxious for him to go to Colombia to evaluate and expedite the operation. Will acquired a pass-port on June 18, 1901. With the revolutionaries still active in Colombia, schisms in the ranks of his company, and the mine still not producing enough to meet expenses, Will had his work cut out for him.

MIXING MARRIAGE WITH MINING   **6**

MINING WAS ONLY ONE of Will Brewster's business interests at the turn of the century. Besides selling mining dredges, he was at least a part owner of an array of real estate properties; and by 1901 he shared ownership with his cousin Lawrence Buchanan in a furniture store. Lawrence started the Buchanan Furniture and Carpet Company located in downtown Kansas City at Twelfth and Grand Avenue in 1900. Later the company name was changed to Buchanan Brewster Furniture Company. Will's office for his Brewster Dredge Company was in the same building as the furniture store.

Will had personal as well as business concerns as he headed for Colombia, South America. He had married Mamie S. Hannah on November 22, 1894. Mamie's parents were Irish immigrants but she was born in Missouri. Her expectations of marriage were conventional. They included companionship, but Will did not fit the mold of a breadwinner who worked close to home and came home for dinner every night. His adventurous nature and his far-flung mining interests kept him traveling a great deal. Perhaps that is why the couple did not buy or rent a home of their own. The 1900 census lists them among twenty-six boarders living at 500 Woodland Avenue. Will's occupation is listed as merchant.

There was discord between Mamie and Will before he left for South America in June of 1901. She thought he would be gone about three months, and it is a safe surmise that she did not want him to go. Responding to a letter that Will wrote en route, Mamie penned:

*Well, Dear, it surely was like old times to have you say such
lovely things to me and made me almost feel like a bride
again. Surely we can get along all right if we are always
honest with each other — but you know where there is a little
fire there is a great deal of smoke. But after three months of
separation we can start all over again. Let us never mention this again. It is all over and there are no bones broken
— just act and think as if everything had always been all
right.*

With no children and no house to look after, Mamie bus-
ied herself with other things such as getting Will's clothes
cleaned and stored in "tar bags." She often had dinner with
her mother who lived nearby. She sometimes visited "the
Store" (the Buchanan Furniture and Carpet
Company). Excelsior Springs, about 40 miles northeast of
Kansas City, was a noted resort and mineral-bath spa in those
days. While Will was away, Mamie sometimes spent weekends there with friends.

Mamie worried when no word came from Will after he was
to have arrived in Barranquilla. John Doggett calculated Will
would reach the La Clara Mine site late in June or early in
July. He wrote to Will July 11, 1901:

*I met Mrs. Brewster last Monday in your store. I gave her
all the consolation I could in reference to receipt of news from
you. I will cheer her all I can for she is a worthy woman and
wife — far above the average. I know you will do your best
to keep up her courage.*

The weather that summer of 1901 was dreadfully hot, up
to 110 degrees at times. All the pastures were dry. Dan and
Win, the couple's horses, had to be boarded rather than
pastured. August came with still no word from Will. Mamie
and a friend named Madge went vacationing in Wyoming,
staying at several different guest ranches. Presumably, the
major part of their journey was by train, but they traveled

between ranches on horseback. Mamie wrote that they averaged about 25 miles per day when they moved from one ranch to another.

Mamie returned to Kansas City happy about her trip but unhappy about the care of her horse, Dan, while she was away. Mamie had left Dan with a Mrs. Briggs who was to pay for his board in exchange for the use of him. Upon her return she learned that Will's cousin, Lawrence Buchanan, had borrowed Dan to be used by his wife, Birdie. Lawrence kept Dan in a livery stable where some of the horses were sick. When Mamie brought Dan back to their home stable, Dan carried the "bug" to Win and the other horses there.

Mamie resented that her horse was borrowed without her permission. Apparently, it was a sore point that Dan was used by Birdie Buchanan. Mamie wrote: "Birdie could ride on streetcars as well as before she married him [Lawrence]."

Birdie went to Fort Madison to visit her husband's cousins, Jim and Daisy Brewster, and their daughter, Starr. Mamie wrote to Will about that visit:

> She [Daisy] did not take a fancy to Birdie at all. She does not say anything nice about her. Birdie made a mistake in going there when so many of Starr's school friends were there. Imagine Birdie with 10 girls right out of college, rich girls at that.

Newspapers reported that insurgents in the interior of Colombia were continuing the war. Even as John Doggett tried to reassure Mamie, he, too, was becoming concerned about the lack of communication from Will. Meanwhile, Will disembarked at Barranquilla, Colombia, with a load of heavy mining equipment including a supply of large steel pipe broken down to half-shell to facilitate transportation.

With traffic on the Rio Magdelena blockaded by insurgents, Will faced the problem of how to transport his equipment 500 miles up river. The prospect of waiting out the war, already in its second year, was unacceptable, but Will was resourceful. Inquiries led him to a favorite hangout of riverboat captains. The American whiskey he brought along proved very useful. It was considered more desirable than the brew the locals were drinking. He shared his booze and struck up a friendship with the riverboat captains. Though his facility in the Spanish language was limited, he was able to learn what was happening on the river.

The Rio Magdelena was a wide, and sometimes treacherous, river. River pilots, with the skill and know-how to safely navigate the Magdelena, were scarce. The Colombian government had wooden, steam-driven gunboats that were about 40 to 60 feet long. When able to operate, they delivered mail and other cargo up and down the river. However, rebels along the riverbanks were targeting the pilots and engineers of the government boats. Pilots were at risk of gunfire from the riverbank, even inside their pilothouses. Operating the engine of a boat was stiflingly hot work. The engineers were targeted when they stepped out on deck to catch a breath of air.

Will devised a plan. He proposed armoring a boat's pilothouse and the door to its engine room with his half-shell pipe. The pilots agreed the plan might work for most of the journey; but there was an additional hazard to be evaded. Insurgents had mounted a canon at a bend of the river. It was impossible for boats to stay out of the canon's range as they skirted the point. Will offered a solution for that dilemma, too, and he convinced at least one riverboat captain to try his plan. In exchange for armoring the gunboat, Will bargained to have all of his equipment taken up river to Puerto Berrio where he could book railway transit to Medellin.

As they began the hazardous journey up river, Will's marksmanship became useful. He brought out his rifle (probably a Winchester) with a telescopic sight. He was able to target rebels who had stationed themselves in trees along the riverbank. Once he had knocked one or two out of a tree, the others usually fled. His pipe armor proved effective against the firepower of the inferior guns of the revolutionaries along the shore. Before they approached the canon-fortified bend, Will was put ashore with a few of the government soldiers. They flanked the rebels, scared them off, and dumped the canon into the river. The gunboat rounded the bend unscathed and finally delivered Will and his equipment to the river port of Puerto Berrio.

Will still had to ship his equipment by rail to Medellin and then about 40 miles by mule train to the mine. His war-related troubles continued once he reached the mine site. Laborers were needed to repair the four-mile canal and make other changes necessary to get the mine into paying production. It was difficult to keep local workers on the job because press gangs roamed the countryside looking for men to conscript into service in the war. When a press gang was in the vicinity, the peons simply disappeared into the undergrowth and did not return.

A fence surrounded the encampment at La Clara. As a press gang approached the mine site one day, Will talked his workers into hiding within the compound. When the gang shouted at the gate, Will strapped on his two revolvers and went out to meet them. Unsnapping his holsters so they could see his guns at the ready, he asked the would-be intruders what they wanted. They must have been impressed, for they backed off their errand saying, "Ah, señor, we mean no harm." "Well, in that case," Will replied, "leave your weapons at the gate and come on in for some American whiskey." So he entertained them and they went on their way.

Near the end of August, Mamie finally received a letter that Will had written on July 13. She responded:

You have no idea how terrible it [Will's letter] makes me feel. Well, Will, we all have our hard times. I hope you and I are having ours now. Possibly when we are older we will know how to enjoy ourselves. Why did they not write you the truth about affairs down there — instead telling about the lovely climate and beautiful scenery. They did not let you know about their being out of money and about the sickness. How sorry I am for them all. Such folly for a little mine. Money — what good would a million do Mr. Chapman now? [Will had reported that Chapman was very ill.] He has wasted life and education and years of practice for what? You are in your prime, why stay there and use up everything. Come home and be contented and try and make the best of things. I know I do not suit you as well as some other people might, but we are married and we ought to make the best of ourselves. I have tried so hard but always fail at the step.

Writing letters to Will seemed very one-sided to Mamie. She wrote to him every week but she doubted if many of her letters were reaching him. Three letters that Will wrote to her in August, September, and October of 1901, were received all at the same time. On December 19, when she wrote to him from Chicago, where she was visiting an uncle, she had heard nothing further from Will. She had been in Chicago for two months awaiting the preparation of new rooms that were being readied for them in Kansas City. She went to the theater often while in Chicago. She worried about Will being sick so far from home and told him that the gold he sent had never arrived.

Back in Kansas City on Christmas Day, Mamie wrote that their new apartment would not be finished until March. She was expecting Will to start home at any time, and she delivered an ultimatum: "When you come home you need not plan ever going back again."

Mamie was not the only one expecting Will to return home. In February, John Doggett wrote that he hoped his letter would reach Will before he left Colombia. Doggett thought Will's associates in the company were trying to avoid repaying his loan, and he was upset over the company's failure to dispose of the dredge stored in Barranquilla.

In May, Will received a cable from his brother, Jim, stating, "Return home at once. Buck in trouble." What sort of trouble Buck (Lawrence Buchanan) was having is not clear, perhaps something in regard to the Buchanan Furniture & Carpet Company. Will also received a letter from an Alma Danby threatening court action if he did not pay rent for storage of another of his dredges, the one that was still out in John Day, Oregon. But Will was too absorbed with what he was doing to yield to pressures to return home. Besides being involved in operations at La Clara, he was also exploring and acquiring 35 other mining sites in Colombia.

Years later, Will wrote to a friend that during his stay in Colombia in 1902, with an investment of only $25,000, he took $76,000 in gold out of the La Clara mine. Probably, he used all or most of the profits expanding his company's holdings. However, the mine produced enough that Will's brother Jim and his cousin Lawrence began to show interest in the project.

As the spring and summer of 1902 came and went with no word from Will, Mamie began to wonder if he were still alive. The originally expected three months' duration of Will's trip stretched beyond a year, and Mamie's tolerance grew thin and finally wore out. On August 6, 1902, Will received another telegram from his brother Jim. It read, "Mamie suing for divorce – September court – come immediately."

A meeting of stockholders of the Colombia Gold Dredging Company was held August 11, 1902, in Colombia before Will returned to the States. It was attended by Will Brewster, J.T. O'Brian, and John Johnston with Will voting a proxy for John Doggett and O'Brian voting a proxy for B. H. Chapman (the treasurer, who remained very ill in Medellin). Apparently, Lanergan, Mathes, one of the Floods, and Kemper had either dropped out or been bought out. Doggett must have accepted stock in lieu of repayment of his loan. They were not able to have a financial report at their meeting of stockholders, perhaps due to Chapman's illness and a neglect of record keeping. They considered changes in the bylaws, nominations for the board of directors (which this time included Jim Brewster and Lawrence Buchanan), and the buying out of stock owned by Taylor and the other Mr. Flood. They set the time of the next stockholders' meeting for March of 1903 to be held in Fort Madison, Iowa.

Will was back in New York by September. John T. O'Brian was again left in charge of the mining operations in Colombia.

IF AT FIRST YOU DON'T SUCCEED, ... **7**

WILL BREWSTER FREQUENTLY TURNED to his older brother when he was in a personal or financial jam. The joint financial legacy that Jim and Will received from their father increased their need to communicate with each other. Jim's role in his brother's divorce proceedings illustrates the intertwining of their financial situations during those early years after Charles' death. Jim, the practical one, was loyal but he was sometimes frustrated when caught in a bind precipitated by Will's actions.

On September 11, 1902, Jim addressed a letter to Will in New York. He advised Will that Mamie's lawyers were seeking alimony. He explained that Missouri's divorce laws required the serving of suit documents in person to the defendant and proof of nonsupport before alimony could be awarded. Jim advised Will to have a cable sent to Mamie from Colombia stating that he (Will) would have to stay in Colombia and did not know when he could come home. He suggested that Will lose his identity until after the divorce. Jim offered: "You might come here in the night and I will take you down to Snag Lake where I have a nice little cabin and would have a colored cook."

As might have been expected, once back in the United States, Will did not choose to stay in a hiding place. Kearney, Nebraska, was one of his destinations. A possible motive for the trip is that Will may have brought messages or gifts for Mary O'Brian from her husband. Also, there was a potential buyer for a farm that Jim and Will owned near Kearney. Will may have worked on that deal while in the vicinity.

Will's travels were vexing to his brother who was sure word of Will's return from Colombia would reach his wife. In an effort to conceal Will's return from Mamie, Jim addressed his letters to Will as Mr. J.W. Zeus, Esquire. Jim advised Will to come to Fort Madison immediately "to plan out the campaign" with O'Grady, Will's Kansas City attorney. Jim wrote:

> *If you should enter your appearance in the case she [Mamie] would be entitled to a personal judgment, if she could prove a case entitling her to a divorce. I should think that matters could be settled so that you would not have to pay her any alimony at all, as even $50 a month alimony would be a heavy burden to carry as long as she lives ... If she should get a divorce from you she would forfeit her dower right to the real property in Iowa, but she would not forfeit her dower right to property in Missouri.*

Mamie wrote to Jim on September 14, 1902, objecting to the handling of the Equity Building that Jim and Will owned at 915 Walnut Street in downtown Kansas City. To help forestall a nonsupport claim, Jim arranged for Mamie to receive half of the rents and the building's expenses were to come out of Mamie's half. Mamie protested that the regular expenses of operating the building would absorb all of her half of the rents. In addition, she was making payments on bills that were in arrears when she took over the accounts. About her marriage, Mamie wrote:

> *I have lived through nearly 8 years of hell with Will — and the last two have made it impossible to keep this up any longer. Am awfully heart sick and sorry this has all happened ... Mrs. Buchanan herself [Birdie] told me of a woman Will had been keeping where she lived and all about her — and of several other things like that.*

Jim attended a meeting in Kansas City with Mamie and some attorneys on September 23. The report of that meeting states that Jim agreed to let Mamie have all the rent from the building, temporarily:

*... to knock out her claim of non-support ...   Mr. Brewster
[Jim] painted his brother's financial condition in the blackest
colors, but we are doubtful whether she [Mamie] recognized
the picture as a good likeness. Mr. Brewster [Jim] asked her to
consult with her lawyers and make to him an offer of a lump
sum which she would be willing to take in lieu of alimony,
and relinquish her dower rights ... She said that she had paid
taxes on a good many properties in Missouri and Kansas, and
believed that he [Will] had considerable property.*

Will took up residence in Chicago during the divorce proceedings. Despite efforts to conceal his return to the United
States, Mamie did learn from friends that he was back in this
country. There is no evidence of any inclination on Will's part
to reconcile with his wife. The divorce became final in 1903 in
Independence, Missouri. Mamie received a property settlement. Sometime later, Will heard that she remarried and that
her new husband was a man of wealth.

No one had foreseen how long it would take to get the
LaClara Mine established and working. During the early years
that John O'Brian spent in Colombia, his wife and son were
often in dire financial straits. O'Brian's wife, Mary, may have
been related to Will and Jim. Her full name was Mary
Brewster Early O'Brian. Mary's letters to her husband and to
Will often reflected her financial worries. However, after Will's
sojourn at the mine in 1901 and 1902, the tone and concerns
of Mary's letters changed. That was probably a result of the
easing of Mary's situation due to the success of the mine.

Mail from Colombia continued to take weeks or months to
reach its destination. Mary relayed to Will some news from
her husband that she received in January of 1903, though it
was written the prior October and November:

*He [O'Brian] was sick with rheumatism in his ankles —
could not mount his horse and was taken to the city [Medellin]
on a stretcher. In the latter letter he wrote that he had discarded his crutches and would return to the mine in a few*

days. He was horribly discouraged, impatient and <u>cross</u>. The mine, I inferred was working satisfactorily but he was anxious about Mr. Chapman [treasurer of the company who had been sick for some time]. Mr. O'Brian wrote in both letters that Mr. Chapman was insane and must be brought to the states, and if he could not get someone to bring him he would do so; that he would cable Mr. Johnston to return at once to relieve him and that he would cable me if he came. But I have not heard from him since either by letter or by cable. I'm rather anxious about him and hope he will not attempt the journey with an insane man. I'm sure he would not leave the mine until someone returns to take his place, but I hope Mr. Johnston will go down soon. Rheumatism doesn't make one exactly placid.

When Mary O'Brian learned of Will's and Mamie's divorce, her sympathies were with Will. Mary had endured much longer absences from her husband than Mamie had. She wrote as follows:

You are altogether too modest in estimating your position as to women, and I beg to remind you that <u>you</u> were not the failure. I think my gray hair makes the "delicately veiled compliment" permissible.

The Colombia Gold Dredging Company was reorganized and renamed in 1903 or 1904. It became the La Clara Placer & Mines Company. Stockholders in the old company were instructed to exchange their stock at double the face value. The new company had offices in Chicago, Ft. Madison, Yuma (Arizona), and Medellin (Colombia). Officers were Will Brewster, president, J. T. O'Brian, superintendent and vice-president, J.C. Brewster, treasurer, and J. A. S. Pollard, secretary. (Pollard was an associate of Jim in the bank at Fort Madison.) Apparently, B.H. Chapman and John Johnston were out of the picture at the time of the reorganization.

Among Will's acquaintances in the Chicago area was Ira B.

Lesh. The Lesh family lived in Oak Park, a suburb of Chicago. Ira and Alice Lesh had a petite and pretty daughter named Edith who was a friend of Will's niece, Starr. Though Will's age was twice that of Edith's — he was 38, she was 19 — they began a courtship.

The announcement of Will's engagement to Edith Lesh about the first of February, 1904, came as a surprise to Will's brother and family in Fort Madison. However, Jim and Daisy Brewster knew the Lesh family, and they extended their congratulations. Though Edith and Will planned a June wedding, Daisy suggested, perhaps jokingly, that Will and Edith speed up their plans and have a double wedding with Starr and Alba Garrott who were to be married that spring. Daisy's suggestion was not taken seriously.

In March, Edith and her mother went to Fort Madison to attend the wedding of Starr and Alba. It was not an altogether happy occasion for Will's future mother-in-law, Alice. Afterward she wrote to Will apologizing for a rumor that circulated during that visit. She told Will that the disparaging remark about his and Edith's behavior, credited to Alice, had actually come from Daisy, Will's sister-in-law. Alice said she also heard Daisy make the same remark, using the expression "slobbering over," in reference to the behavior of Starr and Alba.

Another bit of gossip Alice heard in Fort Madison was that Will might still be seeing Mamie, his former wife. Also, she had seen Mamie's picture conspicuously displayed somewhere. Alice insisted that she did not want to be a meddler, and she assured Will that she believed that he was being true to her daughter. However, she suggested that the picture should be burned or returned to "Mrs. Brewster," meaning Mamie. Alice wrote that she was thankful to be delivered from Mrs. B's (Daisy's) tongue and she was glad to be back home and far from Fort Madison.

Will decided he was not ready to keep a June wedding date. Edith assured him she was ready to set their wedding date but would wait patiently until he was ready. In response to his concern about preparing a place for her, she insisted

that she could be happy anywhere so long as he was
there. During the period of the engagement, Will was traveling, mostly between Chicago and Fort Madison, but Kansas
City and Oklahoma were also on his itinerary. In addition, he
was considering returning to South America. Edith's letters
to Will dealt with her social engagements, Spanish lessons,
tennis matches, shopping, and piano playing. Each letter pro-
fessed her love for him and her desire to be with him. On June
5, 1904, Edith wrote:

> ... We are going to be so happy Oh! so happy ... No, dear, I
> don't care if we don't have a large wedding but I do want to
> have the girls, my best friends here and Starr, if she is able. It
> is hard to know where to draw the line in a thing like that,
> though ... We will discuss it all — pros and cons when you
> come over.

Will and Edith were married September 1, 1904, in Oak
Park, Illinois. Will returned to Kansas City with his new bride.
Two events in the first fifteen months of their marriage suggest that Will was finally trying to put down roots. They purchased the home at 3423 Charlotte Street, and they became
the parents of a daughter, Marguerite, on November 26, 1905.

COLORADO RANCHER   **8**

THE BUCHANAN FURNITURE AND Carpet Company that Will owned with his cousin Lawrence Buchanan was not doing well in 1906. Will hired a Chicago accounting firm to audit the company books covering the years 1900 through August, 1906. The audit report contained a scathing indictment of the owners and of the management of the company. It stated that the books were in a "deplorable condition" and noted "gross carelessness on the part of the bookkeeper." After the audit, the business was incorporated and there was a stock offering. At that time the store's name was changed to Buchanan Brewster Furniture Company. Will's father-in-law, Ira B. Lesh, became an officer in the company. His name was added to the company letterhead and his signature as secretary appeared on the company's stock

Buchanan Brewster Furniture Company, 1204 Main Street in Kansas City, 1906.

certificates along with that of L.J. Buchanan, president.

The store was moved from its Twelfth and Grand location to 1204 and 1206 Main. A ten-year lease was acquired on the building at the new site. An advertising campaign was launched, and there were high hopes for the future. Business was better initially, but the improvement must have been short lived. The next year, the business was moved down the street to the Scarritt Building. Will's letters of 1907 show some discouragement. He wrote to O'Brian that he was thinking of selling the furniture business. Edified by hindsight, he was painfully aware of errors he had made. The Buchanan Brewster Furniture Company listing does not appear in the Kansas City Directory after 1908.

There is a story that was passed down through the family about an importer who rented a building from Will. (Probably the building at Twelfth and Main was sublet to the importer to fill out the lease.) When the importer's business failed, Will received an ornately carved Chinese settee and a pair of very large Satsuma vases in lieu of rent that was overdue. The

Ornately carved Chinese settee, said to have been one of a pair to come out of a palace in Peking during the Boxer Rebellion about the turn of the 20th century.

settee and one of the vases (the other vase was broken years ago) have been in the family since about 1910. The settee was purported to have come out of a palace in Peking, China, during the Boxer Uprising in about 1903. It is said to have been one of a matched pair.

In a letter written in early June of 1907, Will announced to O'Brian that he was expecting the birth of a son and heir. In July he wrote that the baby had arrived but it was not the expected "future president." Will's letter states, "It was just a girl." The new little daughter was named Barbara. Her birthdate was June 25, 1907. A young woman named Mary Wetmiller was hired as a nanny for the two little Brewster daughters. Marguerite, whose family nickname was "Sissy," remembered Mary with great fondness.

Will's mining interests continued in this country along with those in Colombia, South America. In the U. S., his focus turned to the southwest — Arizona and New Mexico. In Colombia, besides La Clara, all of the following names of mines appear in Will's correspondence of 1906 to 1909: Cusuco, Monitas, Mirafloris, La Miel, Rafael, Hormiguero, Ladesma, Raternaro, Vibreal, Combia. Will or his company evidently held interests in these and more.

In 1906, negotiations were in progress to sell the La Clara mine. O'Brian left a G. R. Snover in charge of the mine while he went to Los Angeles, California, to work a deal with investors there. The intention was to have Snover keep operating La Clara so it would not deteriorate before it could be sold. Will considered Snover's salary of $250 per month too high, but they did not expect to pay it for long.

While O'Brian worked with potential buyers in California, R.B. Taylor was in New York working on negotiations there. Will and his several associates wavered between hope and discouragement as they pursued various deals. Investors appeared interested in the Colombian mines, but they were reticent to risk capital in a foreign land. The slow modes of communication (postal delivery) and transportation complicated the negotiations. The sale of La Clara failed to materialize.

O'Brian was still having health problems. While in California, he decided to enter a health spa in the desert for several weeks. He wrote to Will that he was often experiencing numbness for two or three hours during which he could not hold a pencil in his hand. He cited the "remains of beriberi" as the cause.

The distance between Kansas City and the Colombian gold fields complicated all matters related to the mines. Negotiations to buy, sell, or lease interests in many of the mines were ongoing. There were lawsuits related to the unauthorized use of their water sources and to land titles. Some or all of the properties were registered in the name of J. T. O'Brian in order to facilitate various deals. In 1908, Will was worried about O'Brian's poor health. He was afraid O'Brian might die before the titles could be changed.

Apparently Will returned to Colombia briefly in late 1908 or 1909. The La Clara mine was leased to a group called the McGuire Brothers. Because management of business matters related to the mines was almost impossible for a nonresident foreigner such as Will, he enlisted the help of Don Luis Johnson. Johnson was the Colombian citizen who first introduced Will to mining in Colombia. Provided with Will's power of attorney, Johnson had full authority to represent Will in bookkeeping and other business matters related to the Colombian mines.

The response of Edith, Will's wife, to his absence was different from that of her predecessor. Years later their daughter, Marguerite, told the author that Will returned home from South America unexpectedly and discovered Edith "in bed with the governor of Missouri." When questioned as to which governor, Sissy readily responded with the man's name. Research failed to disprove the allegation. He was not yet in office at the time of the alleged liaison, but he did become the governor. Biographical facts — times, places, and ages — for Edith and that soon-to-become state executive left open the possibility that the allegation could be true. Marguerite said that her parents divorced after her father's return from

Colombia. She believed about a year elapsed before they married each other again.

In one of Will's letters to O'Brian, he wrote that he was considering buying a ranch out west and spending the rest of his days there. Sometime before 1910, he did purchase a prize apple ranch near the small town of Fruita in western Colorado. The property included a ranch house and a guesthouse for entertaining. A caretaker named Fred Byers was employed as a foreman to run the ranch with its apple orchards.

In 1910, probably just after the remarriage of Will and Edith, the family prepared to move to the ranch. Household goods and family wardrobes were shipped to the care of Fred Byers. Apparently the shipment arrived in Fruita and was awaiting delivery to the ranch when a fire broke out in the railway storage facility. A list of furnishings lost in that fire covers eight pages and includes more than 200 pieces of household items and about as many items of men's, women's and children's clothing. Among the furniture items were a player piano, a leather couch, a silk brocade divan, four oriental rugs, half a dozen rockers, and many mahogany and silver items. The list of men's clothing included fancy dress items such as a cutaway frock suit, a Prince Albert silk lined suit, silk vests, light striped trousers, a beaver overcoat, an opera hat, and cravats. Women's items included many fur and silk coats, suits and accessories as well as lace, silk, velvet and embroidered dresses.

The shipment to Fruita may have been insured. A lawsuit to recover the fire losses was filed by Omah E. Robinson against the Union Pacific Railway. Litigation was apparently still in progress in 1914 when one of the parties declared bankruptcy. No evidence remains as to what Will and his family recovered. The family's move to Colorado was delayed a year or so.

The city limits of Kansas City moved southward over the years. By 1909, Prospect had been extended to Seventy-ninth Street, but widening and paving had not yet taken place. A city ordinance was passed that year to open and widen Fifty-ninth Street from Stateline to the eastern city limits. There was little development east of Prospect or south of Fifty-fifth Street. In January of 1910, Will bought 17.6 acres of land for development in that area. He paid $22,000 for it. The tract was bounded by Fifty-eighth Street on the north, Fifty-ninth on the south, Prospect on the west and Chestnut Street on the east.

As mentioned earlier, Will was involved in setting up the Midland Investment Company in 1888. In 1910 he was the company president. In 1911, he and Edith signed over the above tract of land to the Midland Investment Company. Then Will, acting for the company,

Edith Lesh Brewster and daughters Barbara, age 3¹/₂ (left), and Marguerite, age 5, 1910.

filed to subdivide. At that time, the subdivision was called Timberland. It was later renamed Brewster's Grove. In 1912, the property was placed in trust to secure a $5,000 promissory note.

The family finally moved to the ranch in western Colorado in about 1912. Mary Wetmiller went along to look after seven-year-old Marguerite and five-year-old Barbara. Marguerite (Sissy) remembered being dressed in white ruffled pinafores for outings. At least once she and Barbara went outside and got their pinafores muddy before their parents were ready to go. The girls had a Shetland pony and a cart. When Sissy was older she was allowed to drive the cart the two miles to the store in Fruita.

Sissy recalled that her parents were not getting along very

well at the ranch. She remembered a quarrel between Will
and Edith one day as dinner guests were arriving. Edith threw
a baked potato at Will just as he opened the door. The potato
missed its mark and hit one of the incoming guests. Marguerite and Barbara witnessed the happening, and Barbara ran
and hid under a bed.

Events in Kansas City confirm that Will was not staying
at the ranch full time. He was often away tending his many
business pursuits. Edith also found occasion to get away. Marguerite remembered feeling very left out at one point when
Edith returned with Barbara to Kansas City, leaving her to be
cared for at the ranch.

John O'Brian returned to South America by 1912, and Mary
and their son Brian joined him there. Mary stayed on in Colombia when they sent Brian back to the States to school. John
was excitedly pursuing more gold mining properties and urging Will to join him. Lawsuits were pending related to water
rights on several of the mining properties, but O'Brian was
confident they would win the suits. Work on some of the sites
was stopped by injunction until the suits were settled. Then
the rainy season set in with a vengeance causing mudslides
that blocked their tunnels and ditches. By 1914, they had won
the suit for the La Clara but lost the others. O'Brian swore
that any future purchase agreements he entered into would
contain a clause requiring the seller to defend any lawsuits
brought against the property. He wanted nothing more to do
with litigation in that country.

O'Brian reported that monetary conditions were very bad
in Colombia due to World War I in Europe. He wrote that banks
all over South America were failing because about 75 percent
of their credit came from Europe, and European credit was
shut off. On a personal level, responding to something Will
had written about his marriage, O'Brian expressed sadness
that Edith was dissatisfied.

John and Mary O'Brian returned to the United States at
the end of 1914. They left Medellin, Colombia, on December
13, and "making just ordinary everyday connections" arrived

in Springfield, Massachusetts, on December 31, in time to welcome in the new year. O'Brian reported that they could have improved on that time by making special effort. He wrote that they brought in a heavy cargo of gold and that "all the gold from the south is coming to New York instead of going to London and Paris as heretofore" due to the war in Europe.

O'Brian was expecting to return to South America, but he passed away in 1915. The titles to the Colombian mining properties had been registered in John O'Brian's name to facilitate the resolution of legal matters. It was expected that the titles would be returned to the company name when those matters were settled. Because O'Brian's death occurred before that was accomplished, those titles passed into his estate and under the control of his widow. All things pertaining to the proceeds from the mines in Colombia were entrusted to Don Luis Johnson, the Colombian national who had first informed Will about mining prospects in Colombia.

SINGLE PARENT   9

WILL AND EDITH SEPARATED again. Their second divorce was apparently finalized in late 1914 or early 1915 in Grand Junction, Colorado. Years later Will wrote to a friend that if he had known Edith would not be marrying the rich doctor she had lined up, he would have "hog tied" her to the ranch.

Edith was given a property settlement but, according to Marguerite, her father was awarded custody of both daughters. Edith pled with Will until he allowed her to assume custody of Barbara while he kept Marguerite. As a condition of that concession, he insisted that neither parent should interfere in any way with the custody of the other. Will was of the opinion that it would be healthier for each daughter not to be handed back and forth from one parent to the other. Will kept his end of the bargain by pretty much ignoring Barbara during her early years.

Edith turned the raising of Barbara over to her parents, Alice and Ira Lesh, while she went to New York City to pursue a career. Edith worked for *Good Housekeeping* magazine for a time. The grandparents lived in Toledo, Ohio, while Barbara was growing up. They also spent time in Fort Myers, Florida, and Asheville, North Carolina. According to Marguerite, Alice Lesh was a very strict grandmother, and she was quite religious. Those qualities sometimes put Barbara and her grandmother at odds. Barbara was not an exceptional student, but she was good at sports and she loved to swim. She told Sissy that she sometimes sneaked out the window to take a swim after being sent to bed in Fort Meyers. Eventually, Edith remarried but she stayed on in New York, and Barbara contin-

Mirror profiles of Will Brewster, about 1912

ued to live with her grandparents. Edith's new husband's name was Ernest Sharp.

Will and Marguerite stayed on at the ranch for a time.Fred Byers, a young man Will hired in 1910, managed the ranch and its orchards. In 1915, Fred married a young woman named Minta, and they continued to live at the ranch, leaving Will free to travel and take care of his other business interests. Fred and Minta remained fast friends with Will over the years. The Byers' first child was named William, a namesake of Will Brewster.

Marguerite adored her daddy. Will often took her along on his travels. She remembered staying in hotels, especially in Chicago. Will had an active social life. Marguerite recalled times when Will was preparing to go out for the evening, and one of his girlfriends came to their hotel room to have the back of her dress fastened by him. Sissy quickly added that she never witnessed any "hanky panky." When Will had business appointments, he either had one of his girl friends babysit with Marguerite, or he dropped her off at a movie theater where she watched whatever was showing until he returned for her.

When Will's travels were such that he could not take Marguerite along, he left her with his brother Jim's family in Fort Madison or with his cousin Anna Brewster Jefferson in Rosedale, a suburb of Kansas City. Marguerite recalled going to school in Rosedale and sitting on the school steps crying for her mama. Anna had a son, Ted, who was about Marguerite's age. Marguerite was not fond of staying in the Jefferson household because Ted sometimes teased her and spied on her.

Will eventually enrolled his daughter in St. Theresa's Academy, a boarding school for girls in Kansas City. Sissy's classmates were mostly from well-to-do families. When Edith learned that Marguerite was enrolled in a Catholic school, she wrote her disapproval to Will but, of course, she had no say in the matter. Marguerite proved to be a good student and did well in school.

Will bought expensive clothes and usually dressed smartly, but he liked to dress sloppily around home. On one of his sloppy days, he dropped by Marguerite's school and waved to her at the window. "Who is that?" her classmates asked. Thinking quickly, Sissy said, "Oh! That's our gardener."

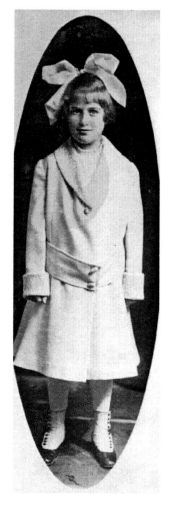

Marguerite (Sissy) Brewster, about 1912

In 1918, Edith wanted to get her two daughters together for a summer visit. Barbara was then age eleven and Marguerite would turn thirteen in the fall. Edith petitioned Will to send Marguerite east, noting that she and Barbara had not seen Marguerite for about four years. She wrote that she could not afford to bring Barbara west. Will's reply follows:

My dear Edith:

Owing to the strenuous conditions imposed by the war I find it quite impossible to send Marguerite to make you the visit this year. Very sorry to have to disappoint you, but in as much as our arrangement for the children was made over four years ago I do not feel that another year will work any greater hardship on them.

I do not write frequently to Barbara for the reason that it might have the tendency to keep her mind unsettled, and I think a few weeks vacation together would have a tendency to work more harm than good for Marguerite's home life here and her school work, and I think that we both must deny ourselves, for I, too, would love to see Barbara, but in as much as our paths lie in different directions, and our arrangements for the future of the children was made I feel that you must abide by the decision you made at the ranch in Colorado. . . I wrote my relatives at Ft. Madison before answering your letter, and they think it would be very unwise to disturb Marguerite's present condition.

I also think that you and your Mother should make your letters less frequent to Marguerite, and confine them to periods of holidays and birthdays...

Thanking you for your good wishes expressed in your letter, and I do regret very much our inability to indulge the girls in a seashore outing this year.

World War I was in progress in Europe between 1914 and 1918. Will expressed his feelings about the war effort in a letter to Mary O'Brian:

I am very glad to hear of Brian's success, and while in many ways it is heartbreaking for mothers to be called upon to give their only sons to the service of their country in this terrible war, still I am sure that in the inner recesses of your heart you must be very proud to have such a son to give, and to know that Brian has the desire and courage to go and help win world-wide democracy. Nothing would please me more than to be with the boys at the Front in France, but I am disqualified in many ways — age limit and eye sight, having been turned down twice.

An opportunity for a role in the war effort turned up near
Junction City, Kansas. Camp Funston was a training camp
with accommodations for 50,000 soldiers. A four-block-long
Federal Activity Zone was under construction there. The con-
cessions in the Zone would include restaurants, theaters, an
arcade, bowling alleys, barbershops, retail stores, tailor shops,
etc. These were being built to government specifications by
private capital.

A Junction City bank was financing the construction of a
drug store in the Zone. The store was about sixty-percent complete when a robbery occurred at the bank. While the crime
was in progress, someone recognized the robber and he went
berserk. He made everyone face the wall and he shot them all
in the back of the head. As a result of the robbery and massa-
cre, the bank was unable to continue its commitment to the
drug store on a prominent corner in Camp Funston's Federal
Activity Zone.

Will learned about the project and agreed to take over the
bank's obligation of almost five thousand dollars. He acquired
a five-year lease on the property and completed the building
according to War Department specifications. He opened the
drugstore in late 1917 after acquiring an additional loan of

**Will Brewster's drug store on a corner of the Federal Activity Zone at
Camp Funston.**

Soda fountain in Will Brewster's drug store at Camp Funston

five thousand dollars. Profits were made during the first few months after the opening. Will made payments on his bank loans during that time, but business fell off after the war ended in November of 1918. Then the government took over the Zone and promised to pay for the losses of the concessionaires. Will discontinued making payments on his loans despite frequent duns from the bank. He was waiting for the government to make good their promise, and he turned his attention to other projects. The bank responded to Will's nonpayment by repeatedly renewing the notes and compounding the interest owed.

Finally, to get the bank off his back, Will offered as collateral two pieces of real estate, a 184-acre farm in Missouri and the ranch in Colorado, along with his power of attorney to deal with the government in the reimbursement matter on his behalf. When the bank checked out the farm, they rejected it because it had a mortgage almost equal to their estimate of its value. The outcome on the ranch is not known.

What is known is that it took an act of Congress to appropriate the funds to cover the losses of the concessionaires. Congress would also determine the size of the reimbursements. In 1925, almost seven years after the government takeover of the Zone, the appropriation came through. Will's portion amounted to about $13,300, but he did not receive the money.

The check was sent to the bank because they had negotiated using Will's power of attorney. Counting all the compounded interest, the bank contended that Will owed them about $20,000.00, so they cashed the check. Will was convinced he had been wronged. As late as the 1930s Will wrote to his cousin, Ted Jefferson, asking him to inquire into the matter when he was in Washington. However, the matter was never resolved to Will's satisfaction.

EFFIE LANORE   **10**

F REDERICK JAMES WAS BORN in England. In young
adulthood he immigrated to Nebraska with two brothers. Fred
was about thirty years old when he married sixteen-year-old
Sarah Jane Dunnehue in 1876. The pair settled on a farm
near Elmwood, Nebraska. The first of their four children died
in infancy. Their three surviving offspring were Mellie, Arthur,
and Effie Lanore. Effie, who was born January 20, 1884, was
just nine months old when death claimed her father. Fred had
diabetes. He died of blood poisoning.

How was Sarah Jane to support her three young children,

Sarah and Fred James, parents of
Effie Lanore, about 1876

The James children: Effie
Lanore (front), Mellie and
Arthur, about 1886

all under the age of six years? In those days of non-mecha-
nized farming, life was hard for most families. Survival was
doubtful for a woman alone on a farm with three small children. Convention and environment heavily circumscribed the
lives of women at that time, leaving few options available.
Whether by preference or because it was the only path in sight,
Sarah Jane remarried in about 1886.

Like most of his generation, the new husband, Elijah Baggs,
was a farmer. And like Sarah Jane's first husband, he was
also an English immigrant. Elijah and Sarah Jane were thrifty
and hospitable. They had no more children, but with Sarah
Jane's three, they formed a close-knit family group. Elijah
was the only father that Effie could remember. The family
moved to Kansas in about 1895. Effie was a teenager when
they moved again, this time to Oklahoma, near Watonga, in
1899. They raised cattle and grew cotton and wheat on their
320-acre farm.

**The house built by the Baggs/James family when they moved to Oklahoma
in 1899. On the horse is Walter Maurer (husband of Mellie), Effie is on her
pony, Mellie and Sarah (mother) are standing, Arthur in the buggy and
Elijah Baggs (stepfather) with hat in hand.**

All three of the James children were small of stature. When Effie reached her full adult height she was just five feet tall. The typical life pattern for girls of her generation was to marry young and start a family. Effie's brother and sister, Arthur and Mellie, followed that tradition. They married and settled down in Oklahoma, but Effie had other ideas. She was about twenty years old when she set her sights on Kansas City. Her parents were dismayed. Elijah told his stepdaughter, "Effie, you're gonna keep flittn' around 'till you land on a cow chip!" But Effie had a mind of her own.

The Kansas City Directories provide clues to Effie's early employment. In 1904 she worked as a seamstress. In 1905 and 1906 she was employed in a dry goods store. The following year her name is missing from the directory because she was attending the Warrensburg Normal Business College. Her maternal grandparents lived in Warrensburg. That may have influenced her choice of that institution. Her work at the business college was given high praise.

When Effie returned to Kansas City in 1908, she worked as a stenographer in the office of John A. Minor, a real estate broker. His office was in the R.A. Long Building but was moved the following year to the Reliance Building at 214 East Tenth Street. Effie was eventually promoted to the position of bookkeeper.

When she came to the Kansas City, Effie quickly became a student of the conventions of polite city society. She learned the popular social dance steps of that day. Typed instructions for the Fox Trot, the One Step, the Broadway Glide, the Four Step and the Waltz Canter were found among the letters she saved on a much-worn page of J. A. Minor stationery. Pictures of Effie and her friends show her dressed in the modest high-necked, long-skirted fashions of the time. Large fancy hats were apparently the mode even on picnics and holiday outings. Property that her employer owned near the red bridge on Red Bridge Road was a favorite picnic site for Effie and her friends. Minor Park in that vicinity is probably named for Effie's employer.

Effie taking dictation from her employer, J.A. Minor.

Effie was usually a happy and optimistic person. Years later, her son described her as loving, sincere, capable, religious, practical, energetic, and talkative. He said, "She had a good sense of right and wrong, was loyal to her friends, neighborly to both strangers and friends, and charitable." Effie's nieces and nephew remembered her contagious sense of humor. She loved to hear and to tell a good joke. Effie once wrote:

> *We live in a world of defects and limitations where there is no character without a flaw and no life without its tempering of pain — bitter is mixed with the sweet. To be cheerful means to make little of the hardships we encounter ... Cheerfulness is a precious treasure.*

Effie's religious background was in the Reorganized Church of Jesus Christ of Latter Day Saints. She found fellowship among RLDS members in Kansas City. A diploma from the

International Sunday School Association credits her completion of the first standard teacher-training course. Among her papers were notes from lessons she taught and talks she delivered. Her religious observance was not limited to Sunday mornings. She was active in Religio, which usually met on Sunday evening. She defined Religio as a school for the development of Christian character, especially for the young.

Effie (left) and Dodie (also in a dark dress) with two friends in white blouses, about 1908.

The friendliness with which Effie met her world netted many friendships that were maintained over the years. There were girl friends from her business college days, from her work associations, and from her church acquaintances. Dora Lowe, whose nickname was "Dodie," was Effie's closest long-term friend. The two young women began sharing living quarters in 1910 to lighten housing expenses for each.

Dodie could be depended upon to carry her share of their financial obligations and household chores. Those are qualities that Effie also demonstrated. The two became like sisters. Dodie was taller and more reserved than Effie. Both were in their middle twenties and still single. Both were more independent than were most women of their day. Dodie was a talented seamstress, a skill she used to support herself. Though Dodie and Effie were very different, their personalities complemented each other.

There were boyfriends, too. In 1906, a friend from Effie's church "set his cap" for her, but she must not have shared his ardor. Later, there was Edwin. His letters present a mystery, tempting one to read between the lines. Edwin obviously thought he was very much in love with Effie, but something happened to cause her to distrust him. In December of 1910 he wrote to her from a hospital where he was a patient:

> *Your two letters came as a great shock to me and as I am situated now I can say nothing. The real situation is somewhat peculiar and will not bear explanation in a letter but I will say this, "I have never been married." Whether or not I am suffering now for past follies, that I alone must judge ... You may lead the Dr. to believe that you called up regarding me simply as a casual friend ... To say that I am deeply grieved expresses my feelings inadequately.*

The next day he wrote:

> *I think you will find that you can tell the folks at the house that I have offended you and drop me that way.*

Effie Lanore James, age 25

Edwin had borrowed money from both Effie and Dodie, so his correspondence continued for several years while he paid it back a little at a time. Apparently, whatever was troubling him was serious enough that Effie did not want to continue their relationship. Though both Effie and Dodie were near an age at which they might have been branded "old maids," neither was ready to enter a marriage just to be married.

The Kansas City Directories again give clues to when Effie may have met Will Brewster. In 1910 the office for his Midland Investment Company was in the Reliance Building where Effie worked. Since Will was dealing in real estate and Effie's boss was a real estate broker in the same building, it seems natural that Will would seek assistance from the Minor firm. Surely Will's and Effie's paths crossed in the line of business. However, it has been reported that Will dated Dodie before he became interested in Effie. Perhaps Dodie had done sewing or alterations on Will's wardrobe. It is not known whether Will's introduction to Effie was through business contacts or through his acquaintance with Dodie.

Will's business interests (and perhaps his adventurous nature) kept him traveling — out west exploring mining projects, visiting, and attending to business in Fort Madison, Chicago, and elsewhere. He corresponded with Luis Johnson and others to keep in touch with his Colombian gold mines, though such communication was slow and unsatisfying. The abstract of title for Will's subdivision in Kansas City contains a document signed in 1916 by Wm. J. Brewster, president of the Midland Investment Company and E. L. James, secretary.

Letters indicate that Will was courting Effie in 1916. This courtship appears different from Will's prior ones. It lasted longer for one thing. He courted Effie for at least two years. A desire for them to be together is evident in Will's letters to Effie, but his letters also include matters of business as well as requests for Effie to check on his daughter, Marguerite, who was attending St. Theresa's Academy. They were building a partnership in which Effie would share Will's business concerns as well as his personal life.

Will was in his early fifties but, by all reports, he appeared and acted younger. He was still a charmer and he loved to tease. Effie was in her early thirties. Years later Effie chuckled as she recalled that the uninhibited Will would sometimes start clowning as they walked down the street together. Rather than show embarrassment on those occasions, she said she simply stood off a few paces and stared at him as if she had no idea who that crazy person was.

Will retained ownership of the home at 3423 Charlotte in Kansas City. While he was at Camp Funston near Junction City, Kansas, in 1917 and 1918, Effie and Dodie lived in his Charlotte Street house. After Will and Effie were married on April 10, 1918, Effie joined Will at Camp Funston and helped him run his drugstore there. When the government took over the Federal Activity Zone at Camp Funston, Will and Effie returned to Kansas City and were at home at 3423 Charlotte. With the exception of part of 1918, Dodie continued to live with them until her marriage to Fred Lowd in about 1923. The Brewsters and the Lowds continued a relationship that was more like family than casual friends.

The newlyweds at home at 3423 Charlotte

THE LONG-AWAITED SON AND HEIR   **11**

UPON THE RETURN OF the newlyweds from Camp Funston to Kansas City, Effie turned her attention to homemaking. Her thirteen-year-old stepdaughter, Marguerite, had missed being mothered and Effie began filling in the blanks in Marguerite's training for domestic tasks, personal hygiene, and social conventions. The relationship between stepmother and stepdaughter was close and affectionate and remained so throughout their lives.

The South American mines did not produce much for Will and his La Clara Placer and Mines Company between 1910 and 1920. World War I, personal matters, and other business concerns absorbed Will's focus. The death of John O'Brian left their mining affairs in disarray. In a letter to Mrs. O'Brian on July 17, 1918, Will wrote:

> *I have been very much occupied with some very hard swimming to keep my head above the war crisis, having been caught with considerable non-productive real estate, and together with taxes, has just about pulled me under. If I had the $30, 000, which I sank in S. A. it would certainly come in handy, but I fear that I will have to consider that investment practically a total loss.*
>
> *Should you have any encouraging news from Luis Johnson relative to the LaClara please write me.*

Don Luis Johnson, the Colombian citizen entrusted with business matters related to the company's mining interests in Colombia, continued to put off making an accounting of the proceeds of the mines that came through his hands. A letter

Will wrote to Don Luis on July 19, 1919, highlighting some of the muddle in management and communication at that time:

> *Regarding the matter of O'Brian dictating to you the dis-*
> *position of the company's property, funds, or receipts ... he had*
> *no authority from the company to do this ... You mentioned in*
> *your letter that you were waiting for a list of the stockholders*
> *in order to enable you to properly distribute the royalties that*
> *were going to be paid in. You will understand that this is a*
> *matter for the LaClara Corporation to apportion ...*
>
> *I hope to have the pleasure of seeing you this fall and*
> *when I arrive we will try to straighten out the affairs of the*
> *LaClara Placer Mines Company.*

It is doubtful that Will ever made that trip to South America in the fall of 1919 to check on his mines. Effie was expecting their first child. Will was probably on hand for the birth of their daughter on Effie's thirty-sixth birthday, January 20, 1920. They named her Billie. She was born at home, but she lived only one day. She was a "blue baby," so called due to a purplish-blue complexion caused by a scarcity of oxygen in the blood. Sadly, Will and Effie buried their first-born on January 22 in the Forest Hill Cemetery in an infant plot, block 16 lot 4 space 17, located close to the intersection of Seventy-first Street and Troost Avenue in Kansas City, Missouri. The grave has no marker today.

With her childbearing years waning, Effie soon became pregnant again. Will did not appear to be excited about the impending birth. He was fifty-five years old. He wanted a son, but he had fathered only girls. No longer trusting a home birth, Effie entered the old St. Joseph Hospital on Linwood Boulevard. The long-awaited son and heir was born there on February 19, 1921. Will and Effie were agreed that the baby should be named William after his father, but Effie favored James for a middle name while Will voted for DeForest. Effie's choice related to her maiden name and to Will's brother's name. However, when Effie learned that the ancestral name DeForest might entitle their son to a scholarship at Yale University the decision was made. They were not then aware that DeForest had to be the sur-name — not just the given name with DeForest lineage — to claim that endowment.

Young William DeForest was called Billy, which was shortened to Bill in his teen years. He was the instant de-light not only of his parents but also of his fifteen-year-old half-sister, Marguerite, and of his childless "Aunt" Dodie who lived with the family. Bill ex-plained years later that he was a child with three mother figures — Effie, Marguerite,

Billy Brewster, age 1 year, one of many photos taken during his early childhood.

and Dodie — and a father who seemed more like a grandfa-ther. Billy immediately became the most doted upon and of-ten-photographed child imaginable. He was registered on the "cradle roll" at Effie's church and was taken to Sunday school as soon as he was old enough to be in one of the classes.

After the end of World War I, Kansas City had continued to expand to the south and east toward Swope Park. The open-ing and widening of both Fifty-ninth Street and Prospect Av-enue made the twenty-acre tract of land that Will had bought — between Fifty-eighth and Fifty-ninth Streets and east from Prospect — prime for development. During the 1920s, he di-vided the property into building lots and named the subdivi-sion Brewster's Grove. An alleyway was plotted between Pros-pect and the next street east, which is Montgall. Apparently, Will sold some of the lots and began building on others. Bun-galows facing Prospect Avenue were among the first to rise. In 1922, Will moved his family into the house at 5823 Pros-

The house Will Brewster had built for his family in Brewster's Grove at 5828 Montgall.

pect. This house was smaller than the family home at 3423 Charlotte, but it had the advantage of being on site for Will to supervise other construction in progress in Brewster's Grove.

Prominent among Will's plans for Brewster's Grove was a new Brewster family residence. He reserved for it four lots on Montgall and two adjacent lots on Prospect. The spacious two-story Dutch colonial home at 5828 Montgall was completed in 1925, and the family moved there from the bungalow on Prospect. A Brewster coat-of-arms was sculpted and mounted on the exterior wall beneath the peak of the front porch roof. On the first floor were formal living and dining rooms along with a music room, a kitchen and breakfast room and a half bath. There were three bedrooms, a bathroom and a wide sleeping porch upstairs. Will had a garage with a loft built behind the house. It was large enough to provide parking space for a car and storage for extra lumber and other building supplies. The house no longer exists. The property was cleared in the 1980s to make way for the Bruce Watkins Freeway.

Billy attended the J. J. Pershing Elementary School at Fifty-ninth and Park Streets. He was forbidden to cross Prospect Avenue except on school days when a policeman was on duty to see students safely across. Many of Bill's childhood memories involved the one square block area bounded by Prospect and Montgall between Fifty-eighth and Fifty-ninth Streets. The extra lots that Will reserved provided space for a garden and a large play area. Billy and his friends played baseball and football under the large elm tree that dominated the area between the back of the house and Prospect.

In the decades of the 1920s and 1930s, small neighborhood stores were common. Three of these — grocery, drug, and dry goods stores — occupied the northeast corner of Fifty-ninth and Prospect. Bobby Briggs, whose family operated the dry goods store and lived in the same building, was one of Billy's playmates. The Kemp family lived in a house behind the drugstore of which they were proprietors. Bill remembered that Effie considered LaRue Kemp a naughty little girl. He said, "Mom didn't want me going into any garage with LaRue. I went into our garage with her once, and did I ever get my legs switched. I don't remember what we did."

Other neighborhood playmates were Roy Wilhelmsen whose family home faced Prospect Avenue. Jenny Wilhelmsen, Roy's mother, was a trusted friend to Effie and a mentor to Billy. Lloyd Broyles, whose father was a doctor, lived nearby. The kids' nickname for Lloyd was "Doc" because his father wanted him to become a doctor. However, Lloyd chose a career in forestry instead. Billy also had a faithful canine playmate named Rex. A cranky widow lady lived between the Kemps and the Brewsters on Montgall. She got after the kids when their ball went into her yard. On Halloween they played tricks on her by sneaking up to her door, ringing her doorbell and running to hide. When she came to the door, there was no one in sight.

Effie was a charter member of the Linwood Child Conservation Club. Its members were young mothers who met monthly to socialize and to study child-rearing methods. The members became lifelong friends, sharing the joys and sorrows of each. They continued to meet long after their children were grown — approximately from 1922 to 1972. The Linwood Club was credited for inspiring some of the training in

social graces and table manners that Billy received. He learned
how and when to use not only the knife, fork, spoon, and linen
napkins but also the salad fork, grapefruit spoon, iced-tea
spoon, etc. He was taught at an early age to be courteous and
to try to think of the needs of others first. (Always say "please,
thank-you, and may I." Pass the cookies to others first and
serve yourself last.) Those kinds of attitudes and forms of behavior became second nature as he grew.

Effie was diligent in her parenting role. She taught her son
how to do household chores such as dusting and sweeping.
Billy's early lessons in economics involved peddling brown bread
that his mother baked. When he returned home with his proceeds, they made an accounting. After he paid for Effie's ingre-
dients, he was allowed to keep the profit. Bill once wrote of his
childhood, "Mom was a trainer of children. I always had chores
around the house. I had limits to observe in time and space."

Bill remembered times spent with his dad, like being taken
to the "picture show" just a block south on Prospect. Will challenged Billy to a footrace on the way and Billy loved it. Admis-
sion cost ten cents and the movie included cartoons as well as
the feature. On occasion, Will took his son downtown in Kansas City to attend to business errands and visit Marguerite at
her work. The two stopped at a small bar and delicatessen on
Twelfth Street called Wachters where they enjoyed a sandwich and Will had a beer.

Will took Billy, and sometimes the rest of the family, on
camping trips in Missouri's Ozarks. They traveled in a tour-
ing car that had panels with isinglass windows. Most of the
roads on which they drove were dirt or surfaced only with
gravel. Creeks, lacking bridges, had to be forded. Road conditions were sometimes scary to a young boy. Billy remembered
the car sliding down a hill on a muddy road. The brakes were
hot when they came to rest at the bottom. Will drove into the
creek and stopped, presumably to cool off the brakes.

On one of those memorable outings, Billy was allowed to
bring a buddy along. On their way, Will hailed a farmer who
was headed for market with a load of watermelons. At the

campsite, he set the purchased melon in the cold water of the Osage River to chill. They pitched their tent and a cook fly on property owned by one of Will's friends. They draped netting over themselves and their cots to bar mosquitoes from biting them as they slept. Will bathed in the stream wearing just his BVDs (undershirt and under shorts all in one piece). He served up meals that he cooked under primitive conditions. The boys explored the creek and ran about the camp playing their games. Billy's friend ran into one of the tent ropes and was "knocked silly." Will monitored the situation and the boy recovered before long. Billy acquired his love of camping and outdoor cooking on those outings.

Among Bill's childhood memories were trips to the farm near Watonga, Oklahoma, to visit his maternal grandparents. On one occasion, a four-wheeled trailer loaded with furniture for Effie's folks was pulled behind the family car. Trailers and their hitches did not always function well in those days. Billy was assigned to watch out the back window of the car and to alert his dad when the trailer began to sway.

Being the only child among older adults, Billy sometimes became bored when visiting on the farm. Grandpa Baggs once entertained Billy by funneling water into cricket holes in the barnyard so they could watch the crickets come out. When they went into Watonga to purchase a Coca Cola, Billy stood in the middle of the one-block-long main street and wanted to know where was the town.

In contrast to trips to the Oklahoma farm were visits to the paternal relatives in Fort Madison. Located on the banks of the Mississippi River in the southeast corner of Iowa, Fort Madison had become a prosperous railroad hub. Jim Brewster and his family lived in a large, comfortable two-story home. Bill remembered his Uncle Jim as a serious, kindly, reliable man. Jim Brewster was president of a bank and a prominent citizen.

Jim's wife, Aunt Daisy, was said to be "uppity" and to "put on airs." Bill recalled that Aunt Daisy had a facial twitch that was "sometimes violent enough to scare the pants off me." Apparently, Daisy was not especially fond of her brother-in-law, Will. She characterized Will as a "male butterfly," probably because he had flitted into three marriages and out of two of them. Jim's handicapped adult son Charley lived with his father and stepmother. Jim's daughter Starr and her husband also lived in Fort Madison.

Billy preferred to be in the company of Angela, the maid and cook, rather than with Aunt Daisy. Angela was "a simple, orphaned country girl" of German ancestry. She had come to serve the Jim Brewster family when she was still in her teens. She was a loyal, capable servant. Bill remembered Angela's good sense of humor and the bountiful meals she prepared.

Will, Effie, and Billy occasionally spent outings in a retreat owned by Uncle Jim, and sometimes Angela and cousin Charley went along. The cabin was built on stilts on a raised bit of land adjacent to the Mississippi River. Driving through the foot or so of backwater that surrounded the cottage was scary to Billy. Angela kept the cabin's one big all-purpose room and two bedrooms clean and comfortable. There were lots of big frogs "the size of a teapot" in the waters near the cabin. They went "frogging" at night with one person rowing the boat, another holding a large lantern and a third managing a bamboo pole. With experience, one could spot a frog when the light was pointed where the weeds and water met. The frog would stay put with the light shining in its eyes. A hook on the line from the pole was lowered under the frog's chin and jerked up. Bill remembered the frog legs that Angela cooked were very tasty. She also introduced him to turtle meat. Bill once said, "Angela liked to show me new things."

The Brewster family in the late 1920s, Effie, Billy, Will and Marguerite

BUSINESS STRESSES 12

WILL'S BUSINESS PURSUITS DID not produce robust returns during the decade of the 1920s. Taxes and mortgages related to his real estate holdings including those in Brewster's Grove were often complicated. Lots were sold or offered as collateral for construction and other loans. Titles were shifted from one relative or investor to another. Some statements of back taxes owed were disputed because the taxing authority did not have the current owner on its records. Even the punctilious Effie was frustrated trying to straighten out and keep up with the complex array of Will's business dealings.

Amos T. Maxwell (Mac) was a friend of Will's with roots in Oklahoma. Mac had apparently worked with Will on various ventures. It is probable that Will introduced Maxwell to mining prospects in Colombia. On July 16, 1920, Maxwell wrote to Will from Medillin, Colombia, that he was sending a package of deeds. He also told of numerous mining sites he was learning about, some of which he thought might interest Will.

Don Luis Johnson had not met Amos Maxwell but something stirred him to action. He finally made an accounting in November, 1920, showing income from the La Clara mine for two prior five-year periods. He reported $32,040.49 in gold taken from the mine between 1910 to 1915, and $39,188.53 between 1915 to 1920. All of the proceeds were reported to have gone to defray mining expenses and to pay amounts that were owed to John O'Brian's widow.

In 1922, Don Luis wrote that he would see to the transfer of the La Clara titles to Will's company but he did not follow through on that commitment. Titles to the mines remained in John O'Brian's name and lawsuits related to titles and water rights continued. Will's brother Jim and others in Fort Madison who were involved in the La Clara Placer and Mining Company were disillusioned by the haphazard way the business of the Colombian mines was handled.

Will's former father-in-law, Ira Lesh, died in 1922 or 1923. The widow, Alice, wrote to Will about several business matters related to property she and her husband owned — forty shares of stock in the La Clara mine, real estate lots in McAllister, Oklahoma, and five lots in Sault Ste. Marie, Michigan. Will replied with suggestions about the land and encouragement that the La Clara stock would soon be paying something to stockholders.

Will gathered from Alice's letter that his sixteen-year-old daughter Barbara was becoming a financial burden to her grandmother, and he suggested that Barbara come to Kansas City to make her home with the Brewster family. He made this proposal to the grandmother rather than to Edith, Barbara's mother, since Alice was the one who had made a home for Barbara "these many years." He asked Alice to give the matter serious and unselfish consideration.

A cousin wrote to Marguerite that Alice had a complete mental breakdown resulting from grief suppression. The letter reported that Edith went to Toledo to try to make arrangements for her mother, but Alice refused help. Edith took Barbara back to New York with her. In response to that news, Will wrote to Edith, addressing her as "My dear Mrs. Sharp" and expressing appreciation that Edith was taking a personal interest in Barbara by taking her into Edith's own home. He had gathered from Alice's letters that Edith had not been in a position to do this earlier. He reiterated the offer made to Alice that Barbara come to Kansas City to visit or to live with him and his family, but his offer was not accepted.

Edith tried again that summer of 1923 to get Will to send Marguerite East to spend a month or so with her and Barbara. She chided Will for his inattention to Barbara. She wrote, "Barbara is just about the prettiest, most attractive girl I have ever seen and you would be very proud of her." It is not known whether Will sent Marguerite that summer, but the sisters did have some limited exposure to each other during their late teens and young adult years.

Will's friend Mac was again in Colombia in 1928 looking into the mining situation and reporting to Will. Will evidently asked Mac to look into matters surrounding the La Clara mine. Maxwell met Don Luis Johnson in January, 1929, before checking out the mine. Mac reported to Will from La Clara on January 31 that the La Clara Placer and Mines Company was not recognized in Colombia. The name O'Brian was recognized because the company's properties were still titled in O'Brian's name. Maxwell recounted a tangled eighteen-year history of claims and lawsuits relating to the mines.

Will's finances were stretched, and he needed the income that he believed the Colombian mines should supply. He was planning a South American trip to talk to Johnson in person and to check on the mines. He had evidently turned to his brother Jim for capital many times. It appears that he may have asked Effie to write to Jim for financial backing for this trip. Jim replied on December 20, 1928, as follows:

Dear Effie:

I am in receipt of your favor of December 18 and in reply would say I have made arrangements to borrow $5,000.00. Which is all the credit I am allowed but I had to take up a note of Will's for $1,000.00 dated August 31st, 1928, and I am sending you the balance which is $4,000.00. This is the best I can do.

I am sorry that you cannot go with Will to South America for I think you have a better business head than he and if there is anything in the South American deal you might bring home the money. I am skeptical about the whole business but if he thinks he can get some money out of his mines, O.K.

Whether due to Jim's urging, or other incentives, changes were made to include Effie and Billy in Will's trip plans. At the time, Will was 63 years old and Effie was 45. To Effie, who had never traveled far, the distance and the ocean voyage seemed daunting. She dreaded leaving loved ones and friends behind. She knew little of what she might encounter, and the language barrier seemed formidable. Though they regretted interrupting Billy's school year, Effie would not leave him behind. Billy regretted leaving his dog, Rex, and his neighborhood buddies; but he was flexible and ready for adventure.

Marguerite wanted to go along but, it was decided that she should stay, at least until it was known how long Will would need to remain in Colombia. She was twenty-three years old, still living at home with her folks and working as a secretary for the Aetna Insurance Company. Will and Effie would depend on Marguerite to take care of their personal business at home while they were absent. She would collect rents, and they would advise her by letter about the selling of one of the houses in Brewster's Grove and the payment of taxes and interest on various properties and loans.

Arrangements were made to rent the family home to a Mrs. Adcock, her son, and three of the son's friends during their absence. One room was reserved for Marguerite. Effie, always concerned about propriety, cautioned Marguerite against "foolishness" regarding the young men in the house and she depended upon Mrs. Adcock and her close neighbor, Jenny Wilhelmsen, to chaperone. Having that many eligible young bachelors so near at hand made Marguerite the envy of her girl friends who were also single.

Effie packed thirteen pieces of luggage, including two steamer trunks and all of Billy's school books. She assigned Billy the job of counting their luggage whenever they transferred from one form of transportation to another. She warned him to be especially watchful of the wicker bag because it was full of canned food and special treats. (No telling what kind of food they would find in a foreign land.)

In later years Bill explained that steamer trunks were so named because they were used for long trips on steam-powered trains or steamships. Plastics and synthetic materials such as nylon were not yet available in those days. Bill described their steamer trunks in this way:

The steamer trunks were metal-covered with extra heavy brass corners to stand up to rough handling. They had sturdy leather handles on each end, and were hinged in the middle. The inside of the trunks were wood boxing covered with cloth. They stood on end when opened, thus creating two compartments — one for hanging clothes, the other with three drawers for folded clothes. Mom's rule number one: Never put liquids in the steamer trunk. You put your best clothes in there.

THE VOYAGE 13

WILL, EFFIE AND BILLY left Kansas City by train on February 5, 1929. Effie mailed a postcard home during a two-hour layover in Memphis before they bedded down in the Pullman coach on the night train to New Orleans. Effie wrote letters in great detail about what she wore, the food they ate, the people they met, and scenes along the way that were new to her. She wrote, "I like New Orleans better than any strange place I was ever in." She described it as the quaintest place with little narrow streets, funny little shops, 250-year-old buildings, and "lovely" cemeteries with above ground burials. She loved the unfamiliar accents of the local speech and marveled at the pretty green yards during that winter season when things were drab at home. She sent perfume made from magnolia blossoms to Marguerite.

Will took Billy along when he visited an oyster bar in New Orleans. Years later Bill described that event as follows:

The [oyster] bar was housed in a small building like a carnival booth — one side was folded open. A customer could walk up to the bar that filled the open side with a brass rail for the feet like bars of the old West of the 1800s. Behind the bar were several men cracking open oysters on order of the customer. The oysters were served raw on the half-shell with condiments such as Worcestershire sauce, Tobasco sauce, etc. Most eaters of raw oysters do not chew them. They shake on the sauce then, using a small two-pronged fork, put the freshly opened oyster shell to their mouth, hook the fork into the oyster to push it into the mouth, and swallow it whole — an experience I only tried once, but Dad ate his dozen.

On February 9, the three Brewsters and 20 other passengers boarded the *S. S. Suriname*, of the "Great White Fleet" owned by the United Fruit Company Steamship Service. These ships carried passengers to various Caribbean ports and brought cargoes of bananas and coffee back to the United States. Fog delayed their departure until late in the day. Effie was disappointed that darkness veiled the scenery on the hundred-mile route to the Gulf of Mexico. She was impressed with the food aboard ship (crabmeat au gratin for dinner the first night) and the way the stewards strove to please the passengers. At daybreak, they began to see dolphins and flying fish and great flocks of white pelicans.

After they left the mouth of the Mississippi River, the water suddenly turned from a greenish color to blue black, like ink, as if there were a line between the two colors. As the ship rose and fell in rough twelve to eighteen-foot waves, Billy and Effie were plagued with seasickness, but Will continued to eat three square meals a day without discomfort. While Effie reclined in a deck chair nursing her queasiness, Billy played between intermittent bouts of nausea. Will used the time to study his Spanish.

Their fellow passengers were friendly, especially the Friday family that included a ten-year-old boy who played with Billy. Dr. Friday, a U. S. Government employee, was stationed in the Panama Canal Zone at Balboa. On board also was a woman from Tennessee who kept them all laughing. A young woman in the next cabin was attractive and had a following of several of the men on board. Once she stayed out all night attending a "drunken pajama party" which set the other passengers' "tongues wagging."

Will and Effie gathered information about current conditions in Colombia from two of the passengers who lived and worked there. One young man, who would also be going up river on the Magdelena, told them the riverboats were dirty, the beds were poor, and the food was poor. They were advised to take their own water and drinking cups. With tips to all the stewards, they could expect to pay about $70 per person

United Fruit Company steamship

to go up river. (They had planned to pay only $50.) Dry weather could extend the river trip from the usual seven days to two or three weeks. Medellin was reported to be the only decent place to live in Colombia.

With her seasickness, back pain aggravated by the motion of the ship, and bad news about conditions ahead in Colombia, Effie was having second thoughts about the trip. She wrote, "I would be satisfied to just see the good old U.S.A." She wanted no more boat rides, even for pleasure. She wished they could afford the eight-hour plane trip up river instead of the riverboat. Effie was thinking they might try to return home sooner than planned.

They docked in the breakwater at Cristobal, Panama, late at night on February 13 but had to wait for a doctor to come aboard for an inspection before passengers could debark the next morning. Effie reported that her stomach soon righted itself when the ship stopped moving. Billy was busy taking in all the new sights and sounds and wandering as far as Effie's watchful eye would allow. He saw natives loading bananas on to a United Fruit Company ship. Each worker carried a huge cluster of the fruit, his bare back protected from his abrasive burden only by a burlap sack. Billy was startled when one of the bearers suddenly threw his load to the ground. Listening, he learned the man had discovered a scorpion among the bananas he was carrying.

Will had shipped freight that did not arrive in New Or-

THE VOYAGE   83

leans in time to get aboard the *S. S. Suriname* with them. Included among the freight items were a stove, a large trunk full of tools and work clothes, and a "grafanola" with records to help them study the Spanish language. Using the ship's radio, Will learned that his freight would arrive in Barranquilla, Colombia, on February 22. So he scheduled their passage to Colombia for February 21 which allowed them a weeklong sightseeing stay in Panama.

Dr. Friday and his family were especially friendly and hospitable during that week in Panama.They invited the Brewsters on a drive with them around Cristobal and Colon. Effie described houses built up off the ground for air circulation with children's playgrounds and parking space under the houses. After the drive, they accompanied the Fridays across the isthmus by train to Balboa, a distance of 45 or 50 miles. In Balboa they were able to stay in a room that a friend of Dr. Friday made available for $10 for the week. They felt fortunate because both the Atlantic and Pacific U. S. fleets were in the area for biannual maneuvers, and the hotels were crowded and charging higher rates than usual — $7 to $12 per day.

Effie's optimism returned as she enjoyed the majestic palm trees and the tropical flowers and fruits of Panama. The relaxed pace of life and the friendly transplanted Americans in the Canal Zone made her think it might not be a bad place to live. As they watched large ships go through the locks, they were amazed at the engineering feat that was the Panama Canal. Walking across a bridge over the locks scared Billy and made Effie's knees shaky. They were taken on drives through Panama and visited an old cathedral with an impressive gold altar. Effie noted a sad contrast between living conditions in old Panama and the rich quality of life in the Canal Zone with its deluxe facilities.

Billy had a very uncomfortable eighth birthday in the Canal Zone on February 19. The reason for his discomfort is told in Effie's words written the next day to Marguerite and Dodie:

Billy went in swimming yesterday. I told him he must not

go in unless his Daddy was going along and he said he was, so I went on over to Mrs. Friday's and ate lunch, thinking Daddy was looking after Billy. After lunch I came back home and found Dad lying down and had never been with Billy. I was peeved at Dad and Bill both, Billy for storying and Dad for not taking care of him. I hurried on over to the pool and Billy was still in — 4^1/$_2$ hours — with sun boiling. I hustled him out, but he is terribly sunburned ... I greased him good with face cream, his legs and arms, and shoulders are awful. I put him in bed and he is still in bed today — kind of a poor way to spend his birthday ... I guess it will teach him a lesson, but rather dear.

On February 21 they went back across the Canal Zone to Cristobal where Will had booked a second class cabin on the French liner Pellerin de La Touche. Effie objected to those accommodations, and she upgraded to first class for herself and Billy. Will remained in second class, and he dreaded what was ahead for Effie. If she thought the second class cabins on this ship were poor, what would she think of the accommodations on the riverboat? Again, rough seas brought on seasickness for Effie and Billy. In her nausea, Effie was made nervous by the chatter in French, Syrian, and Spanish around her, none of which she understood.

They docked at Puerto Colombia, fourteen miles by rail from Barranquilla. Dredging, in progress at the mouth of the Rio Magdelena, would eventually enable large steamships to dock at Barranquilla, but not yet. Effie described Puerto Colombia as "a god-forsaken place with sand streets and white concrete houses with grass roofs." She noted that a goat or a native on a mule with a barrel on each side of the mule was a common sight on the street. "Little Italy or 18th Street [in Kansas City] are magnificent in comparison." She judged the population of Puerto Colombia at 1000, while Barranquilla had 130,000.

When they came off the ship, there were many Colombians "hollering" in Spanish to carry their luggage and, of course, get a tip. Will was off somewhere checking on the status of his freight shipment. Effie was always conscious of their limited financial reserves. The clamor and the strange language of porters all about her wanting to handle her bags was upsetting. Finally, a hotel employee who spoke both Spanish and English rescued their bags and guided them to the "dinky" car and train that took them to Barranquilla. He directed them to the Hotel Inglesia where Will had stayed years before. Effie wrote:

> *I must tell you of a little incident I saw on the train — a woman with her tiny baby were on the train. The baby had no diaper on, only a little knitted coat. I kept wondering just what would happen as the baby kept nursing most of the time, mother's breast exposed all the time, so I didn't wait long before I saw. It began to wet and the mother held it right out in the isle with its little knitted coat held up until it got through ... There was a very dignified young man sitting facing this lady ... He was Swiss. I am sure he must have wished he were anywhere but there. He looked out of the window most of the time. The mother must have been used to doing this as she didn't act like that was anything [unusual].*

The Hotel Inglesia was an old converted mansion on the outskirts of Barranquilla. They learned too late that two other, more modern hotels in the city would have been a cheaper, more comfortable choice. Effie thought some young man just beginning to shave would have been proud to have a mustache like the one on the old English lady who ran the hotel. The chambermaid who could have been "Methuselah's wife — old and wrinkled as a witch," spoke only Spanish. Effie could not understand her but guessed she was a "good old soul." Effie thought the grounds of the hotel might be beautiful in the rainy season but everything was covered with dust because the dry season was in progress.

The interior of the hotel left much to be desired. Effie wrote that the rooms were terrible looking — walls of "compo" board, the "hardest looking old furniture," and floors of wide pine boards covered with a square of linoleum. The beds were lumpy and sagged in the middle like hammocks. The windows had no glass or curtains, only shutters. Large mosquito netting hung from the ceiling to cover the beds.

The dining room was an open porch with "the rattiest looking old tables with dirty table cloths." Flies had first choice of the food while the mosquitoes dined on the diners. Effie was so bitten by mosquitoes as she sat at breakfast that she had to escape to their room, take off her stockings, and dot herself with "Mercurochrome."

From the veranda of the hotel, Effie watched four women washing clothes in a place about ten feet square like a small swimming pool. They had large wooden tubs and were washing their clothes in cold water with soap and lots of elbow grease. One bathed her baby along with the clothes, then nursed it and put it to sleep naked on a mat on the grass. The clothes were spread on the grass to dry while the winds continued to blow dust over all. Another woman heated several irons on live coals and used them to press the clothes. Effie assumed the women had never seen a washing machine or an electric iron. It reinforced her opinion that the "good old USA" was luxurious and a land of "milk and honey."

Their freight had arrived in Barranquilla but getting it cleared of red tape for the trip up river proved a lengthy process. They opted to continue their journey and have the freight sent along later. The mounting costs of the trip and the uncertainty of pay-off from the mines were a constant concern. Effie believed the course of their future rested on the financial outcome of their trip.

They were able to book passage on a boat that carried mail. It was smaller than most of the riverboats — fifteen or twenty cabins for passengers. Only one other woman was on board. The heat on the river was oppressive. They had unwittingly booked the cabin just above the ship's galley. The heat rising from the mammoth cook stove made the air in their cabin stifling. The low water level made it unsafe to navigate after dark, so they tied up at night. Will arranged for a cot on an upper deck while Effie and Billy tried to sleep in the cabin. However, the last two nights mother and son escaped to cots on the top deck where the officers' quarters were located. About twelve or fourteen men were also sleeping there. Effie wrote:

One good old Papa Jew, with whom I had previously talked, saw I was rather nervous about sleeping in an open room with so many strange men with only a mosquito net over me, told me not to be afraid that he would watch out for me, and I believe he was the loudest in the chorus of snorers. He told me the next morning that he kept his eye open all the time for me. I had to smile to myself, but told him that I felt real safe with him there.

The river trip was not easy, though it was not the dire hardship they were led to expect. Effie was grateful not to be troubled with seasickness. She found encouragement among passengers and crew as she worked on her Spanish.

I talked and studied Spanish all along the way. I would say a noun or verb, throw in a lot of motions with my hands and do some gymnastics and they would supply the rest and laugh at me, but we had a good time.

Sternwheeler on the Magdalena River

Sights along the riverbank included several larger riverboats stuck on sandbars waiting for rains to raise the water level and lift them off. Little native huts made of mud with grass roofs dotted the landscape here and there. Men without shirts, and naked babies and children were commonplace. Most went barefoot or wore slippers with soles and toe covering (no heels) of twisted grass. Effie wrote:

> *I hardly see how they keep [those slippers] on ... Some of the worst looking feet you ever saw. They would make you sick at your stomach. They do not look like feet anymore, toes stubbed or broken off, and bottoms of feet look worse than the thickest old piece of leather ... One boy about nine years old came down with many others to see the boat come in to a little village and, while standing there before the boat and all the other natives, urinated.*

Effie was shocked that the boy seemed unconcerned about doing so.

Prevalent attitudes toward race in the United States in the 1920s are evident in Effie's observations. She was astonished when a black man, with whom Will had some business, shook hands with Will and acted "as if he were an equal." She was surprised when she observed a white man with "lovely manners" sitting and talking to a "Negro" woman. However, it did not seem to bother Effie that Billy made friends with a black boy who worked at their hotel in Barranquilla. She wrote:

> *White looking people seem to mix with the blacks ... I don't understand. There must not be any class distinction, only between the rich and the poor. I must keep my mouth shut and eyes and ears open. The people who looked like Negroes to me ate at the same table as the rest of the people.*

On the riverboat, the Brewsters had the good fortune to meet a young Spanish man, Eduardo Greiffenstein, who

Native thatch-roofed huts, naked toddler in the doorway

worked in Barranquilla and was headed home to Medellin for a visit after a three-year absence. He was fluent in both Spanish and English and translated for them. When they arrived in Puerto Berrio on March 2, Eduardo arranged for the transport of their luggage to the hotel and negotiated the hotel bill and the necessary tips to baggage handlers for them.

The train ride to Medellin was in two parts. Eduardo's family met him at Limon, where they all transferred to an auto to get over the mountain to Santiago and the final leg of their trip by rail to Medellin. It was customary for friends or family to meet travelers on the way and travel the last leg of the journey with them. Don Luis offered to meet the Brewsters at Limon, but they declined that offer and asked that he just meet them when the train arrived in Medellin, which he did.

The Brewster family and Eduardo's family got acquainted on the train from Santiago to Medellin. The father ran a hardware store in Medellin and had sold supplies to the McGuires who were leasing Will's La Clara mines. Eduardo had two sisters, ages 8 and 14, and two brothers, ages 17 and 20. The twenty-year-old had studied in Indiana for a time and was eager to return to the United States, much to the consternation of his parents. Effie was impressed by the demonstrated affection of the parents toward Eduardo and his siblings. The mother did not speak English, but she was friendly and invited the Brewsters to come to tea one day soon.

MEDELLIN 14

THE JOURNEY FROM Kansas City to Medellin, Colombia, South America, took a full month. What a relief it was to enter the pleasant climate of Medellin after the heat of the river and the lowlands! The weather was delightful — quite cool at night and comfortable during the day. Will wrote:

> *We had a fine night's rest after our tiresome journey. It was hot as hell on the Magdelena River at Puerto Berrio last night but it is cool and fine here — had to have blankets.*

The Hotel Bristol in Medellin boasted of "all the comfort of the best European and American hotels." Its beds actually had bedsprings, not just wooden slats or canvas as was common in other local accommodations. Effie described the five courses that were served at each meal in the hotel dining room and worried about what they would do to her waistline. The portico outside their room offered a view of great mountains to the east and to the west.

Effie reported that Billy missed his dog Rex terribly and that he was full of "unused explosives" because he was not getting the exercise to which he was accustomed. One day he climbed up on the water closet in the bathroom, and its cover broke into six or eight pieces. Effie was anxious to get Billy back to his studies so he would not be behind his classmates when he returned to school; but it was hard to get him to settle down to his schoolwork in the hotel environment.

Billy liked to visit with the Spanish boys who helped about the hotel. After chumming with them one day, he returned with five dimes in his pocket. Effie was dismayed to learn that some

of the Spanish boys had taught her eight-year-old son to
gamble. She did not know how Billy managed to communicate, but he seemed to understand and to be understood. He
told her the Spanish boys made lots of motions and he did, too.

The building across the street from the hotel seemed so
close that one could almost reach out and shake hands with
someone over there. The narrow cobblestone streets were
barely wide enough for an automobile to drive through. If two
people met on the sidewalk, one had to step into the street to
allow the other to pass. The cobblestones were hard on shoes,
and Effie soon had to look for a repair shop to keep her foot-
wear looking respectable.

Houses were built flush with the sidewalk and were joined
together in a row. They were constructed of mud and plastered inside and out. Only the different colors of paint enabled
one to tell where one house ended and the next began. Bars
guarded windows and the front entry was often of glass and
ornamental iron. Typically, just inside the front wall of the
house was a patio open to the sky and planted with flowering
shrubs. Courting took place with the señor outside and the
señorita inside. If he entered the house it was considered a
declaration of engagement.

To Effie, the streets of Medellin seemed crowded with terrible looking creatures — beggars, barefoot peons carrying
great loads of produce or laundry on their heads, and little
boys who thought nothing of urinating in the parks and open
places. A streetcar ride to the end of the line allowed a closer
view of the mountains beyond. They could see haciendas dotted here and there on the mountainside. Effie thought she
would surely slip off the back of the mule if she tried to ascend
the steep slope to one of those dwellings.

The town seemed dead at night. There were no shop windows to interest one on an evening stroll. Movie houses were
showing films that Effie judged were three or four years behind those available in Kansas City. Fleas were a problem in
the hotel and in the movie houses. These did not seem to bother
Will and Billy as much as they did Effie. She reported her legs

This man with his burden of bed and rocking chair had to stop to let an auto pass. The new building across the street is near the apartment the Brewsters rented in Medellin.

were always red with the "Mercurochrome" she used to quell the itching, and it was not very effective. She and Will soon developed a circle of friends among mining associates and other foreigners. They spent evenings playing cards.

Always concerned about finances, Effie wanted to find cheaper living accommodations — she embarrassed Will by bargaining with the clerk at the hotel and getting their room rent reduced from $240 per month to $200. Their search for rental living quarters was frustrating. The few available accommodations were unfurnished; and furnishings were much more expensive than in the States. Most items cost about four times as much as they cost at home.

Early in April, after a month of living in the hotel, they rented one of the small apartments above a warehouse. Most of their furnishings were purchased second hand from Americans who were returning to the States. Effie cited the cost of each item in a letter to Marguerite. One happy advantage to the apartment, besides the rent costing less than the hotel, was that it was free of fleas except when some of their visitors brought the bugs in on their clothing. Rats were sometimes a problem because grain was stored in the warehouse below them.

Billy was in third grade when he was taken out of school for the trip. Effie brought along third and fourth grade books

for him. She worried that her supervision of Billy's studies
and her letter writing were suffering because she was spending so much time cooking (with small pans on a two burner
stove) and hosting the steady stream of guests who dropped
by for tea or a meal. Finally, they found a tutor who worked
with Billy.

Effie wrote that Billy was being spoiled rotten by all the
adult attention he was getting. She worried that he was growing lazier each day because he had no place to play except the
corridor outside their apartment. A German boy about Billy's
age lived in a neighboring apartment. He spoke no English
and Billy knew no German, but they both spoke a little Spanish as they played together.

A trip to the market, Effie noted, could make one want to
vomit. The venders in the market stalls appeared to be mostly
people of mixed Indian and African blood, and they looked dirty
to Effie. She observed a vender working butter with her hands
and picking out flecks of dirt. Effie once observed a peddler
with his wares spread out on a big mound of small rocks left
by a street repair crew. The peddler's merchandise consisted
of yards and yards of ribbon all mixed and piled together on
an old rag.

The meat stalls were bloody with carcasses hanging on
great hooks and covered with flies. The butcher would carve
from one of the carcasses whatever cut the shopper ordered.
The shopper carried newspaper to market in which to wrap
her meat purchase. There were no containers such as we have
today. Bags were made of leaves. Effie mentioned buying small
tomatoes the size of marbles packaged in a leaf bag. Another
time she saw a truck unloading salt in bags made of leaves. It
was hoped that washing and cooking would rid the foods of
contamination.

In a letter to Marguerite, Billy wrote:

*Mother gave me some worm medicine yesterday and [it]
made me sick in bed all day. I vomited and vomited. But got
up feeling peppy this morning. Mother said she guessed she*

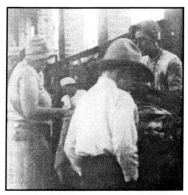

Effie and Billy in a Medellin meat market

Pottery market in Medellin

got the worm all right. They tell us here that one must take worm medicine every six months, as one gets worms through food. Mrs. Maldonado and Alicia [a neighbor and her toddler] took it too, but they didn't get sick ...

Don Luis Johnson dropped by their hotel several times, and they visited his office a time or two. Effie wrote that Don Luis was very nice to her. He brought her a box of candy and he and his daughter sent her roses. Effie appeared to take some initiative in business matters. She suggested that Don Luis have a meeting of stockholders before she and Will went out to the mine. Don Luis did have that meeting, but no apparent enlightenment came to Will as a result. Effie reported that Johnson was like a flea, never anywhere for more than a few minutes. He always seemed to be busy, but she had heard that he never did much.

Don Luis lived with his daughter and her American husband, or they lived with him. The son-in-law was also involved in mining, and Will suspected that most of the royalties that should have been sent to him had been invested, instead, in the son-in-law's mines. The daughter finally invited Effie and Will for tea, but still Don Luis was not forthcoming with the accounting that Will was seeking. Effie thought Will should "make that old chap stay put and get some things done."

SUSPICIONS CONFIRMED   **15**

A REVIEW OF THE status of Will's company is in order here. At the stockholders' meeting that was held in 1902, after Mamie filed for divorce and before Will returned to the United States, several changes to the company were enacted. Jim Brewster and Lawrence Buchanan were added to the board of directors. The shares of capital stock were increased and the name was changed from the Colombian Gold Dredging Company to the La Clara Placer and Mines Company. Though two of their mines, the La Clara and the Barbero, had been producing gold for many years, the La Clara Placer and Mines Company, was not registered in Colombia in 1929.

In those early days, titles to the company's properties were put in John T. O'Brian's name so O'Brian could expedite legal matters related to the company's mining in Colombia. It was intended that the titles be changed to reflect the company's ownership once the litigation was cleared. A new set of legalization papers reflecting the name change was sent to O'Brian to be filed in Colombia, but O'Brian did not get them filed. Instead he brought the papers back to Will when he returned to the United States. The titles could not be changed until the company's name change was legalized in the United States. Will apparently should have acted but did not, and lawsuits in Colombia were still unresolved when O'Brian died. As a result, O'Brian's heirs — his widow, Mary, and his son, Brian — still held the titles in 1929.

Will wrote home to Marguerite and to Jim in Fort Madison to search for the paperwork that had been done in the United States related to the name change. He also asked Jim to send an attorney to Kearney, Nebraska, to obtain powers of attorney from the O'Brians. Jim Brewster was disgusted with Will for not having seen to the paperwork matters himself before he left for Colombia. Failing to find the papers, they wrote for notary-certified copies from Prescott, Arizona, where the original filing was made. After those documents were received, amended, and signed for the name change in Fort Madison, they had to be registered in Washington before they could be sent to Will in Colombia. Also, Jim grudgingly sent his attorney to Kearney, but Mrs. O'Brian and her son were not ready to cooperate. So Jim had to foot the $75.00 attorney expense with no benefit received.

Will was not given to monitoring the details of his entrepreneurial pursuits, especially after his focus turned to a new venture. To use Effie's words, Will tended to be "lax in his business dealings." One can see why Jim Brewster's patience with his brother was running short. Will had used up his own inheritance while Jim had conserved and increased his. Will continued to turn to Jim when his needs for capital were pressing. Jim usually came through with enough to get Will out of a jam but he kept threatening to end the flow of cash. However, with typical charm, Will still managed to talk his brother into meeting his requests. In his June 21, 1929, letter to enlist Jim's help, Will signed off with a teasing "Your darling brother."

The McGuires, who had operated the LaClara mine since O'Brian's death, lived within walking distance of the mine. No longer were pack mules needed to get from Medellin to the mine. A rail line now passed about two miles from the McGuire's home. Will's expected freight shipment still had not arrived when the Brewsters went out to spend a couple of days with the McGuires and to visit the La Clara mine about two weeks after their arrival in Medellin. They rode the slow-moving train. The McGuires sent horses for them to ride the final two miles, up hill and down, to the McGuire home. Effie wrote to Marguerite about her sore muscles after that horseback ride.

The Brewsters were able to watch a cleanup of gold from

Effie, Will, Billy and Don Luis on horses. Mr. McGuire standing. This house near the La Clara mine contained machine shops and an ice plant.

the LaClara mine. Effie and Billy saw for the first time the slurry of water, mud, gravel and large rocks in a basin-like pond. Machinery, like Will had designed, sucked up the slurry to a header on a slide-like sluice with riffles (slats) in its bottom. With the opening of a valve, the mass was propelled down the sluice box by waterpower so strong that it could kill a man a hundred feet away. The rocks and the mud were washed away while gold and iron ore were caught in the riffles of the sluice. When the slats were removed from the sluice the remaining wet mass was carefully collected in buckets and poured into a large copper kettle on a tripod over a fire. Water was boiled off until only a dry powder was left. A huge horseshoe magnet was used to remove and discard the iron ore. The gold dust and nuggets were then taken to a kiln to be melted and formed into bricks. Will handed Billy one of the gold bricks and Billy nearly dropped it. He had no idea that gold was so heavy.

Laws in Colombia were such that only a small percentage of the value of the gold could be taken out of the country. The manager of the mine, however, gave Will two vials of gold dust. Effie safeguarded that small cache, brought them home in her luggage and used them when times became very difficult during the Great Depression.

The McGuires were hospitable on that visit in April, 1929. Will and Effie learned that the McGuires considered Don Luis

Johnson "a crook." They also learned that the Homeguero mine, which Will sold in 1906 for $15,000, had produced more than $2,000,000 in gold. Willis McGuire appears to have been honest enough, but he lacked an understanding of the relationship between O'Brian and Will's company. McGuire had been authorized by O'Brian to operate the mine. After paying the expenses, McGuire had turned the proceeds over to Don Luis as agreed.

Willis McGuire reported that the LaClara had produced $101,262 worth of gold in the three years from 1926 to 1929 alone. Will's take should have been thirteen percent ($13,164) of that, less a commission for Don Luis. Instead, Will received about $3,500.00. Later, the Mcguires produced the figures for the years 1909 to 1926. During that time period the LaClara mine produced $1,223,442.50 in gold. Will had received very little in royalties for those years.

Johnson continued to dodge requests for his accounting. Will arranged to receive future royalties directly from the

Flume on La Clara mine where Effie and Billy watched them extract 26.49 pounds of gold worth $6,357.60 one day in 1929.

McGuires, avoiding Johnson as middleman. Ongoing litigation, O'Brian's untimely death, Johnson's apparent conniving,
and Will's neglect all seem to have contributed to the confusion of ownership and accounting. Some of the funds, to which
Will and his company were entitled, were thought to have been
sent to the widow O'Brian.

To say that Will and Effie were upset with Don Luis
Johnson is putting it mildly. Will wanted to sue Johnson but
could not do so while titles to the mines were still in O'Brian's
name. In addition to the title matter, it appeared that Don
Luis no longer had assets to pay what he owed them even if
they were to get a judgment against him. Will wrote to Jim, "I
feel like filling his [Johnson's] carcass full of holes." Effie hid
Will's guns at one point because Will was so angry she was
afraid he might do something rash.

Effie estimated that Will's laxity in his various business
dealings probably cost him a fortune of close to $400,000.00
over the years — this during a time when $400,000.00 was a
very hefty sum. She wrote to Marguerite:

> Well, if only a lesson has been learned not to be lax in
> business we may yet make a fortune. I certainly want to pound
> in Billy's head <u>thoroughness</u>.

FURTHER EXPLORATION   **16**

WILL WAS EAGER TO get out to examine some mine sites he had bought thirty years before and to survey other sites on which he had working-lease options; but he had to wait for his freight shipment to arrive with the trunk containing his tools and work clothes. The terms of his lease options provided Will the right to establish whatever claims he chose among several available properties with two years to make his final decisions. Don Luis Johnson represented the group that controlled those properties. It was ironic that Will had to deal with Don Luis in these matters when he had come to so distrust and dislike the old gent.

Effie wrote that Colombia was very much a "mañana" place. Nothing seemed to happen in a hurry. Will sent wires inquiring about the freight. When he finally received a reply, it contained a request for more shipping fees. Almost three months after it was shipped, the freight arrived on April 27 at a total shipping cost of about $200. The long-awaited "graphanola," that was to help with their study of Spanish, was broken and scarred from its travels.

Will and Mac (Amos T. Maxwell) left Medellin in May after the freight shipment arrived. The first sites they explored were the Ledesme properties. These consisted of eleven claims of about 2500 acres each. With a crew of fourteen men — seven of them natives who poled their canoes — they ascended the Rio Miel (a tributary of the Magdelena) to the mouth of the Rio Samana and up that river to the Rio Ledesme.

Will reported that both the Miel and the Samana were very rapid with many falls and lots of fish. It took about two days to get to where they cleared a three-acre campsite. Will thought they could have made it in a few hours if they had had a fifteen horsepower outboard motor. The tropical forest was so dense — with 150-foot trees, briars, thorn ferns, and vines — that it took them another two days to cut a trail through the remaining five miles to the mine site. Will wrote that the humidity of the wet woods was "a fright for an old one like me." The flies, mosquitoes, and biting insects were always in evidence.

In a letter to his daughter Barbara, Will wrote that his mines had lain there with no one in the region thereabouts for 20 years. The natives wouldn't go into this region because of the bad water and climate. About the only white men that had been there before were the Spaniards who had worked out the creeks and small streams in the sixteenth century. One could see the old Spanish rock piles with trees four feet in diameter growing out of them. However, there was plenty of gold left to be worked by modern methods.

Monkeys were thick in the trees, screeching, "hollering" and throwing sticks at the intruders; but the men became accustomed to that and paid little attention. Will reported there were plenty of wild animals in the jungle — tigers, wild hogs, turkeys, "Guaguas", ant eaters, and numerous others that the natives had names for. He shot at a "tiger" but missed.

The party remained at the site fifteen days, walking daily the five miles from their camp to the claim site. Will wrote that the long walks "brought back my piles in the old fistula wound Dr. Minor made in 1894, so I was laid up in camp for three days." They learned later that they could have camped just two miles from the mine site.

The numerous test holes they drilled in that site revealed "very satisfactory gold values" in each one. Will talked to an old man in the vicinity who had been mining with pick and shovel and taking out $250.00 in gold per month. Will was excited about the potential for mining there with hydraulic machinery. He thought developing a mine on the Ledesme properties would be much less expensive than the LaClara site had been. No freighting by rail or pack mules would be needed. Riverboat and canoes could transport the equipment. A drawback to those sites was that the water supply was not abundant.

Nearly worn out, Will returned to Medellin to raise money to continue their exploration while Mac went on to a second site. Will returned one of their crew members, a Canadian Indian named George, to Medellin to release him because he was lazy. They could not afford to feed and pay one who failed to do his share of the work. Effie reported that Will had lost about a foot off his waistline when he returned, but he seemed in good health otherwise.

Will's enthusiastic report of his findings lifted Effie's spirits and her letters took on an optimistic tone. Will was dreaming of forming a new company, incorporating under Colombian law for $100,000 with a par value of one dollar per share of stock. He anticipated selling 40,000 shares and retaining 60,000. He hoped much of the financing might come from his brother Jim and/or the Dr. Friday, resident of Balboa in the Panama Canal Zone, who had befriended the Brewster family on their journey to Colombia. In her letters, Effie urged family members and friends to talk up the investment opportunity among their acquaintances. They were now sure the gold was there. Funding seemed all that stood between them and striking it rich.

Their immediate need, however, was to get enough money for Will to continue his explorations. Will had already spent $600 on the survey of the Ledesme sites and their bank account was reduced to $200.00. Royalties from the LaClara mine were tied up in lawsuits. What little income they had from rentals at home was not equal to their expenses. Will took a calculated risk. He wrote a check on the Fort Madison bank for $300, figuring that his brother Jim would honor it. While he returned to the jungle where Mac had set up another camp, he instructed Effie to write to Jim requesting a draft for another $700. Effie was reluctant to do that. She felt beholden to Jim, and she hoped they would soon have a mine operating so they could repay all they had already borrowed. Jim came through with the total of $1000, but he complained that he had to sell Schaffer Pen Company stock at fifty cents on the dollar to do so. Will doubted that statement.

When Will rejoined Mac to explore a site called San Antonia in Colombia's San Juan region, Mac was cranky and had not done all that Will had expected. On July 7, Will wrote to Effie from San Juan:

> *The climate here is delightful, altitude about 2000 ft., cool nights and about 80 in day time. Have a good place to stop, and little milk, but a long distance from the mines we want to examine, as yet there are no trails or roads over to the falls on San Antonia. Mac was there two times, but it takes three hours to go by trail, and he did not try to set up a camp ... So his 3 weeks here is of no use, except to hear his report on where he has been ... Monday I am sending two men to make shortest road into the falls and below and [I] will go with them. It may be hard to get a road in for mules from this side ...*
>
> *Mac is about played out in his legs, wore them out going too hard in Ledesme and has done little walking here. He found a rich streak of gravel near the house here, and has been having men work there taking out gold at a 50% loss for two men ... but this mine has no water for machinery, so why waste time here ...*
>
> *These Peons are so dammed inquisitive and curious they won't even have the common decency to leave you alone to take a bath, so one old woman (40) stood in the door while I stripped for a bath and remained there until I took my bath, she seemed to enjoy it, too ...*
>
> *Mr. Escobar who was to show us all these mines and was supposed to know all about them doesn't know any more about this group than he did on Ledesma. He has never been to the falls on San Antonia and has lived here all his life, and owns the land, has never been on the falls of Inglesia Creek, where he says is the best mine. These falls are so far away it will take 3 days to see them, but first I will see the San Antonia.*

On August 7 Will wrote to Marguerite from Puerto Trumfo:

My darling daughter — (also send copy to Babs, please. I write so little.)

I woke this A.M. at 5:30 to the music of the monkeys. They sound much like distant thunder, big red ones and holler like a Bull. I shot one yesterday as we had no meat but he was too old to eat. I have been down here in the wilds for 7 weeks and am fed arapa and beans until I'm groggy and been working mostly on one cylinder and that very much constipated. The young girls and boys run around without any clothes but they all have the fever and rotten teeth ... There is a girl here 16 without any teeth left that's sound. I had to look at her mouth as her cheek was all swelled up with toothache.

They mostly have buckteeth and bowlegs — but I finally got the fever stopped with most of them but my medicine supply is running short. I haven't found anything that looks like a mine with the necessary requirements and have covered 200 square miles territory. I spent $600 in the Ledesma region and $700 down here in San Juan region. The climate there is better with nice bathing conditions which helps as we come in every night with wetness from perspiration, even our pants are wet to the skin, and a cool bath is heavenly.

I have been here on the River Magdellena a week waiting for the mules and cargoes as we are now going into the Corcorna region down the River from here. This is a hell of a hole to stay in. Mosquitoes, man-eating flies and 140 different varieties of ants, wasps, and bees ... The woods are full of them. They ate all the rim out of my Panama hat, nothing left but the crown. They are so fond of salt. I am sleeping in a barn with the pigs, chickens and animals, air is full of B.S. The ants (little ones) drop down in the night thru the mosquito bar and light on one's whiskers and hair but finally you fall asleep.

I haven't had any vegetables to eat since I left Medellin. I brought a sack of cabbage with me but that didn't last long as we have to feed the whole dammed family with our provi-

sions. Mac was too dammed tired and lazy to cook and I don't intend to do it all. I have been resting up this week here in Puerto Trumfo doing my own cooking on 3 rocks and wood fire. I walked 3 miles yesterday in the woods hoping to find something fit to eat but drew a blank. I caught a fish today so will not starve. I'll have a swell time cooking it on one of these pieces of Indian pottery, one has to do everything in this business, now laugh.

I took a steamer up the river 40 miles the other day to phone Ma to keep her from worrying for me. The town La Dorado was all up in arms from a report that there was a gang of bandits camped in the graveyard nearby. I told them I thot it was a lie as no dammed peon had the guts to camp in a graveyard. They gave me a pistol and a handful of cartridges to take to bed with me as I told them they could sit up all night but I was tired and was hitting the cot and to call me when the fireworks started. I was staying with Sr. Carrisquilla in his store. It seems the night before they raided the stores in Honda, 20 miles away. I wasn't called during the night but the gang of storekeepers were all drunk and looked like they spent a bad night. I left next day for here.

I left Mac in San Juan to put down some more holes in the river bars as the tests we made were not satisfactory and the water supply lacks head (fall) to hydraulic, some gold, yes. I like Ledesma better as it would cost less to install machinery. I would like to go back there and go over on another river. They report muy rico [very rich], who knows until I go and see it.

I may go back to Zone [Panama Canal Zone] with Ma and see a bunch of men there about capital to prospect further. Then I just had a bath in the room or barn. The tall dark haired, blackeyed tango female that brought the water has been throwing burning glances at me when I was taking my bath. She had the nerve to stop in the doorway and burn me up with her googoo eyes but when finally I let go of the last half of my BVDs she shoved away — all of which shows they have some modesty. I didn't want to shock her by saying get out. They are so timid, they sure go "nertz" about white boys — you know I have grown a cute German mustache and it makes me look around 24 its so reddish blonde.

Well, Sis dear, I do hope you had a good time — rest — on your vacation and you sure needed it with all that worry paying taxes and interest and everything. Sorry to have let you in for it all, though it seems we had to get this S.A. fever off our chest. No? We came 10 years too late to profit any, or even 3 years would have meant $10,000 but that old crooked agent Johnson can't repay anything. He lost his dough, and mostly all of mine, financing his sons in a poor mine. Those Colombians just go and mount a mine because someone says its muy rico. They don't test it out first.

I know this letter is written like a crazy one but you should see the hell and torment of the insects hovering about my seemingly sweet self. There is a big green fly that bites through your pants and what a wallop they give me. They call it the Kongo. It makes you do the Tango. And then there are little ones like nats that sting like a mosquito. They get through the mosquito bar.

I expect the mules and cargo in today, thank God. Anywhere but this hole on the river with monkeys amid God's great outdoors, that's the helluvit. Well, Sis dear, I hope you get a great deal out of this inspiring letter. You know there are no news items to read here and its all the same—pigs, chickens, dogs, mules and starved children one has to listen to. Lovingly, Dad.

P.S. Mac is a dammed poor camping partner, is disagreeably argumentative — no humor left in him and you know one must have it to keep sane in this country. I am clear off him as an agreeable companion. He expected to take up the gold in hunks and he must think I am to blame for his disappointment. We finally got rid of George Lemas, a Canadian Indian — nutty.

I wish I could hand this letter to that plane just passing over. It would reach you quicker perhaps.

They cut a trail through to the Inglesia Falls where even the natives had never been. Will reported having three gusaños (skin worms) in the calf of his leg making sores that looked like boils. He had stomach discomfort due to food he ate en route. After all that effort and hardship, Will was disappointed with that site. The holes they put down to test for gold did not show good values.

Will continued on to the third group of sites called Corcorna. He described that expedition in another letter to his daughter:

I left Puerto Trumfo on a raft and floated down to the Corcorna River and up that river two days in canoe, thence 4 days mule back as the river was too swift for us. We made camp and explored the mines on several rivers or creeks, that flowed into the Corcorna, with three natives. The district was as new to them as it was to me; but it was not so difficult to get about as was the Ledesma where we had to cut our trails thru dense forests and jungles to the sources of the streams to get the fall by barometer and quantity of water depend-able for mining. While there I found a three foot quartz vein that has gold all thru it. It lay in the bed of a creek where the Old Spaniards had worked the stream bed and taken the placer gold out; but the ledge or vein they had overlooked as it was not even disturbed or picked into. The samples I got run over $200 per ton. I am going back to get more as I did not have any drills or powder with me. It will take me 10 days to go up there if I have good luck with the boats going up to Buenavista. From this town of 500 population I take canoe up the Miel River to the mouth of the Samana River. Thence up Samana to to Ledesma takes two to three days and five days in camp and three days to come down to Buenavista where I can get river steamboats back to Puerto Berrio.

Will picked out three sites that he wanted to develop in the Corcorna region. He also wanted to develop a site in the Ledesma region but figured that could wait until later. He thought it would still be available when he got around to it because no one else had been there in the prior twenty-five years.

On the evening of August 27, he arrived back in Medellin so bewhiskered that Billy thought he looked like Santa Claus. He was much thinner but he had stood his travels well despite all the hardships. Effie took his picture the next morning before he shaved off his beard. Will returned with tales of many long days on mule back, sleeping on cots, hammocks, or hard boards with no mattress, of rats overhead gnawing corn above him while he slept, of being nearly eaten alive by bedbugs one night. Domesticated animals had the run of the native huts where he sometimes stayed overnight. One night when he "stepped out to gaze at the moon" he stepped in a cowpile.

Effie wanted their new company to be handled in a businesslike manner to avoid some of the pitfalls of Will's previous ventures. She insisted that they file the incorporation papers in Medellin before they went off to solicit investors. They had to wait for Don Luis Johnson to return from a trip to begin that process.

While they waited, Will took Billy up into the mountains to examine a quartz mine. "Billy had a glorious time, dressed in his cowboy suit — hat, long boots and all — he took his saddle and rode all over the mountains most of two days." At one point "he was off the horse going down a steep mountain, got started running and couldn't stop, got scared and began to cry, then fell full length flat on his face, and turned a somer-sault and that stopped him."

Will expected that foray to last only one day so they carried food enough for lunch and supper. By late afternoon he realized they could not make it back to Medellin before nightfall, so father and son stopped at a native hut and arranged to spend the night there. When they entered the hut, Will walked over to the bed and suddenly flung the mattress off into a corner. Billy was startled and asked his dad why he had done that. Will told him to go look closely at the mattress. When

Billy enjoyed the attention he received whenever he wore the cowboy suit that Marguerite sent along for his eighth birthday. He wore it when he went down the street to pick up the mail and any other time he could manage.

Billy did that, he found it crawling with bedbugs. They put their saddle blankets over the gunnysacks that covered the roped undergirding of the bed and they used their saddles for pillows.

Billy did not know where the residents of the hut slept that night. He was very hungry when he got up the following morning. He remembered that the natives prepared "arapas" (flat corn cakes) and "masamora" (soup made of hominy) for them. He also recalled that the menu was new to him but it tasted good.

Will did not think much of the mine they explored, but Billy was full of his story when he returned to Medellin. One memento of the trip was a new crop of freckles on Billy's nose.

HOMEWARD BOUND   **17**

WHILE WILL SPENT MOST of the months of May, June, July, and August trekking through jungles testing for gold, Effie spent her time in Medellin stewing about their time schedules and their next course of action. She could not make definite plans for their future, but she continued to formulate various scenarios to conserve their dwindling resources until they could realize sufficient income from the mines. Her letters to Marguerite reveal some of the strategies she considered — sell the Brewster home at 5828 Montgall and move into a small apartment, or share their home with another family for rent and shared expenses. Perhaps they should spend the winter in Watonga, Oklahoma, with her parents.

Billy's schooling was among Effie's top priorities. She wanted him to have a "thorough education" among "associates from good families." Her loyalties to and concern for Will were also strong. She didn't want to leave Will in Colombia alone. She thought of various possibilities for Billy's schooling if Will should need to stay in Colombia to oversee mining operations or in Panama to raise capital. Billy could be enrolled in a school in Barranquilla, but Effie had heard that there were bad Spanish boys in that school. Besides, the climate in Barranquilla was miserably hot and mosquitoes were bad there. The American school in the Canal Zone was another possibility. No decisions could be made until they learned the final amount of their royalties from the LaClara and Barbero mines and what would be required to mount the new mines Will was exploring.

It was a lonely and anxious time for Effie. She longed for home and loved ones. Early on she expected to leave for home by the first of August. That would allow Billy to be back in school at the beginning of the new term. Their departure date, however, was slowly shifted later and later. Billy, too, was eager to return home to Kansas City. One can see a reflection of Effie's concerns in a letter Billy wrote to Sissy:

> *Gee, I was surely mad when I found out we couldn't start home by the first of Aug. I want to get home before school starts. I will feel like a bird out of a cage when I can run and play. All I ever do is to study in the morning, go to the post office and Hotel to see if there is any mail and then in the afternoon I go to see Alicia, [a neighbor's baby daughter] she just lives on the mismo [same] floor we do in the apartment. She has a big pen and I get inside and she likes to play with me. She took her first step for me. Her Mother and she are going back to the States the 19th of September, starting from here the 12th. I hope we will be gone by that time too for I surely would be lonely without her. I will be glad when Daddy comes back, so we can start, even [if] we don't go any farther than the Zone, for there I would get to play outdoors, and have American children to play with. If Mother stays there with daddy I would go to school there. I expect it will be pretty hot there to study. The rainy season has begun. I am still wearing my cowboy suit. It is so nice and cool here I can wear it and not feel too hot. It has been so cool in this house today Mother had to close the door. I suppose Roy and the rest of them are home by now. Did Bobby Briggs go to stay with his grandmother this summer? And how is Bobby Moore, as bad as ever? I suppose Loyd will be so big when I get home I can't play with him. Are the children nice in 5828 Prospect? How is Aunt Dodie, Uncle Fred, Fred C., Mr. Dodson and Lola? I go up to the American Consul's house quite often. How is Rex hope all right? If you see Maurine tell her I will send her a card from Balboa. I am having a fine time. Lovingly, your Big Brother Bill*

One day, while they awaited Will's return, Effie and Billy

were taken on a drive about 30 miles down the Medellin Valley. Effie described it as a beautiful valley with mountainsides covered with green tropical shrubbery and dotted with Spanish style houses surrounded by stately palms. They saw coffee trees in bloom and producing their fruit, the coffee bean. Many fruits — bananas, papayas, lemons, oranges, and several others, the names of which Effie did not know — were being grown. There were quaint villages of "little huts with steep grass roofs, babies without diapers, and men and women dressed in good suits and dresses but barefoot."

Effie reported that Billy had grown a little taller and was less heavy than when they left home. Whenever Billy went to the post office to get their mail he wore the cowboy suit that was Marguerite's gift for his eighth birthday. He seemed to enjoy having people stare as he passed by in that outfit with its chaps, holsters, and toy guns.

As they anticipated their departure from Medellin, the tutor who was hired for Billy finished his work; but Effie continued having her son review his lessons. Effie wrote that Billy was a little scamp about studying, for he wanted to play and waste time. They reviewed his arithmetic, including the multiplication tables and short division. He had finished his speller, had read through his geography book and several times through his readers. She thought he hadn't done much with his language book and was missing out on music. She was gratified that he had found some little Spanish boys for playmates. She hoped that would help him advance his Spanish. She wrote to Marguerite, "It would tickle you to hear Billy out in the corridor talking to the little German kid who speaks Spanish. They manage to understand enough to play for hours together."

After Will's return to Medellin on August 27, Don Luis Johnson continued to be hard to pin down. He was again out of town. Will and Effie believed that Johnson no longer had assets to repay their royalties that he had siphoned for his own use. However, because Johnson headed the group that controlled the properties on which Will wanted to set up mines, "the old crook" was a necessary party to the contract for the mines Will expected to mount. Effie wanted to get the new mining corporation set up properly before they left Colombia so they would have something definite to offer potential investors. Effie kept after Will about completing his business so they could get started home until he let her know that he wanted to hear no more of it. She wrote to Marguerite that she would have to watch what she said about that matter.

While they waited for Johnson's return, Will used some of the time to inform the U.S. Consul about the history of his ventures in Colombia in case he needed future help. They suspected that Johnson had been home for several days before he answered their messages. Finally, a contract with the Society of Mines of Corcorna, Rio Clara and Santo Tomas, of which Johnson was president, was signed on September 29. It gave Will options on six mining properties. The terms of the contract required him to start mining within two years. After that, if operations ceased for a period of at least six months, any equipment mounted on the sites would become the property of the Society.

The Brewster family left Medellin to return home on October 4, 1929. They had been in Colombia seven months. Improvements in the rail service made their route back to the Rio Magdelena easier than their inbound trip. During their stay, a tunnel through the mountain was completed. They were able to return directly on one train from Medellin to Puerto Berrio — no more transferring to an automobile to get over the mountain and then boarding a second train. The ride was also more pleasant because the trains were converted to run on oil so live cinders no longer pelted the passengers.

The riverboat took them from Puerto Berrio to Cartagena rather than to Barranquilla, the seaport at which they had arrived seven months earlier. The trip down river took four days. The final day was spent traversing an old Spanish-built canal that branched off the Rio Magdelena. There were barges on either side of the riverboat and they kept bouncing off one bank and then the other of the narrow canal. Billy kept saying, "Dad, Dad, we're going home!" Effie shared Billy's enthu-

This tunnel through the mountain between Medellin and Puerto Berrio was built during the time the Brewsters were in Medellin.

siasm and she thought Will was just about as anxious to get home as she "although he wouldn't let on."

Effie reported, "If it had not been for the mosquitoes it would have been a delightful trip." They saw iguanas, wild monkeys, flocks of wild turkeys, one "tiger," and lots of ducks. Also mentioned were animals called "ponchas" that looked like a wild pig with a head like a squirrel. They saw women "sitting flat down in the muddy water washing or pounding their clothes." Huts along the banks often had three or four naked children standing out watching the boat go by. Even in Cartagena there were hundreds of little naked children, apparently oblivious to their nakedness. Effie wrote that the riverboat was "real nice but the food was awful—old bull meat, fried plantanos and the *eternal* rice." She was glad she had brought along plenty of marmalade, sardines, butter, papayas, pineapple, cookies, coffee, and chocolate.

Effie described Cartagena as a quaint old town populated by at least 75,000 and much more "cityfied" than Medellin. After the cool climate they had enjoyed in the mountains, the

Effie was impressed by these ancient walls at Cartagena.

heat bothered her. Their hotel, the Via Del Mar, was on an arm of the sea where they could catch any breeze that blew. "Darling little parakeets" played nearby and "squeaked" at the tops of their voices. They toured the old fortresses and walked the underground passageways left by the Spaniards. The old city wall was "so thick that three cars can drive along abreast." Cartagena was a port from which many of the Spanish treasure ships had sailed. As she walked there Effie "wondered what fear they [the old Spaniards] must have felt as they knew the pirates were just outside of their fortressed city."

When they arrived at Cristobal in the Panama Canal Zone they learned that Dr. Friday, from whom Will expected to solicit capital, was on an extended trip to Venezuela and would not return for four months. This changed Will's plans about crossing the isthmus to Balboa, so he returned to Kansas City with Effie and Billy. They were on the final leg of their journey homeward when they heard news of the stock market crash that signaled the beginning of the Great Depression. Surely Will realized immediately that huge spasm in the nation's economy would adversely effect his efforts to raise capital for his new mining ventures. What he could not have known at that point was how long-lasting or how far-reaching that economic downturn would be.

The family arrived back in Kansas City on October 26, 1929. An excited Marguerite ran down the halls of Union Station to greet them. She thought that Billy "seemed older but just as sweet." Because the family home at 5828 Montgall was still being rented, they had to stay with Fred and Dodie Lowd until the renters moved elsewhere.

THE GREAT DEPRESSION   18

THE *WORLD BOOK ENCYCLOPEDIA* records more than twenty recessive periods in the economy of our nation during the past two centuries. However, the magnitude of the Great Depression that extended over the entire decade of the 1930s dwarfed all other recessions in our history. Trends at work during the "Roaring Twenties" are given as causes for the economic collapse. The cost of farm production exceeded the price received for the produce. Many people purchased stocks on margin (with borrowed money), and there was a general abuse of credit. A group of wealthy investors manipulated certain stocks, driving prices to highly inflated levels and then selling, leaving others "holding the bag." When stock prices plunged, margin investors could not cover their losses, and a bank panic ensued. The huge stock market losses that occurred in late October of 1929 confirmed the fears of investors and sent the nation into a drastic spiral of declining production and increasing unemployment.

The *World Book* states: "The Great Depression affected almost every nation. It caused a sharp decrease in world trade because each country tried to help its own industries by raising tariffs on imported goods." From Colombia, Amos Maxwell wrote to Will and Effie that the prices of coffee and cattle there were so low that farmers could not afford to grow and market them. The Colombians were looking to England for needed financial aid.

Back in Kansas City, the Brewster family eventually settled back into their comfortable home at 5828 Montgall. Marguerite was glad to have them all home again. It must have been quite a relief for her to shift the handling of Will's local business matters back to her dad's shoulders. Marguerite, then in her mid-twenties, was interested in a young man who was employed in the insurance office where she worked. His name was George Wilcox.

Will set to work seeking capital to develop the new mining properties for which he had contracted in Colombia. On February 13, 1930, Will wrote to Don Luis Johnson that he had duly formed the Colombia Placer Gold Mining Company on December 12, 1929, with an authorized capital of $300,000 — well ahead of the March deadline set in their contract. In that same letter Will wrote the following:

> *I have just returned from an extended trip into San Antonio and Brownsville, Texas. I am very well pleased with my interview with my connection there. They are all men of ample means and I am assured that the final quota of capital will be forthcoming from Texas. However, [I] am to be in Chicago next week to confer with parties there also.*
>
> *I find the Country in general to be reacting from the November stock panic and many are shy as to foreign investments and those near at home as well. I have no hesitancy in saying that the outlook is not encouraging for large capital; but as [I] do not approach the larger capitalists I have been doing very well.*

Financial problems were mounting, not only for the Brewsters but for most of the citizens of our nation. Real estate values were dropping by fifty percent or more. Will reported that a house he built and sold in Brewster's Grove for $10,500 in 1919 was offered for sale by the current owner in the 1930s for $3,000. Will kept expecting the values to rise again but that was a long time coming.

Billy was especially happy to be back with his dog Rex and his neighborhood playmates. An assessment of Billy's academic progress after the months of his absence found him to have outdistanced his class. He was placed in a program that was advanced half a year ahead of his former classmates. When he looked back in later years, he thought that placement was probably a mistake. He was one of the youngest in his class and he sometimes felt out of step with his new classmates.

One of the things Effie regretted having Billy miss while they were in South America was training in music. She tried to fill that void by hiring a piano teacher to come to the home for lessons. Bill remembered those times as follows:

> When I was about age 10 or 12, Mom set my piano prac-
> tice schedule each week. My piano teacher was an older man
> of German ancestry who spoke with an accent. He wanted
> me to learn technique. I hated those finger exercises with no
> melody. He finally relented and taught me to play "The Star
> Spangled Banner."
>
> The biggest drawback to my learning to play the piano
> was that I memorized quickly, including skipping notes and
> playing a wrong note. Another problem was that my base-
> ball-playing buddies would come to the window [usually open
> in summer, no air-conditioning in those days] and wait for
> me to finish practicing. Their patience was short when they
> needed me to make a team. Mom usually told them in a kind
> but firm way that I could come when my practice was fully
> done. One hour of practice on a pretty summer morning
> seemed like forever.

There were few developments in Will's South American interests. A letter from Willis McGuire, who managed the La Clara mine in Colombia, indicated that he was insulted by the tone of a letter that Will wrote to him inquiring about the settlement of the lawsuits and the subsequent distribution of the released mine proceeds. McGuire reported that those proceeds were used up in court costs and other expenses.

The clock was ticking away toward the deadlines outlined in Will's contract with Don Luis Johnson's group for the anticipated new mining ventures in Colombia. Will remained unable to meet the capitalization requirements, and it is assumed that the time expired and the contract was voided.

Hopes of ever reviving the mining interests in Colombia apparently died.

The year 1932 was especially eventful in the personal lives of the Brewster family. They were apparently sharing their home with roomers to save expenses. After school was out, Will, Effie, and Billy went to spend the summer in Iowa. Marguerite remained in Kansas City to work for the Aetna Insurance Company and to plan her marriage to George Wilcox, which was scheduled for August 24. A letter to her parents outlined her plans and revealed her excitement and concerns surrounding those plans.

The Aetna had a company policy not to employ two people of the same family. Since Marguerite and George worked in the same office, their marriage would violate that ruling, so they petitioned for an exception. A letter written by the manager of the Kansas City office to the home office of the company is interesting:

> *George Wilcox tells me that he and Miss Marguerite Brewster desire to get married ... The trouble is that Miss Brewster has been handling her agency work so very efficiently that it would be difficult, perhaps impossible, to find someone who in a short period could without considerable training handle her work. The question arises therefore, whether or not the Company would sanction continuing her employment after her marriage.*
>
> *Miss Brewster's father, who has been a man of considerable means and who still owns quite a bit of unproductive real estate, has suffered reverses and is at the present time in very stringent financial condition. This makes it necessary for Miss Brewster to maintain a young brother and otherwise contribute to the support of the family. How long this situation will continue, no one knows.*
>
> *While we have had, and still have, in our employ several married women, we have never had a case where husband and wife are both employed in our office. I know that the common experience of having man and wife or other relatives*

employed in the same office is a bad practice but I am strongly inclined to believe that this case would prove to be an exception to the rule ... My personal inclination would be to give the proposition a trial. I certainly would not want to do anything to postpone what seems to be a well considered and well timed matrimonial venture.

Please see that this case has careful consideration and advise me of the Company's position so that I can tell these young folks what they may count on in making their plans for the future.

Companies were reducing wages and cutting other costs in efforts to keep afloat in the deteriorating financial climate. The Aetna was no exception. Marguerite wrote to her folks that the Aetna had announced that it would cut all employees' salaries by ten percent beginning in December of that year. She had been contributing to the family's support, and she was concerned about the financial impact her marriage would have on the family. She and George offered to live in the family home with the rest of the family and the roomers after their marriage and to contribute to the expenses of the home.

When word came that the company would allow Marguerite to continue working on a trial basis after her marriage, her plans were put in high gear. Costs had to be kept to a minimum. She would have only one attendant, her special friend, Dorothy Hall. The ceremony would be held in the "garden" at 5828 Montgall. The yard would be decorated and lit with Japanese paper lanterns. An artificial moon would be hoisted into the big elm tree to add to the romantic atmosphere of the occasion. An open window would allow the piano to provide the wedding march and to accompany the soloist as he sang "Oh Promise Me" and "I Love You Truly." An arching rose trellis would frame the bride and groom during the ceremony. One hundred eighty-five guests were invited.

On August 10, 1932, just two weeks before the wedding, the family was rocked by the death of Will's brother Jim. He was seventy-one years old. Jim's obituary took up most of a column on the front page of *The Evening Democrat*, the Fort Madison newspaper. It appeared under the large headline, **"James C. Brewster Dies Today."** The only larger headline on that front page was **"HOPES TO GET CHANCELLORSHIP,"** referring to Hitler's bid for increasing power in Germany.

Jim Brewster, brother of Will

The newspaper account noted Jim's career as president of the Fort Madison Savings Bank and his interest in other businesses including the Fort Madison Chair Company, the Fort Madison Street and Railway Company and the Sheaffer Pen Company of which he was an officer. Survivors named in the obituary were Jim's wife, Daisy, his daughter and son-in-law, Starr and Alba Garrott, his son Charles (mentally handicapped) and his

brother Will. No mention is made of his sister Martha who was a patient in a mental sanitarium in Iowa at that time.

Jim's fortune was left in trust for his wife and children. His bank became the trustee. Jim had been the trustee for the Kirkland Trust, that Charles Brewster (father of Jim, Will, and Martha) had granted to take care of Martha and her son Charles Kirkland. Will was named successor trustee for the Kirkland Trust. After Jim's death Mr. Pollard, attorney for Jim's bank, sent a legal form for Will to sign declining the successor trusteeship. Will refused to sign the form but wrote a letter saying that he would be willing for the bank to act as his agent in Fort Madison in matters of the trust. Before Mr. Pollard could have received Will's reply, Will received notice from him that the court had appointed the bank as successor trustee. Will did not assert his right or responsibility to succeed as trustee at that time, but four years later he needed to question the bank's actions.

Jim's death was undoubtedly not just an emotional blow to Will but a financial one as well. The bank and Jim's widow, Daisy, were not likely to be as amenable to help Will in a financial bind as Jim had been.

The wedding of George and Marguerite proceeded on schedule. Edith, Marguerite's biological mother, wrote her regrets that she was not able to come, and she urged Marguerite to come visit her and her husband for a low-cost honeymoon. The

Wedding of Marguerite Brewster and George Wilcox, August 24, 1932, in the garden at 5828 Montgall. Maid of Honor on the left is Dorothy Hall, then George and Marguerite, Will and Effie and George's parents.

couple, however, chose to honeymoon in Denver. Upon returning home, they moved in
with Marguerite's parents so
they could continue her support
of the family. Later, they took
up residence in one of the
Brewster's Grove houses
nearby.

Billy continued to be the absolute "apple of the eye" of the
adults in his family. Effie's
friend, the childless Dora Lowd,
remained very close to the family. Her relationship to Billy is
shown in a flowery poem that
she asked a friend, May Liddel,

**"Aunt" Dodie, Billy's third
mother figure. The first two were
his mother and older sister.**

to write. Dora had it framed for Billy's twelfth birthday in
1933. It is inscribed, "To Billy Brewster from Aunt Dodie":

Twelve Years Old Today

How rapidly the time goes by!
'Twas twelve short years ago.
I held you as a baby fair
Within my arms, and oh!
How precious every feature was,
In slumber or awake!
How tenderly I loved you, dear,
So much I would not take
A Croesus' treasure in exchange
For my rich joy to hold.
It's hard to realize you're twelve
I've watched those years unfold;
Your first school days,
The friends you made –
The jolly fun – the cares –
The honor of your manly heart –

The way you said your prayers;
When you were happy, so was I
And when you lay so ill
My soul was tortured –
For each pain I'd gladly spare you, Bill.
Although you're not my very own,
I feel you are — I do!
God let me know how wonderful
To have a boy like you!

The illness referred to in the poem was undulant fever, also called Malta fever, that Billy contracted in the early 1930s. This disease was very serious in those days before antibiotics. Recurrent fever with night sweats, weakness, and painful joints are its symptoms. Undulant fever was the impetus for regulations regarding the pasteurization of milk because its cause was traced to raw milk from infected cows. Billy was quite sick and his body wasted away to skin and bone. He missed a semester of school, but with youthful resilience, he eventually recovered.

During the decade of the 1930s, as hope dwindled and died for the implementation of the Colombian mines, Will turned his attention to the Western United States — Colorado, New Mexico, Arizona. He surveyed and considered various mining opportunities, but he was unable to raise capital to implement his findings.

Bill recalled his father one morning suddenly slamming down the newspaper he was reading. Will exclaimed, "I just lost seven and a half million dollars!" He had been reading a news item about a large strike of gold in a mine that he had once owned somewhere in the Northwestern United States.

Counter to the norm for women of her day, Effie began working outside the home to help meet her family's needs. She joined a real estate office headed by a woman named Merle Brewer. An article about the firm appeared in the *Kansas City Journal Post* on November 10, 1935, under the headline, "Manless Realty Brokerage Does Brisk Business." Specializing mostly in homes in the Country Club district, the Merle Brewer organization included ten women and was thought to be the only all-female real estate firm in the country at the time.

During the 1920s Effie had adopted the use of her middle name in business correspondence. In the 1930s she became known as "Lanore" among business associates and new friends, but old friends and family members continued to call her Effie. Her name is misspelled "Lanora" in the newspaper article.

During the Great Depression, few families had sufficient resources to purchase houses even at prices that were a fraction of what it had cost to build them. In the absence of buyers, many would-be sellers opted to try to rent their properties. Effie handled mostly rentals. Years later, on a drive through Kansas City's Country Club district, Effie pointed out house after house offered for sale during the Great Depression for less than $3,000. Those same houses might sell for more than $100,000 today.

Will and Effie sometimes collaborated as she pursued her real estate deals, and he tried to sell or rent his many real estate properties. Those that were rented brought very little while others sat vacant with overhead costs accumulating. Will was accustomed to negotiating real estate matters with the local government. He became an advocate for financially pressed folks who needed to have their property taxes adjusted in those difficult times, but income from those activities was minimal.

Businesses as well as individuals were being hit hard by the depressed economy. Banks and loan companies, overloaded with defaulted mortgages, tried to work with debtors so payments could be made. Many nice houses rented for as little as $25 per month. Even so, many properties stood vacant. More than one family often occupied a single house, or families took in roomers to share housing costs. Homelessness and starvation were the reality for many and a very real threat for many others.

Meeting obligations for taxes and mortgages on Will's real estate holdings and providing family necessities proved increasingly difficult for the Brewsters. Effie's small and inter-

mittent income combined with the minimal proceeds from
Will's activities and Marguerite's contributions fell short of
their needs. One after another the real estate properties were
lost to foreclosure or taxes. It must have been devastating to
watch one's assets eroding to nothing.

In September of 1932, the month following Marguerite's
wedding, the Brewster home at 5828 Montgall was foreclosed
due to delinquent interest. Will had built the house in 1926,
the largest house in the neighborhood, when building costs
were high. For two years before the foreclosure they offered
the house for sale for less than its intrinsic value with no success. After the foreclosure, the family was allowed to rent the
house for $40 per month, and they continued to live there.

The Prudential Insurance Company evidently owned the
property after the foreclosure. A letter that Will wrote to the
Prudential on May 31, 1934, alerted them to a possible all-cash
sale of the family home. It is not clear to whom the house was
sold. However, the sale of it enabled Will to acquire another
home loan on one of his other houses "to save a home for myself and my family, for at the age of 68 one must do the best he
can." By 1935 the family had moved to 5819 Prospect, one of
the smaller Brewster's Grove houses.

**5819 Prospect, one of Brewster's Grove houses. The Brewster family
moved here after the home at 5828 Montgall was foreclosed.**

KIRKLAND ESTATE   **19**

WILL'S SISTER, MARTHA JANE Kirkland, never remarried after being deserted by and divorced from Port Kirkland in the 1880s. Later in life Martha contracted scarlet fever, and complications from it affected her mentally. She died May 5, 1935, at age 75. At the time of her death she was living in a state asylum at Mt. Pleasant, Iowa, reportedly of "unsound mind." Her son, Charles Kirkland, was an invalid being cared for in California.

Martha's passing marked the legal termination of the Kirkland Trust that her father had granted to take care of his daughter and grandson. After Martha's death, titles to the real estate properties in Fort Madison and Chicago, that comprised the corpus of the Trust, should have been transferred to Martha's son and only heir. The bank, however, did not execute those titles — probably because Charles Kirkland was incompetent to care for his financial affairs.

Charles Kirkland died January 7, 1936, at age 55, eight months after the death of his mother. Charles was "deficient of mind" and partially paralyzed due to Infantile Paralysis (polio) which he suffered in his teens. He had been confined to a wheelchair. Jim Brewster, as trustee of the Kirkland Trust and compassionate uncle, had seen that Charles was cared for. On occasion, Will had also helped with the care of their nephew. Charles Kirkland never married. Incapable of seeing to his own legal matters, he died intestate (without having made a will).

Charles' estate was limited to the properties still held in the Kirkland Trust. The Fort Madison properties in the trust included a four-unit apartment building labeled lot 433 and a brick house, a brick cottage, and two flats on a corner labeled lot 434. Heirs to those holdings, according to Iowa law, were Will (one-half interest) and Jim's two children, Starr and Charley (one-quarter interest each). The Chicago properties included a service station with a fifteen-car garage at 1739-1743 Lake Street and a series of apartments at 3365 and 3401-3407 Prairie Avenue. Illinois law made Will the sole heir to the Chicago properties.

Will called into question the handling of the properties in the Kirkland Trust during Jim's and the bank's tenures as trustees. Jim had floated loans and mortgages in Fort Madison to build and furnish the four-unit apartment building there. The original trust did not provide for the encumbering of trust properties. Will charged that the bank had illegally usurped the trusteeship upon Jim's death.

There was an adversarial relationship between Will and Mr. "Bud" Pollard, the bank's attorney. They clearly disliked each other. When Will went to the Fort Madison Savings Bank to discuss estate matters, Pollard was included in the conference. At least once Pollard stipulated a time limit of five minutes for their conversations. Pollard became noted for long, long letters explaining the legal aspects of everything, always in favor of the bank's position.

As trustee of Jim's Trust, the bank held delinquent loans and mortgages (an aggregate of $11,155) on the Fort Madison properties. Will charged that after Jim's death, the bank had intentionally and unnecessarily used the Kirkland Trust income to maintain and improve the Fort Madison properties rather than to pay principal and interest on the loans. He believed the bank's intention was to foreclose on the properties, eliminating Will's half interest, and to have the properties in good condition when the bank acquired ownership for Jim's heirs. The Fort Madison holdings were probated and estate tax was paid. Because titles to the properties were still held by the trust, Will contended that the titles should have passed directly to the heirs without probate.

Will further charged that the bank did not use due diligence in managing the Chicago properties. The bank's agent in Chicago allowed the tenant of the Lake Street property to default on rent payments for four years while the defaulting tenant sublet the property and kept the rents from the sublease. Subsequently, the agent leased that property to another lessee for half the deemed rental value. The Prairie Avenue properties were in "deplorable" condition and the taxes were in arrears.

The legal wrangling and clearing of titles went on for years during which time Will and his family had great need for the tantalizing resources that lay just beyond their reach. In 1936 the small house in Brewster's Grove into which the family had moved was apparently lost to back taxes or defaulted loans. Will, Effie, and Billy moved in with Dora and Fred Lowd who were renting the three-bedroom house at 1314 East Twenty-ninth Street in Kansas City.

Will consulted with attorneys in Kansas City and in Iowa and was sure he had grounds to sue the Fort Madison Bank, but he was advised against it, and he lacked the resources to do so. Meanwhile, Will's financial situation continued to disintegrate. At his niece Starr's behest, the bank agreed to lend Will $40 a month against the final settlement of the estate.

It is difficult to sort out the rights and wrongs of the handling of the Kirkland Trust. From the voluminous correspondence over several years, one gets the impression that officers and attorneys for the bank may have considered the Kirkland estate too complex and time-consuming and the income too small to be worth stewarding closely. Was Will negligent when he did not assume the trusteeship of the Kirkland Trust when Jim died? Rather than sign the legal form declining the trusteeship, Will wrote a letter to Mr. Pollard dated September 1, 1932, which reads in part:

> ... I wanted to know if you think that the matter [administering the trust] can be turned over to the Bank thru a Power of Atty or appointment of Agent and be taken care of that way. ... I have no knowledge of the condition of the affairs of

this estate. .... If the charge of the bank for handling the
Kirkland Estate is reasonable, which I am sure it will be, I
would gladly leave the whole matter in the bank's hands ...

Pollard's position was that Will had indicated at the time
that he was in Fort Madison for Jim's funeral that he did not
want to assume the responsibilities of the trusteeship. Pollard wrote:

> *Someone had to be appointed Trustee in order to collect*
> *the rents of the Fort Madison property and pay the cost of*
> *operating this property, ... [I] advised him [Will] that the ap-*
> *pointment of a Trustee for the Martha J. Kirkland Trust could*
> *not be made through a Power of Attorney or the appointment*
> *of an Agent executed by him ... Call it what you will: a decli-*
> *nation to serve; a refusal to serve; inability or unwillingness*
> *to qualify as Trustee, they all have substantially the same*
> *legal effect ...*

Fortunately, Will's niece Starr was friendly to her uncle,
but Starr was in fragile health and needed, at times, to be
protected from controversy. After years of wrangling, Will negotiated a reduction of some of the expenses leveled against
the Kirkland Trust and paid his share. In September of 1938,
Will accepted a cash settlement of $614.77 and dropped his
claims against the bank.

Almost three years after the death of Charles Kirkland, a
letter was received from a California resident named Gillice.
The letter acknowledged receipt of the payment of a bill Gillice
had submitted for services he rendered to Charles Kirkland
during his final illness. In addition, the Gillice letter contained
what Will considered "fantastic fairy stories," including a claim
that Charles had fathered an illegitimate child with a black
washwoman, a shooting scrape with a pimp, and an alleged
payoff of $750 to the black prostitute. Will believed Charles
was physically incapable of having fathered a child. Will considered the allegations to be an attempt at blackmail to ob-

tain money from the Kirkland estate. The charges were neither answered nor proven.

The Iowa probate of the Charles Kirkland estate was finally concluded in 1939 with Will receiving an undivided one-
half of the Fort Madison properties and his brother Jim's children receiving one-quarter each. A letter Will wrote to A. M.
Lowrey, president of the Fort Madison Savings Bank, gives
insight into some of the stresses Will faced during those difficult times:

> *The present Mrs. Brewster was a business girl when I mar-*
> *ried her in 1918 and has been active in the Country Club*
> *real estate business the past five years, her earnings however*
> *are materially cut through the practice of 'Split Commissions'*
> *prevailing but without this income we should not have been*
> *able to eat regularly.*
>
> *This personal confession is due to the fact I wish to im-*
> *press, that this income from the Estate of Charles Kirkland*
> *is duly appreciated ...*

Management of the properties was an ongoing concern with
expenses and maintenance eating up most of the income. Will
went to Fort Madison from time to time to check on the properties there and to help with their maintenance. A new agent,
whose name was G.D. Daisy, replaced Mr. Tobias, who had
managed poorly the Chicago properties. Though the net income from the properties was small and by no means met the
needs of Will's family, whatever amount came was gratefully
received.

EDUCATING BILLY   **20**

BILLY ATTENDED KANSAS CITY'S old Paseo High School, which sat high on the hill overlooking the forty-seven hundred block of the Paseo Boulevard. Schoolwork was not difficult for him; but social relationships seemed more important than top grades. He soon dropped the "y" from his nickname and became known at school as Bill. Later, during adulthood, he liked to quote the first two lines of Eugene Field's poem, "Jest 'Fore Christmas:"

> *Father calls me William, sister calls me Will,*
> *Mother calls me Willie, but the fellers call me Bill!*

Bill had a circle of friends with whom he hung out, played tennis, and started smoking. Effie was disappointed when her son began smoking, but his dad was a moderate smoker so she felt powerless to do more than complain. The health consequences of smoking were not yet defined. In many social circles in those days, smoking was considered acceptable or even desirable. Young people often regarded it as a mark of sophistication. Most homes were equipped with ashtrays for guests who smoked even if there were no smokers in the family. It was considered inhospitable to deny a guest the privilege of smoking in the house.

Bill was in his junior year in high school when the family lost their home at 5819 Prospect and moved in with Fred and Dora (Dodie) Lowd at 1314 East Twenty-ninth Street. Sharing the rent and other household expenses reduced the financial burden for both families. Sharing household chores was something Dodie and Effie had done before. Bill continued to attend Paseo High School but had to take a city bus to get there.

An ushering job at the Isis movie theater in the shopping area at Thirty-first and Troost Avenue provided Bill with pocket money for dates and cigarettes when funds were so scarce at home. That job also cultivated in him a life-long fascination with the cinema.

Taking a date to the Midland theater in downtown Kansas City was an occasion to "pull out all the stops." One had to dress up not only to impress the girl friend but also because everyday clothes were considered inappropriate for downtown. Teenagers did not own cars. They often double or triple dated so the boys could take turns providing rides for the group. Bill's turn involved obtaining special permission to drive the family's old Franklin roadster that he thought was a sorry relic. (In later years he considered it a classic and wished he still had it.) He washed and polished the car to lessen his teenage embarrassment after the show when the valet parking attendant delivered his vehicle before the waiting crowd.

During Bill's high school days, Will was at home more than he had ever been during his adult life. Except for work he had done for his father during his youth, Will had never been employed by anyone. Though he occasionally helped Effie with her real estate business or helped someone get their taxes reduced, most of his time and energy were spent on his own projects. He cultivated a garden on a vacant lot nearby; he worked on problems surrounding the Kirkland estate, and he kept in touch with mining contacts in Colombia and in this country.

He continued, throughout the decade of the 1930s, to hope that he could get some new mining projects started, if not in Colombia then in the western United States. The prospect of riches from the Colombian gold mines had seemed so close to realization. He knew the gold was there ready to be mined. If only economic conditions had not turned against him just at the time he sought backing. The Kirkland estate represented some hope for eventual help but legal matters and prior mismanagement were delaying its realization.

Dodie was employed as a seamstress doing alterations at a dress shop downtown. She received a phone message at work one day from Will. The message simply stated, "Come home." When Dodie tried to return the call, there was no answer. Alarmed, she immediately made arrangements to leave work. When she arrived at home, neither Will nor anyone else was there. She knew that Effie was probably unreachable as she moved about the city taking care of her real estate business. Fred was at work and Bill was at school.

As Dodie entered the kitchen, the meaning of Will's message became clear. A bushel of fresh peaches rested beside the workspace. Knowing Will, she realized that he had purchased peaches to be canned, and he had strategically made himself scarce to avoid repercussions. Though somewhat disgusted with Will for his subterfuge, she dutifully waded in on the canning. There was no use returning to work for the rest of the day, and an investment in fresh produce was not to be wasted.

Will was no stranger to the kitchen. In those days of Depression and Prohibition, he sometimes made home brew. He bottled whatever grog it was and stored it in the basement until the first bottle blew its cork. Then it was ready for consumption. Bill came home more than once to find his dad in the kitchen with flour all over his apron and the kitchen counter. The filling of the pie in progress was not limited to one fruit but contained a combination of all fruits available, including raisins. When the emerging masterpiece was ready for the oven, Will placed it there with a flourish; and, as he slammed the oven door shut, he exclaimed, "Nox vomicus, e pluribus unum, damn-it-to-hellibus, BAKE!!"

Bill recalled that he never heard his father take the Lord's name in vain, but his exclamations sometimes verged on the irreverent. Will often quoted or misquoted snippet's of Shakespeare. He rolled the initial "r" as he proclaimed one of his favorites: "Rrrripped me from me mother's womb before me time! Scarce half made-up I was!"

As the middle of the twentieth century approached, three-score and ten years were often considered an average life expectancy. Any time beyond seventy was a bonus. After Will passed his seventieth birthday in 1936, he began having some health problems. His recuperation from an appendectomy was prolonged by complications, and he began a series of tooth extractions. As a teenager Bill, was very much aware of the aging of his parents. As with most matters, he was open about his concern for them. He asked that they have their pictures taken so he would have that record if they should pass away.

Effie, too, was having some health problems during Bill's high school days. A condition that she called arthritis and neuritis caused her discomfort and pain, especially in her hands and arms. She was beset by worries that made it difficult to maintain her characteristic jovial, optimistic attitude. She was worried over having lost their homes. She worried about their inability to repay a personal loan that friends had cosigned with them. She worried about the shortfall of her income to meet the family's basic needs. She felt guilty having to accept Marguerite's charity. She doubted their ability to stay in their rental house if the Lowds should move. But above all else she worried about finding a way to send Bill to college.

During that time of struggle for economic survival, Effie was having a crisis of the spirit. Sundays were prime time for her real estate business. She needed to work when customers were available to look at properties. So she stopped going to church, and she ceased making sure that her son attended services as well. Her faith that had been such a rock of assurance for her seemed to have faded, and there were times when she felt desperate. She was encouraged by friends to look into Christian Science, and she subscribed to a course called "Psychiana" offered by Frank B. Robinson, a doctor of divinity in Moscow, Idaho. The following is quoted from a letter Effie wrote to Dr. Robinson on October 9, 1937:

> *I have read and reread each lesson, and have made an intense effort to digest all that has been said, as I have for the past five years been HUNGRY for the TRUTH which would*

satisfy the longings of my soul ... I do not believe I have fully caught the clear method of using the GOD LAW because I have not had any distinct demonstration, other than what I have always had—that of life, family, friends, something to eat and wear — for which, of course, I am dearly grateful ...

He [her husband, Will] has been studying the lessons with me, and has enjoyed them very much, as they agree along the lines he has always thought. He has always been a 'radical' disbeliever in the Bible stories, and ever since we have been married (20 years) he has always credited me with good sense — with this one exception, I believe in them and he didn't. However, with the periodical "clashing" of our opinions, he set my mind to THINKING, which resulted more or less in me losing MY God. He is a very free thinker ...

My husband, son and I came out of the depression — if it is over — penniless ... I had been trained in office work — so ventured out into the real estate and rental field — commission basis — and have been in it ever since, but owing to my exhausted nerves, and slow business during these years, life has been indeed strenuous. So, I have been searching for HELP — something that would lift me out of discouragement and despair. I have always been active — even in my own home — and would not be content to sit down. But to work from nine to fourteen hours a day showing and listing property and not be able to make a reasonable salary — sufficient to take care of us — does discourage me.

Now tell me please, Dr. Robinson, is there any definite help outside of one's own strenuous effort and capacity to do? This may seem to you unnecessary to ask in the face of all those wonderful lessons, and from them I do catch glimpses, which give me hope for the things I need and desire. When one thinks of the magnitude of the creation of the GODLAW it seems silly to ask this — but I have been going along so long doing my level best to make a living, and I have always tried to live by the Golden Rule — was brought up that way by good parents, but still I am in need of strength and good health to carry on. I am in need of a home of our own, and money enough to care for it and us, in need of money to finish my boy's education—he is sixteen, and will be out of high school this coming year. This does not seem like too much to ask for and desire.

My reason for pouring out my troubles to you is that you might catch what is hindering me. My thought is along this line of reasoning — The God-Law does not work, I suppose, in miraculous ways. It cannot work with one beyond that one's capacity — hence my schooling and training and capacity is limited, and not sufficient in these trying times, for me and my family to have a comfortable, happy living. One cannot be happy with such a pressure of needs. Will you kindly write me if I am wrong? ...

However, I would have been sunk with this reasoning during those first trying years of our loss of home, etc. had not some kind friend given me her church literature — which was Christian Science — and it brought comfort and courage and hope, and I began to find a Source, I felt, on which I could rely. May I say here that I have found that Psychiana and Christian Science agree about many, many things. In Christian Science I could never seem to figure out about the existence of the human body, and why. I believe your 7th and 8th lessons are clearing my thought somewhat on this line ...

Knowing that you are a very busy person, and in a great work, I should have not taken so much of your time, but please believe me, I am in need of this God Power, and its enlightenment, that I may go on courageously, fervently trusting and expectant ...

Bill graduated from the Paseo High School on June 7, 1938, among a class of more than 500. He had remained very thin after his bout with undulant fever some years before. In fact, his parents were so concerned about his health that summer after his graduation that they insisted he quit his ushering job at the Isis. They considered his late shift-work injurious.

As the summer progressed, it was decided that Bill should enroll in the small church-sponsored junior college called

**Wiliam D. (Bill)
Brewster, 1938**

Graceland (now Graceland University) located just north of the Missouri border in Lamoni, Iowa. His sister Marguerite stepped in to meet the major cost of his tuition, room and board, which was $415 for the year. This represented no small sacrifice on her part in those still-dark Depression days. Bill was well aware of his sister's generosity and often expressed in his letters to her his appreciation and his hope to repay.

Beginning his college career required quite an adjustment for Bill. Lamoni was very small compared to his native Kansas City. Graceland's entire student body was about half the size of his high school graduating class. Living in the small frame dormitory called Marietta Hall on the Graceland campus without the constant supervision of his parents was new. His first year roommate was William Williams who was congenial but more quiet and religious than Bill. The emphasis on church activities was a change for him — he had not attended church during his teens. The discipline of studying for college courses was more demanding than high school had been. His grades remained in the average range.

Though he was serious about getting a college education, he saw no need to study to the exclusion of social and recreational pursuits. His letters often mention his participation on various committees for planning social events. His more liberal attitude toward activities such as dancing and smoking, upon which the church frowned, sometimes set him apart. But Bill was a flexible, social person, and he adjusted in his own time and way.

When he entered Graceland that September of 1938, he had not yet gained his full adult height of six feet. He weighed only 130 pounds but that began to change almost immediately. Food was a major topic in his letters home ("Thank you for the cake, send more!"). A hot plate in his room soon provided help to supplement what he ate at the commissary. Two months into the school year, he had gained twenty-three pounds and probably an inch or so in height. He wrote to his folks an urgent request for new slacks because his were getting too tight to button at the waist and his pants' cuffs were revealing his ankles. He wrote that the fellows were suggesting that he throw a party for his ankles and invite his pant legs to come on down.

Bill began to find special friends among his classmates. He was initiated into a social club called the Sixes. He soon found kindred spirits in Fred Robbins and Earl Dipple. Fred became his second-year roommate. Though Bill usually complied with college rules, he sometimes had trouble agreeing with them. When he disagreed, he could be vocal about his point of view. For example, he did well in speech class until he chose as the subject of an oration the proposition that dancing be allowed on campus.

Awareness of the limited financial resources of his parents and his sister is also very evident in Bill's letters to them. He expressed gratitude for the occasional dollar or two that each of them sent to him. One of his letters gave an accounting of his personal monthly expenditures as follows:

Laundry	$1.20	per month
Haircut	.35	every three weeks
Cigarettes	.50	per month
Cleaning and pressing	.40	per month
Misc. expense (such as shoe polish, hair oil, soap)	.50	per month
TOTAL NECESSARY EXPENSE	$2.95	

Two shows (stag)	.50
One show with date	.50
Eats afterward	.20
	$1.20

In 1943, William John (Will) and Effie Lanore Brewster complied with their son's request that they have photo portraits made.

Finances were so tight that an extra "mouth to feed" would be an added burden. When Bill wanted to bring Fred Robbins home with him for the weekend, he wrote to Marguerite requesting that Fred be allowed to stay with her and George rather than with his folks at 1314 East Twenty-ninth Street. Bill's reasoning was that Fred Lowd might want his parents to pay extra for having to feed an extra person in the household over that weekend.

He declined the possibility of working out of town the summer between his two years at Graceland College. He said he wanted to be with his folks because he thought he might not have them much longer.

Attitudes toward guns and hunting were different in those days. Bill took a shotgun to college with him. He was a fair marksman, and he enjoyed hunting game in the woods around the college. One of his letters noted that he saw a red fox and located its den. He reported having shot sixteen rabbits one day, and he bagged twenty on another occasion. No mention is made of what he did with the rabbits he killed. Perhaps the college cooks made use of them.

As his two years at Graceland progressed, the topic of girls began to compete in Bill's letters with those of food and finances. Typical of Bill, his letters were very open about his dates, supplying details to his parents and his sister. Dating was very tame in those days. Transportation and entertainment opportunities were limited and curfews and morals were strictly defined. Bill noted some hypocrisy in the behavior of some of his classmates who condemned "necking" while he knew they were engaging in some of that activity. He admitted to "pitching a little woo" himself, which meant he sometimes hugged and kissed a girl.

In a letter to his mother dated May 8, 1940, Bill explained the meaning of "going steady:"

> *Well, I have done it! Something that I said that I would never do. I am going steady. Nothing serious, however, just being practical about the whole thing. I found out some things about this steady business — some practical things. First of all, one doesn't feel that he has to spend money on the girl every time he takes her out or wants to be with her, then too, if you want to hold her hand you don't have to be embarrassed because people just look at you and say, "Oh, he's going steady." Quite a system, isn't it! She is a very nice girl, with blue eyes, brown hair, very nice complexion and lovely figure. She lost her father this year, poor thing, and she needs someone to comfort her and so I am the one. She isn't too prissy and she isn't too brazen, just right. Another nice thing about this steady business, each one has the other to keep him or her in check and, too, you never have to worry about a date. (Going steady means that no one else is to date the said party lest one be looked down on.)*

The name of his steady girl friend is not mentioned in the letter. The night before graduation, Bill broke the curfew rules by keeping his date out after their dormitory hours. This was considered a serious infraction. He was punished by being handed an empty diploma envelope at graduation. He had to appear before a committee about the matter. The committee's findings were quoted in a letter from the college addressed to Bill's father on June 11, 1940:

> *In the opinion of the committee, the students concerned represent in general wholesome patterns and no precedents seem to be involved. The committee, therefore, feels that these incidents may be closed with the conversations held between the student and the committee. It seems evident that these students are, on the whole, people of good judgment and merit our confidence in future decisions.*

The diploma conferring Bill's Associate of Arts degree was mailed to him.

WORLD WAR II   **21**

As BILL BEGAN HIS second year at Graceland College in September of 1939, events in Europe seemed far away and of negligible impact on his life. That same month, under the leadership of Adolph Hitler, Germany moved to expand its domain in Europe by attacking Poland. Poland fell quickly to the well-planned and executed might of the German army. Though Germany divided Poland with Russia, the relationship between Germany and Russia was an uneasy one. Early in December that same year, Russia invaded Finland in an effort to strengthen her northwestern border and to obtain more naval bases on the Baltic Sea. After three months of intense fighting, Finland surrendered. In the summer of 1940, Russia also seized Estonia, Latvia, and Lithuania.

While Russia was expanding its boundaries during that winter of 1939-1940, the rest of Europe was poised awaiting Germany's next move. The uncertainty ended in April. The targets were Denmark and Norway with their strategic access to the North Sea. France and Britain came to the aid of the Scandinavians but Germany prevailed. In the next two months, Belgium, Holland and Luxembourg also fell to Germany. Then France was attacked in June, and Italy joined Germany to share the spoils.

As Bill graduated from Graceland College in June of 1940, the conflicts in Europe still seemed remote but they were becoming harder to ignore. This was the second time in twenty-five years that Germany had fomented a world conflict by moving aggressively on her neighbors. The parents of Bill's generation had witnessed or fought in World War I. They were not eager to become embroiled again in Europe's struggles or to expose their sons to the trenches and poison gas typical of that prior war.

About the time Bill returned home after his two years at Graceland, Fred and Dora Lowd moved out. The Brewsters remained in the house they had shared with the Lowds, and Effie looked for roomers to help meet the rent and other household expenses. The roomers she found were Bill and two of his college friends, James Harlan Beatty and Edith Barr. The young folks all found jobs in Kansas City after graduating from Graceland. Bill Frye became a fourth young person to share room and board with them. Effie was a good cook, and she kept her expanded "family" well fed. She knew the cost, down to the penny, of every dish she put on the table, and she imposed certain house rules. One of her rules: If a boarder soiled her white linen tablecloth, he or she was expected to cover that spot with coins. Fabrics were not treated for permanent press in those days. Ironing a linen tablecloth was quite a chore. Despite, or perhaps because of, her rules, the young boarders soon bonded with their genial landlady and all began to call her "Mom."

Meanwhile, Europe's war clouds continued to threaten. On June 22, 1940, France surrendered to Germany and Italy. Three months later, Germany began bombing Great Britain while Italy turned its sights on Africa. When the Italians were being pushed back in Africa, Hitler sent German troops to support them. Canada quickly allied itself with Great Britain. The United States stopped short of joining the war but offered support under a "lend-lease" plan to those nations allied against Germany and Italy. Though reticent to intervene, the United States began to build defense plants and to expand its armed forces. Germany deployed submarines, called U-boats, in "wolf-pack" groupings in the Atlantic Ocean to prevent supplies from Canada and the United States reaching Great Britain.

The war continued to escalate with more nations joining on both sides of the conflict. Germany, Italy, Japan and the nations joining them were labeled "Axis Powers." The nations opposing the Axis Powers were called the "Allies." Japan had attacked China in 1937, and by 1940 it occupied Indochina. The United States reacted by stopping its shipments of steel and gasoline to Japan. The Germans anticipated a ready conquest when they marched into Russia in June of 1941. Their invasion force included three million men, and the battle line stretched over two thousand miles — from the Arctic to the Black Sea. The United States and Great Britain began shipping supplies to Russia, and the Russians proved relentless in defending themselves against the Germans.

In the United States, the uncertainty about entering the war ended on December 7, 1941. Japan launched a surprise bombing attack on Pearl Harbor in Hawaii that day, and the war suddenly became personal to Americans. President Franklin D. Roosevelt immediately asked Congress to declare war on Japan. Three days later, Germany and Italy declared war on the United States and Congress responded with return declarations. As the United States joined the ranks of the Allies, her efforts at preparation changed to full-scale mobilization for war.

Back in Kansas City, Bill left his job in the mailroom at Avon Products Corporation to work for North American Aviation, a war-related industry in Kansas City, Kansas. He celebrated his twenty-first birthday on February 19, 1942. Being healthy and able-bodied, he knew he would soon be called to serve in the armed forces, and he began to explore ways to exercise some choice as to where and how he would serve. A retired Navy warrant officer, a friend of the family, advised him to join the Navy before his number was drawn in the draft lottery, and that is what he did.

On September 23, 1942, Bill spent a tiresome day sitting around the Navy recruiting office waiting to sign papers. He was sworn in late that day and was immediately assigned to a troop train bound for boot camp in California. While on the train, he wrote a postcard to his folks telling them how the day had gone and where he was headed. He asked them not to worry and wrote that he had already struck up a friendship with one of the other recruits.

Boot camp in San Diego was shortened from two months to four weeks to meet the urgency of the war effort. Bill wrote to his parents in great detail about his experiences. When he arrived at camp, he received a second physical examination, several immunizations, and a regulation hair cut ("I look like a shorn sheep!"). He was issued regulation Navy clothing, including underwear and toilet articles, and he mailed his civilian clothes home. Bill reported:

> *Everything is done on the double and then wait about two hours before doing something else ... [like] learning the fundamentals such as washing clothes, drill, guard duty, semaphore, and how to pack our bags. We have to do everything a certain way and no other. There are a thousand rules, but I guess we will learn them in due time ... We sleep with our heads a certain way ... All of our belongings have to be kept in two canvas bags, the large one called a "sea bag," the smaller one called a "ditty bag"...*
>
> *The lingo here is different in many ways, for instance to eat is called "chow." When we get up in the morning it is "hit the deck." Everyone is called "Mac" if you don't know him.*

Fellow sailors were referred to as "shipmates." The walls were "bulkheads." One day Bill and his shipmates were issued gas masks, and they were herded into a chamber filled with tear gas. All of them came out shedding tears, and any exposed skin was stinging, but they had no ill effects after about an hour.

Only about four in Bill's company of 160 men had any college education, and some had not completed high school. Many were having difficulty learning the exercise and semaphore (signaling) drills that the whole company was to do in unison. The battalion commander chose Bill and one other recruit out of 320 men to lead the physical drill and parade. The typing skills that Bill had honed at Graceland came in handy for writing letters and probably helped him land duty as an orderly for an officer while others in his platoon drew duties like cleaning sewers. However, Bill did his share of guard duty, cleanup of the barracks, and vigilance to avoid the outbreak of crab lice that occurred in his company.

Food is a recurrent topic in Bill's letters home:

> *We all march over to the chow line in single file. We get a tray and a mug. Everything is rush, rush, rush ... [He lists various vegetables and meats they were served] and lemon juice — tastes just like water, but someone told me it was lemonade so we call it that ... And BEANS. Don't let anyone ever tell you the Navy doesn't feed you beans. I can blow a candle out at forty paces if I lean over.*

The next step after boot camp was assignment to ships or to various training schools for specialized jobs. Aptitude tests were given to screen candidates for the schools. The logistics of moving such large numbers of men and preparing and equipping them for battle must have been a mind-boggling task. Uncertainty is often evident in Bill's letters. Where would he be sent next? What would he be doing? Rumors were rampant. When three large ships were lost in the war, it was rumored that more than the expected number of those in boot camp would be tapped for sea duty.

As it turned out, Bill was assigned to electrician's school at the University of Houston, Texas. He arrived there November 1, 1942. He found the officers easy to get along with. The residents of Houston, missing their own sons in the military, went out of their way to entertain and to be helpful to the servicemen in their midst. Civilian volunteers manned the recreation center of the United Service Organization (USO). In Bill's words:

> *On Sundays many families with patriotic intentions would call in to invite one or two servicemen to their homes for Sunday dinner. Looking for a change from Navy chow I showed up at the USO on Sunday mornings early to put my name on the invitation list. Note: most Navy men were not*

Bill Brewster in the Navy in World War II, 1943

seeking a dinner with the "old folks" but I had grown up dining with old folks. I often found at the table a young daughter ever so often eager to meet, even under their parents' watchful eyes, a young serviceman. I thanked my mother for having taught me great table manners that let me be at ease in such circumstances.

Christmas of 1942 was the first Bill had ever spent away from home. A couple invited him and nine other sailors to stay in their home overnight Christmas Eve and to have a feast on Christmas Day. And what a feast it was! The hosts also provided gifts for each of their sailor guests. Bill was very impressed. He estimated that at least forty percent of the residents of Houston had servicemen in their homes as guests that Christmas.

Bill remembered an old chief petty officer in Houston who probably had been called back to be "dorm mother" to the troops. He had stripes and insignia all down one arm of his uniform for his long service. The man had a voice like a foghorn as he got the troops up every morning at 6 A.M. and out on the parade ground for calisthenics.

Bill was seeing himself in relation to a broader world than he had previously known. He found buddies to pal with or to double date with when on liberty. While in Houston he wrote to his sister Marguerite about his relations with his classmates:

They are all good boys but they lead a mighty simple life.
My vocabulary evidently is too big for them and I have to be
careful what I say or they razz me. One time I used the word
"ambiguous," quite in its place, and the whole class shouted.
Some of them call me the "Society Kid." Don't misunderstand
— I'm not having a hard time. In fact, I'm quite well known
and, I think, liked.

Brewster family finances were still very tight at that time.
Will was receiving a small pension. Effie had retired from the
real estate business in 1941 because of health problems but
continued to take in two or three roomers. Will had required
prostate surgery but his wound was slow to heal. Bill's sister
and brother-in-law were married almost ten years before their
son George was born on May 7, 1942. It soon became apparent that Georgie, as they called him, had developmental problems. He was eventually diagnosed with cerebral palsy.
Georgie was subject to frequent medical emergencies, including seizures. Though Marguerite and George continued to help
her parents as much as they could, their focus needed to be on
their own family needs.

The Kirkland estate properties that Will had inherited were
another possible source of income but they were not producing much. Rent controls were imposed during the war. Land-
lords who raised rents could be prosecuted. Will had only a
half interest in the Fort Madison properties, and he was re-
alizing little or no income there. The 1942 monthly statements
from the property manager of the Chicago properties indicate that all the rents were used up in repairs to the sixty-
year-old apartment buildings. That state of affairs apparently
continued through the war years. It was later learned that
tenants of the Chicago properties were sub-leasing portions
of their apartments and were making profits while Will, the
landlord, realized little or none. Tenants damaged the apartments by subdividing and otherwise misusing their quarters.
Will was not physically or financially able to repair the buildings for sale, and he could not increase the rents until the

controls were lifted.

In order to assist his parents, Bill applied for a family allotment from the Navy. That allotment finally materialized in
May of 1943. Part of what his folks received was deducted
from Bill's pay. The allotment relieved him of much of his worry
about his parents' financial needs. He requested that they
use as much as possible of the allotment to pay off the note
friends had cosigned with them some years before.

When he completed electrician's school, Bill was awarded
the rank of petty officer third class, also designated as
electrician's mate third class. On February 26, 1943, he was
sent to the Algiers Naval Station across the Mississippi River
from New Orleans. Smaller ships such as PT boats and LSTs
were repaired or retrofitted at that base. LSTs were only about
300 feet long. Huge doors in the bow could be opened, and a
ramp lowered to off-load men and cargo on a beach. LSTs
were manufactured in the Ohio valley and were delivered to
the Gulf of Mexico by way of the Ohio and Mississippi rivers.
Masts lay flat on the decks for the trip down river so they
could pass under the many bridges en route.

Once an LST reached the Algiers Naval Station, the mast
was set in place. Stabilizing cables were attached from the
top and middle of the mast to the ends of the yardarm. Then
Bill's work began. He climbed the masts (some as tall as sixty
feet) and installed the signal lights on the yardarm while
standing on the lower cable. A red light was wired on one end
of the yardarm and a green light on the other.

At first Bill worked under the supervision of experienced
electricians. Gradually, he was given more responsibility. The
amount of work to be done varied. At times they were intensely
busy, and at other times there was nothing to be done. During
the slack times, the men read, wrote letters or played cards or
chess. The quantity and quality of food always caught Bill's
notice. He considered the food at that Louisiana post especially good.

Bill watched somewhat impatiently the progress of the war,
relating it to the shipping he saw pass through their port. In

the late summer and fall of 1943, he wrote that the ships were being armed more heavily. He thought that a big invasion was sure to happen in Europe before long, and he estimated that the war should be over in a year. He conjectured about what form of work he would pursue after the war. In September of 1943 he wrote to Marguerite:

> ... After this war I'll come home, of course, but if K.C. can't offer me some good electrical job I'm going to strike out. It's hard to explain, but living near Mom and being so conventional all the time has made a sissy out of me. I've got to get out and toughen up a bit. I've got to be satisfied from within before settling down ... If I don't write for a long time to you or Mom you'll know I'm in the brig for fighting. I can't stand the razzing much longer.

About December 1, 1943, in Kansas City Effie and Will finally managed to finish paying off the note that friends had co-signed with them. Once that was done, they were free to negotiate the purchase of the home they were renting at 1314 East 29th Street. Bill thought if they paid as much as $2500 for that two story, three-bedroom brick and frame house, they might lose money on it when they sold it. They closed their purchase of the house on December 30, 1943, for $2487.90. It provided a secure, low-cost place for them to live, and it proved a good investment. It was finally sold in about 1958 when prices had escalated after the war. Predicting the course of the economy was as uncertain then as today.

During the last half of 1943, Bill worked toward upgrading his rank to electrician's mate second class. He studied hard, passed all of the required tests and received his new rank about the first of December. He was glad to have that behind him as he headed home for a much-anticipated second furlough early in January.

In the Pacific Theater of the war, besides occupying parts of China, the Japanese took over the Netherlands East Indies and parts of the Aleutian Islands, but the tide of the war in

the Pacific was changing. Names of Pacific islands like
Corregidor, Midway, Guadalcanal, and Tarawa became household words as the Japanese were defeated in those places at a
terrible cost in lives, ships, and equipment.

In Europe, the Russians were having some success repel-
ling the German invaders. Allied forces, including the United
States, had prevailed in North Africa and had moved on to
conquer Italy. The Germans continued their bombardment of
Great Britain, but the British were hanging tough. German
factories became prime targets for the bombs of the Allies. An
Allied invasion of Europe was expected, but the timing and
the location for that assault were top secrets.

The war seemed to drag on and morale was not static.
Though Bill's attitude was usually upbeat, there were times
of fatigue, of boredom and discouragement. Even though his
situation was considered "good duty," he began to experience
burnout on his job. He felt guilty when he contrasted his situation with the hardships so many others were enduring overseas. Finally, he volunteered to go overseas, but his orders
did not come.

As he waited, he explored the possibility of entering officers' training school but was ruled out on two counts: his near-
sightedness and an already-filled quota. Then he learned that
a sailor with his same rank wanted to transfer out of a base
near Memphis. Bill applied for a transfer to trade with that
man. Returning from liberty one day, he was surprised to learn
that his name had been crossed off the draft list for sea duty
because of his pending application for transfer. While he awaited
a decision on his transfer, he was sent across the river with a
four-man crew to do a different kind of wiring job that piqued
his interest. The matter of the Memphis transfer remained unresolved for several weeks before it finally fell through.

In Kansas City all that winter of 1943-1944, Will was
troubled with a wound from surgery that did not heal as it
should. By March a new surgery was planned, but before
that operation took place, events took a different turn as explained in one of Effie's letters to a friend:

*Mr. Brewster passed very suddenly with a heart attack
on March 26. He had gone to his room to recline on his bed
and read the Sunday paper about 7 p.m. I was in his room
writing a letter. When I finished I started downstairs to hear
the Charlie McCarthy program and I asked if he didn't want
to go as he always enjoyed the program. But he said he didn't
believe he would go back down, that he wanted to rest and
read. He had put a pillow up to his back, his visor over his
glasses to protect his eyes from the light. I stayed downstairs
to read a story but I sort of missed him calling me to come up
to bed, which was his custom if I stayed down late to read.
So at 11:30 I finished my story and rushed upstairs to ask
him if he wanted a glass of milk or a grapefruit, which also
was his custom before really retiring. As I went into his room
I thought he was asleep. He had removed the pillow from his
back and was lying down, relaxed, with his glasses and visor
still on. Then I sensed that he didn't look quite normal and I
presume he had passed on an hour or so before I discovered
him, as his flesh was cold and his fingernails were blue. You
can imagine how shocked I was to find him gone. We had
been married almost 26 years. He was always so cheerful.
His life had been full and colorful ... I miss him dreadfully.
The days and nights are too long.*

Bill was granted a leave to go home for his father's funeral.
While at home, he helped his mother sort out some of his dad's
belongings. Bill gathered up and discarded a bushel basket-
ful of patent medicines that Will had tried in his effort to solve
his health problems. Will had accumulated more than thirty
new shirts in his dresser that he had never worn. Though financially strapped in his declining years, Will had not completely shed the spending habits of his affluent years. During
his growing-up years, Bill sometimes felt his father was too
far removed in age to understand his son's needs, but he remembered his dad as an honest, principled man who was kind
and energetic.

While in Kansas City at that time, Bill and his mother dis-

cussed options for her future now that her life was changed
by the loss of her mate. They considered putting in storage
the furnishings that she wanted to keep and selling the house
and the Franklin automobile. They discussed the possibility
of Effie coming to Louisiana and renting a furnished room or
apartment for a month or so while Bill continued to be stationed there.

Back on the Naval Base after the funeral, Bill resumed his
duties. He began to have second thoughts about the tentative
plans for his mother's visit. The weather was already becoming uncomfortably warm in New Orleans. Rooms were scarce
and rents were high. There was also the possibility that he
could be drafted for sea duty at any time. Effie decided to
stay on in her home. She had business matters to tend to.
Probate procedures had to be met in three states — Missouri,
Iowa, and Illinois.

During May and June, Bill welcomed a couple of varia-
tions in his work routine. He was sent with a small crew to
ferry a tugboat from a Mississippi port back to his station.
On another occasion, he was suddenly assigned to go to
Galveston with a group to help control a strike in a shipyard.
That turned out to be more of a vacation. The need for their
services had passed by the time they arrived, so they enjoyed
a brief liberty in Galveston.

D-Day, June 6, 1944, saw the beginning of the long-
anticipated invasion in Europe on the French coast of
Normandy. Several thousand ships and planes were used to
deliver the invasion force of nearly 3,000,000 men on five
beachheads. German forces resisted strongly but the Allies
finally gained a foothold. They pushed on toward Germany
from the west while the Russians marched toward Berlin from
the east. As the Allies gained the upper hand in Europe, the
United States prepared to launch even more of its resources
against Japan.

On July 12, Bill wrote to his mother that he was to board a
troop train that evening for a three-day and four-night trip to
San Bruno, near San Francisco. The racetrack at San Bruno

was being converted into a staging area for troops bound for the battlefields in the Pacific. Sailors were bivouacked in temporary quarters while barracks were being built. At one point Bill was bunked in a horse stall. They were moved from one barracks to another as new facilities were hastily completed.

Dust, mud, and a shortage of water were some of the inconveniences that existed while construction continued. True to Effie's training, Bill always tried to keep himself and his clothes very clean. Laundry took ten days when sent out so Bill preferred to do his own. Clothes driers were not yet in use in those days. When Bill brought his first wash in off the line at San Bruno, it was dirtier than before he washed it, so he had to use the laundry services at least temporarily.

While he waited for his orders, he wrote home about his expected overseas assignment:

> *I haven't the slightest idea of where I'm going but I am sure it will be in the Pacific area on an island. My duties will be to keep in operation all electrical equipment in our hospital unit. You see a hospital has lights, hot plates, sterilizers, a power plant, its own laundry, its own kitchen, heads (toilets) — in other words it is a complete unit. Besides the wounded, doctors, (maybe nurses), and corpsmen, there are motor mechanics, carpenters, metal smiths and electricians who keep things running. We will always be in a safe position for we are not a frontline field dressing station but are well behind the lines.*

While at San Bruno, Bill's company consisted mostly of pharmacist mates but also other auxiliary personnel for hospital units. He was assigned platoon leader, so he was again leading daily exercise drills. They hiked up into the mountains for a weeklong primitive camp. The worst part was the long hike up and back. Other than that, it was easy duty and the chow was great. He attended training sessions in seamanship, gunnery and other skills aimed at preparing the men for situations they could meet after being shipped out. Bill was awarded a sharpshooter's medal for his gunnery skills.

After about six weeks, the personnel that would staff Bill's hospital unit were assembled and moved to a base called Shoemaker, about 40 miles from the San Bruno racetrack. The unit then included doctors (general practitioners, anesthesiologists, surgeons), corpsmen, male nurses, medical technicians, pharmacists, a warrant officer, cooks and helpers, drivers, a carpenter and helper, a plumber and helper, and Bill the electrician. Rumors were rampant as to when they would be shipped out, but the orders did not come for more than six months.

While they waited, the men were assigned various duties. For a brief period, Bill was assigned to shore patrol duty. Shore patrol is the Navy's police department charged with patrolling shore areas that are frequented by naval personnel. Their uniforms and equipment included a yellow armband with "SP" on it, a guard belt, boots, and club. Bill had night patrol on the streets of Stockton, California, about 50 miles from his base. He explained two of his patrols as follows:

Last Friday I had the restricted area patrol with an M.P., of course. My, what a filthy place this is. It is a part of Stockton where all the bums and low class hang out ... One can see and usually does see anything and everything happen down there. The night I was there we were involved in a stabbing in which I chased the assassin but lost him in the dark streets. There was also a fight, a negro sailor with a white woman, innumerable drunks, 'whores by the score' and all around us filth. It is disgusting.

The other night I was assigned to the city police squad car. That was fun. We got a call on a robbery, pulled in several drunks and 'covered' the dance in the Hall. Getting to ride was a pleasure for a change. Then, too, we got to cruise over a good-sized area. That nite except for the robbery it was very quiet.

The sailors were encouraged to help out where there were civilian manpower shortages nearby. Bill worked for a while in a tomato cannery. Tomato soup and puree were cooked in four huge vats that were seven feet deep and five feet wide. The products were cooked by steam that ran through copper pipes in the bottom and sides of the vats. There were valves to regulate the flow of steam in the pipes, the flow of raw materials into the vats, and the cooked products out of them. It was very important to turn the correct valves on or off at the right times. After each batch, the vats and pipes were cleaned with coarse steel pads and a garden hose to remove any scorched product so the next batch would not be polluted. Usually one of the vats was cooking while the others were being filled, emptied, or cleaned. Bill was the only serviceman to become foreman of the operation during his four-hour shifts. He later took a job ushering in a movie theater. Those jobs produced extra pocket money that he could readily use.

Rumors about when Bill's company would be shipped out continued to surface. Finally, their commander went back to Washington D.C. and found the papers for his unit buried in a paper logjam. On his twenty-fourth birthday, February 19, 1944, Bill wrote:

> *I would hate to be premature in saying so but I think this last bunch of rumors are somewhat true. We are going to do something fairly soon. Today they took clothing measurements of us all. I understand they are calling back all men on temporary duty — this means something is afoot. We will probably reassemble and then take a short training, to toughen up, here or at our port of embarkation.*
>
> *I was just over to our unit's office and my buddy Downs showed me an allotment list for a 200-bed S.A.H. (hospital). In this particular list was named electrical gear, also carpenter's gear and by the looks of the items listed we will be a permanent based outfit. Among some of the items were 2000 bags of cement, also several thousand feet of lumber and wiring. Don't misunderstand me, we had not received this but we are supposed to. Besides don't tell anybody what I tell you.*

There was a saying during the war, "Loose lips sink ships." This meant that the enemy could have spies anywhere, so citizens were warned not to talk about anything they heard that might be useful to the enemy if they knew it. That is why Bill warned his mother not to talk about what he told her.

WARTIME AND MATTERS OF THE HEART **22**

Our NATION WAS VERY unified during World War II. Most families had someone serving in a branch of the military. Those left at home did all they could to support the war effort and the service personnel. Most homes had a small pennant hung in a window. A blue star on the pennant signified a family member serving in one of the armed forces. A gold star stood for a loved one killed in the war. Families of servicemen dreaded a telegram notifying them of the loss of a loved one, but such notices were received in nearly every community.

The roles of women changed dramatically during that war. Before the war, acceptable roles outside the home for women were primarily those of teachers, nurses, secretaries, or domestic help. Women teachers who married were expected to stop teaching. Married women were expected to become homemakers and mothers. Pregnancies were to be kept out of the workplace. A teacher shortage resulted when most men teachers were called into the armed forces. Married women were then welcomed into the schools, especially those who were teachers before they married. Necessity revealed that women could do all sorts of jobs previously considered the exclusive province of men; and they were encouraged to fill every possible position that might free men to fight in the war. Women were also welcomed into the military but not to serve in combat. They served as nurses or other support personnel.

Townspeople did all they could to help and to entertain the servicemen in their midst. Picking up a hitchhiking man in uniform was considered the patriotic thing to do. Letter writing was another way that adults and children tried to keep up the morale of the troops. Bill received lots of letters from his family and from friends — both male and female. When several days passed without mail, he lamented it. Letters were his lifeline connection with home. He was kept busy in his free time answering the letters he received so his correspondents would write to him again. His parents alone received almost 250 letters that he wrote home during the time he served in the Navy.

While in Texas, Bill wrote to his folks that southern girls were "cold as ice" unless they were properly introduced. But being introduced was apparently no problem to Bill. He met girls through the USO or through the girl friends of his buddies. Marriage was on Bill's mind though not in his plans until the war was over. In one letter, he wrote that he would like to put off marriage until he was age 28. However, he was analyzing the qualities of each of the girls he met, developing his list of prerequisites. One of his strategies was to observe a girl's mother to get an idea of what the daughter might look like in middle age.

Many of the girls he mentioned in his letters to his folks were in their late teens and had just finished high school. However, Momo (a nickname for Margarita) was a twenty-one-year-old college graduate that Bill met while in New Orleans. She was born in Germany of a Russian mother and a Dutch father who was an American citizen. Bill found Momo fun to be with, though he sometimes considered her his intellectual superior.

Momo invited Bill to a crab dinner at home with her family. He was surprised when he saw their dining table covered with several layers of newspaper in preparation for the meal. Once they began to crack the shells of the boiled crabs, he saw the wisdom of using that table covering. He was always ready for new experiences, especially those involving food. Bill remembered that evening as being special. Momo was scheduled to join the WAVES, the female branch of the Navy. After she left, Bill exchanged letters with her for a short while.

After his first furlough in April of 1943, the name "Jean" often appears in his letters. Jean was connected somehow with the Avon Products firm where Bill had worked. They dated while he was home on leave, and he returned to his post believing she was the girl he wanted to marry. He hoped Jean would wait for him until the war was over. He told his folks that she was not only physically attractive, she was very sweet, unselfish, and she was not moody. The two began writing letters and anticipating his next furlough.

During the last half of 1943, Bill curtailed some of his social life to save money for the furlough he would have in January. Gasoline was one of the items being rationed during the war. He wrote to his folks asking them to try to save gas stamps so he would be able to use the car when he got home. By January 6, when he headed home on leave, he had saved about $100.

Bill had a great time while at home — eating his mom's home cooking and going out with Jean. After returning to the naval station, however, he was filled with doubts and discouragement. Effie apparently wrote some items for consideration if Bill were really serious about Jean. He replied that Jean was the finest girl he had ever gone with and that she had all the traits a man could ask for in a wife. However, Jean had not actually expressed her feelings for him. He noted, "This war does mix one's feelings." He wondered if he was really in love with her or was he just lonely and unsettled because of the war? He hoped the intervening eight months before his next furlough would clarify things. Meanwhile, he planned to save money for engagement and wedding rings.

Less than two weeks after Bill returned from that much-anticipated leave, Jean wrote that she was going to California to see a young man she had dated earlier named Norman. Bill protested, first by telegram and then by telephone. Jean admitted she might still be in love with Norman. Bill wrote to his mother, "Perhaps I'm not in love with her but I nearly went crazy thinking about the situation ..." He admitted being very disillusioned about women. A day or two later he wrote to his mother:

I love Jean, Mom, but perhaps it's now loved for I'm try-

ing to forget, but I'm doing a bad job of it. She's on my mind constantly ... I feel all gone inside ... Received your last two letters and appreciate your comments. Yes, I admit it was all my fault. All I was thinking about was Jean's and my future. I wanted a secure future and a good start in marriage and not a hasty affair ... What I can't figure out is that if Jean didn't love me, or didn't even have a tendency, then how come our closeness during my leave and the letters before. I can't help but believe she would have accepted my proposal if I had made one. I could kick myself for not being able to see this when home.

Bill wrote a final letter to Jean and enclosed a note to her mother. The mother replied with the following letter:

Dear Bill,

I hardly know how to write you what I feel, but I know you must be anxious to hear from Jean and I am going to try and not hurt you any, if possible. I received a wire this AM and Jean is getting married today the 12th of February. This is the happiest day of her life and I try to think of it in that light, but I feel very sad today.

I have never thought of her getting married so far from home. I feel as though I have been cheated. I have always pictured her getting married in a church, but wars change everything. I had great hopes she would settle down here so we could be with her and see how happy she really was. Today I tried to send a wire to congratulate them but Uncle Sam said no wires for foolishness. So I sit here all day wondering and trying to imagine what time today it will take place.

I received your letter and sent Jean's on to her. I am sorry if she has hurt you but she wouldn't do it intentionally. She never could hurt anyone on purpose. You may feel like she should of told you, but if she had you might think she was trying to make you jealous or wring a proposal out of you.

Jean never did have to dig for dates or a proposal either. She has been a very popular girl and she tries never to talk of one boy while out with another. You only underestimated her popularity. Most girls are looked upon as trying to capture people's sons but Jean never went with a boy but his folks were also very fond of her. We are very proud of her and everyone seems to fall in love with her sweet disposition and gentle nature.

I want you to know how very much I admire your pleasant personality, and your morals are some of the highest I have ever seen in a young man. I can't say I wanted Jean to marry into money, but I did want him to have high morals and plenty of ambition.

I am writing to you because I know how waiting is, and I was pretty sure she hadn't written. I don't hear as often as I would like. Here is part of her last letter: 'Mother, I haven't written as often as I intended, but I have not even thought of anyone since I arrived. I really should drop all my friends a card, but am so busy.'

Jean may not tell you anything about Norman so I will try and tell you. He went to William Chrisman [High School] and graduated the year before she did. Then he attended Graceland [College] one year and three years at M.U. He signed up for two years foreign service as a civil engineer, so he has spent two lonely years on the islands where our bases are now operating. He doesn't drink or smoke and is very ambitious, as he saved over half of what he earned in the two years. His mother is a widow since he was eight years old, so he has brought himself up under one of the greatest handicaps. Everyone has the greatest admiration for him.

If Jean writes you please don't mention anything I am saying. She would say you didn't want to hear anything about all this.

I hope we will remain good friends. I know this is hard to take now, but I would like to give you a little advice. The next time you fall in love, tell the girl by all means, and let her be the judge as to how long she will wait.

I would like to hear from you again. I am hoping Jean will write to all of us soon, but they are going to San Fran-

cisco for a few days and I don't look for mail until they re-
turn. I remain your friend. Mrs. Earl Thompson

Bill was not one to stay downhearted. He resolved to put
thoughts of Jean behind him, and he soon found other girls he
enjoyed dating. One of those was a pre-med student named
Connie. As had been true of his acquaintance with Momo, Bill
found Connie an interesting conversationalist. The friendship,
however, was simply a temporary diversion. Connie had a doctor friend of whom she was very fond, and she returned to
college to complete her degree. Bill's friendships with Momo
and Connie helped confirm his thoughts about furthering his
own college education after the war. After dating them, he
wrote home about going back to college. He considered going
to a Colorado university to study mining engineering. He
thought he might return to South America to try to rejuve-
nate his dad's mining interests there.

After he was sent to California, he became acquainted with
Marilyn Pein and her family who lived in San Mateo, one of
the towns near Bill's base. He wrote to his mother numerous
times about them:

> *Marilyn is only 17 years old, but she's got her share of*
> *brains and a good sense of humor and is not lazy ... she's*
> *unspoiled and quite modest about her physical appearance*
> *which by the way is <u>mighty</u> nice.*
> *   ... she is a real blond, 5 ft. 5 in., 115 lbs., a lovely long*
> *pair of legs and cute shape to match. She is so innocent and*
> *unspoiled and clean that I enjoy just being with her ... She*
> *lets me forget the Navy for awhile. I'd sure like to see her 4*
> *years from now — boy, what a little gem she is! Her mother is*
> *young looking (not fat either Ha!) and is good-natured. There*
> *are three children — one brother (age 21 and away in the*
> *military), one sister (age 19) and Marilyn. She is very pretty*
> *and healthy. The father is about 40, I guess — likes to fish —*
> *makes his own flies, etc. He has an electrical shop/garage com-*
> *bination. They have a very nice home in a good location.*

I have to hitch-hike over the San Mateo bridge [bus routes did not cross that seven-mile-long bridge] to get there. From here the trip takes 2 hours but it's worth it ... I only get to come over once every two weeks. Mrs. Pein invited me to come over for Sat. nite and Sun. when I come back next time.

And in another letter:

I really had a swell weekend!! ... I hitchhiked over and got 4 rides, one right after another so it only took me two hours. I got there before Marilyn did. Mr. and Mrs. Pein always greet me like they are glad to see me. Mr. Pein mixed up a drink before dinner then we went to the bus line to pick up Marilyn. She works in a department store in Frisco on Saturdays. Then we all had dinner. I helped with the dishes although they insisted I sit down. Georgina, Marilyn's sister, washed them and I wiped them. Marilyn and I and another couple double dated. The other guy had a big car. We danced all evening — from 8 to 12. The other fellow was a young guy ... and we hit it off swell ...

Sunday morning we all slept late but I was first to get up of us three "kids." The girls just love to sleep. Mrs Pein had some fresh, homegrown rhubarb for breakfast and I had three dishes of it — after a bit of coaxing. Ha! Marilyn got ready as we had planned to go to Frisco to the beach where they have a heated swimming pool. Mr. Pein really surprised me when he said, "take the car." I put up a feeble protest but after all, I had gotten a license some time ago thinking I was going to rent a car but never did. They have two cars and we took the older one but it sure felt good to drive again!! Then we had our swim and then stopped at a roadside inn and ate dinner. We had a table by one of the fireplaces. It was real cozy. We got home about 8 o'clock and I left at 10 o'clock.

And again he wrote:

Last Friday I had a date with Marilyn. I got a ride to

Hayward, which is halfway so I got over in good time. I called from San Mateo (downtown) ... and Mrs. Pein invited me for dinner. She had some good old home-cooked hash, a crabmeat salad, some tasty green beans and a swell pudding cake. Boy! Did I ever eat. Mr. Pein told me some time ago that Mrs. Pein liked to see a boy eat 'cause she was used to her son eating a lot so since then I haven't restrained myself. Of course I've been careful to see that everyone else has had all they're going to eat before I dive in, etc. So you needn't worry about me — you've taught me well, Mom, and you needn't worry about me doing anything tactless.

The Pein family continued to welcome Bill into their home throughout his stay in California. He spent his weekend liberties with them, went fishing with Mr. Pein and was offered the use of their car on several occasions. Bill's dates with Marilyn were spent in San Francisco nightclubs and restaurants or at Marilyn's high school dances or swimming and sunbathing at the beach. Because their birthdays were within ten days of each other — February 19 and 28 — Bill and Marilyn celebrated together at a noted restaurant on Fisherman's Wharf in San Francisco. Jack Dempsey, the heavyweight boxer, was there that evening. Bill managed to get his autograph for himself and for Marilyn.

The bronze sharpshooters medal that Bill was awarded for his marksmanship with firearms was about the size of a half-dollar with a target impressed on it and the words "Expert Rifleman," and it was hung on a blue ribbon with green stripes. He was not allowed to wear it with his uniform but instead was required to wear a small ribbon of the same pattern. So he gave the medal to Marilyn and wrote to his mother as follows:

I gave my large medal to Marilyn with the proviso I could take it back in case it didn't remain in the family! Ha! When I said this she asked, "Why, Bill, is that a proposal?" I said, "I wish it could be." Quite tactful, eh? I wasn't kidding her. The way I feel now I wish we could be married. It's a good thing

I'm poor!! Ha!

Marilyn and I went out last Friday nite. It was a nasty day and nite — rained all the time — off and on. We went out to dinner and to a show. We spent a few intimate moments on the divan (clean muggin'!), spoke a few endearing words and then I went back to the base 'till next Saturday. Marilyn is quite fond of me but not in love with me. She's still young and a bit fickle. She goes with her high school friends on the weekends I'm not there. Always tells me about it if I ask. She doesn't throw it in my face. I don't mind for she always reserves the days I can get off which is every other weekend and every other Friday.

Altho she has a good many of the traits I want in a girl there seems to be something lacking. I can't quite describe it. I think it is due to her age. Remember how Jean was — so feminine and lady-like, yet not prissy? Well Marilyn has not yet developed to this stage, nor has she learned all the social graces. I realize that she can learn these things and probably will in the next two or three years. That is what I'm anxious to see when I come back from overseas. When a girl is in high school this type of learning is limited — but after she gets out into the world — either college or a job — she will follow and imitate the girls with whom she associates — right? In short the apple ripens on the tree quicker than in the basket so I intend to leave it there! Ha!

On one of the last weekends Bill was with Marilyn and her family, he and Marilyn had a heart-to-heart talk that Bill reported to his mother:

We had a long talk all day Sunday and it seems she thinks I'm awfully nice and good to her, but she has lost interest. I already knew this so it didn't come as a surprise. She didn't know why she didn't like me as much as she used to altho she did mention another fellow also her folks interfering. She said she misses me when I'm gone. Her letters between weekends have been full of nice things, etc. I told her not to worry

about it as she was young and this was her trouble, Ha! I
also told her that I didn't love her but could have — maybe
— had I been encouraged at the right time. It all ended that
we better understood one another and are still good friends.

As Bill was preparing to leave for his overseas assignment, he asked his mother to write to the Pein family. He suggested that she thank them for treating him so swell — for all of Mrs. Pein's dinners and Mr. Pein's generosity with his car and treating him almost like a son. Bill wrote that she could quote him as saying that the Peins had two fine daughters but cautioned her against making any reference to his feelings for Marilyn. He noted that Marilyn was "mighty good company and very thoughtful of my money and time. But she doesn't love me nor I love her ... Maybe in two or three years she might change and grow older in mind — her body is OK right now — ha!"

Bill sorted his belongings and mailed all non-essential items home to his mother. In the special issue of clothing and gear for the overseas tour of duty he received the following: fur jacket, fur lined pants, rain parka, rain pants, three sets of light weight shirt and pants, a green coat-jacket, two pairs of field shoes, overshoes, two pairs of work gloves, a whistle, two green caps (like ball caps), utility belt, canteen with cup and cover. This was in addition to his regular Navy clothing.

Though departure seemed imminent by March 10, 1945, the men were still filled with when and where questions. Bill conjectured that they would be going into a temperate climate — probably to an island off the China coast and below Formosa (now called Taiwan). A sea voyage of thirty days with a convoy was likely. He confided to his mother that he expected to be gone by St. Patrick's Day.

Knowing that censorship would be enforced and secrecy would be crucial, Bill and Effie agreed on a personal code to let her know where he was once he arrived at his overseas destination. He would write suggesting that his sister Marguerite take her son Georgie to see a doctor. The first letter or two of the doctor's name would be the beginning of the name of the place where he landed.

On March 15, Bill's group was sent to a detention barracks dubbed "Treasure Island" where they were housed in quarantine to await orders to board ship. Bill wrote that they were cut off from everything and everybody outside the barracks. Bill managed to conceal several rolls of film in a false bottom of his ditty bag, and they made it through the bag inspection. The brother-in-law of one of his buddies was stationed on Treasure Island. Bill had that man hold his camera during the inspection so it would not be thrown out. In the interest of secrecy, the letters they wrote while in the detention barracks would be posted five days after their ship sailed.

They boarded the ship early on the morning of March 19 but did not sail until that night. Bill explained that convoys intentionally embarked under cover of darkness. The news of the war in the Pacific at that time was full of reports of fierce battles and ships being sunk. One can only imagine the anxiety that Effie must have felt with her only son heading for the battle zones and Will no longer there to share her concerns. Bill wrote to his mother on March 21 from shipboard:

We've been out for several days and I've been sick nearly all the time. We are pulling into port and I believe everybody is happy about it.

Living conditions aboard aren't too bad, but they aren't like home. We have cold salt water to wash in and for all the lather it makes one might as well not wash at all. If I could only get used to the roll and toss of the ship I'd feel better. I sure hope I do.

Our ship is a fairly new one and thus is more comfortable than most. Our chow has been pretty good, but so far I haven't been able to keep any of it down.

This letter will be censored so there isn't much I can say. We are in smooth water now so right now I feel fine.

I haven't received any mail from anyone since we went to

Treasure Island but keep on writing as it will eventually catch up with me.

Don't worry about me as I'm quite well and safe.

Bill was glad to put his feet on solid ground when they docked in Seattle for four days. Dora and Fred Lowd had moved to Seattle where Fred found work in a war-related industry. Given a shore leave, Bill was able to visit his "Aunt Dodie" briefly.

On the next leg of the voyage, which took them to Hawaii, Bill's seasickness disappeared after about two days. It was difficult for him to know what to write in his letters because of censorship. He resorted to describing the daily routine aboard ship. The men mostly shared a little KP duty [kitchen police — washing dishes, etc.] and they passed time playing cards — Pinochle and Hearts. He told his mother he was avoiding the poker and crap games that were always in progress.

On the final leg of the voyage, Bill's letters began to have holes of various sizes cut out of them. What remained after the censor's scissors had done their work was mostly his personal schedule and instructions about his allotment checks that were being sent home to his mother while he was overseas. He later described that segment of the voyage as seeming long. The men were very much aware of the possibility of encountering Japanese submarines. The troop carrier held several military units — Bill's unit alone consisted of a couple hundred men. Their bunks were strung six or seven high, each consisting of a canvas covering over a frame. Bill was seasick when the seas were rough. The ship would roll, taking water in the deck scuppers on one side and then on the other. He learned to find a spot in the center of the deck where the least movement was occurring.

The men often passed the time by playing cards. It was on that leg of the voyage that Bill learned to play contract bridge. They used the hatch covers as card tables, and when the wind blew, they had to hand the cards to each other rather than lay them down. Sometimes he read a book or he found a partner for a game of Chess. The ship's company was selling cold Cokes, a special treat. They were getting regular reports on the progress of the war, and Bill was hopeful it would all be over soon.

Effie wrote to Mr. and Mrs. Pein in San Mateo as her son requested and she received a lengthy reply from Mrs. Pein, part of which follows:

> *We all missed Bill so much when he had to go over, for we all looked forward to his little weekend visits with us. Bill is a grand boy and we all got such a kick out of the tales he used to tell. We would all sit and laugh and talk for hours when he would come over and was just like one of our family.*
>
> *Bill enjoyed his food so much it was just a pleasure to cook for him. One day he mentioned the swell lemon pies his mom used to make, so the next time he came over I had lemon pie for him and he smacked his lips and said, "O boy this is good, almost as good as my mom's," but of course I knew it wasn't for I am not a good pie maker.*

OKINAWA   23

AFTER THE INVASION OF the Normandy beaches in June
of 1944, Allied armies liberated France and fought their way
from the west toward the capital of Germany. Russia finally
repelled its German invaders and marched toward Berlin from
the eastern side. As the year 1945 dawned, several "Axis" nations in Europe — Italy, Romania, Bulgaria, Hungary —
changed sides by declaring war on Germany.

　　　　　While the war in Europe was nearing an end, the
war in the Pacific was raging furiously. The vast Pacific Ocean
is dotted with islands and Japan had extended control over
most of them.　Fierce battles were fought both on land and at
sea in "island-hopping" campaigns to drive back the Japanese.
In 1942 Allied troops had been captured or were driven off the
Philippine Island of Luzon.　In January of 1945, the Allies returned to retake that lost territory and to free the surviving
war prisoners.

Iwo Jima and Okinawa were the last two islands to be liberated from the Japanese before the planned assault on Japan itself.　The Japanese were aware that their homeland
would be the next target if those islands fell. Determined not
to give up, they committed thousands and thousands of troops
and conscripted native residents to protect those last two
strongholds. Caves were utilized and extensive tunnels were
dug for underground fortifications. Many Japanese defenders
were willing to die in kamikaze aircraft, suicide boats, and
manned bombs in their efforts to stem the invasions.

Iwo Jima is a tiny island of only eight square miles.　The
Japanese had a base on the island with airstrips for fighter
planes that were harassing the Allied B-29 bombers.　Marines

landed on Iwo Jima on February 19, 1945, (Bill's 24th birthday). Of the estimated 22,000 defenders of the island, only about 250 surrendered; the rest were lost in the conflict. About 5,000 Marines lost their lives before the island was secured a month later. The picture of Marines raising the American flag on Iwo Jima's Mt. Suribachi is perhaps the most famous of the World War II photos.

Okinawa, one of a group of islands known as the Ryukyus, is much larger than Iwo Jima. A long narrow island of about 463 square miles, it is halfway between Formosa (Taiwan) and Japan, only about 350 miles from the Japanese mainland. Low rugged mountains dominate the northern part of the island. The invasion of Okinawa began on April 1, 1945. One pilot described the invasion armada as incredible, reaching from horizon to horizon. There was initial optimism that the conquest would be an easy one, but when the Japanese opened up on the invaders, the northern hills became known as the "Meat Grinder." It is said that 700 kamikaze planes attacked in a single day. Estimates place Japanese military and civilian fatalities between 110,000 and 150,000 in the three-month battle that ensued. Allied losses numbered nearly 13,000 dead and tens of thousands wounded.

Bill's unit, SAH#6 (Special Augmented Hospital Unit 6), landed on Okinawa about the first of May using landing vehicles called "ducks" that could operate both on water and on land. The first night was fearful and was spent sleeping on the ground using just their sea bags and hammocks. During the night, Japanese planes flew over while Allied ships' companies followed them with searchlights and took pot shots at them. Though the invasion had begun a month earlier the island was far from secured. That would take another seven weeks.

The content of Bill's letters was limited mostly to camp and personal events due to two constraints: 1) He wanted to minimize his mother's worry and 2) censorship was strictly imposed to avoid informing the enemy of Allied war strategies. He wrote:

Boy, what a talking ole time we will have when I get home. There are so many things I would like to write which are not permitted. I sometimes think I will burst with having to keep them to myself.

Bill's hospital unit was improvising a temporary camp while they waited for more permanent facilities to be built by the Seabees, the Navy's construction battalion. Bill's unit was well behind the battle lines but they were aware of the constant air attacks not far away. He believed that shrapnel from their own anti-aircraft guns posed the greatest danger to his unit.

The men were warned about infiltrators, so they were armed and on the alert. The appearance of snipers was an ever-present possibility. If anyone appeared suddenly, survival seemed to demand that they "shoot and ask questions later." Bill told of one time when a native soldier came through their camp. He was chased into a rocky thicket of trees. When he saw that he was surrounded, he blew himself up with a grenade. On one occasion Bill fired a shot but didn't think he hit anyone. Once those who pursued a sniper returned with gold they had hacked out of the dead sniper's teeth.

As the war in Europe was ending, Okinawa became a focal point in the preparation for the final assault on Japan. Germany's unconditional surrender to the Allies was signed May 7, 1945. When the news reached Bill he wrote:

The War in Germany is over or so we hear, but this war isn't over by any means ... We spent most of yesterday constructing a shelter and we have one of the best. I sure dug a lot of mud! ... Our particular location (camp) is in what was a native garden. We are on a hill and so get a breeze during the day. This location is only temporary for as soon as all our supplies are off the ship we will move to our permanent place. This will mean more work, thus few letters.

We are eating C rations and they are pretty good. They come in two boxes and are for five men ... There are sixteen men in our tent. Yesterday we built us a swell fireplace by

*digging a hole in a mud bank, lining it with brick and put-
ting two smokestacks and using sheet tin on the top. All of
this material was found in the ruined buildings scattered
near here ...*

*As yet there isn't any place to go to spend our money. The
Red Cross has a free canteen where one can get toothbrushes,
cigarettes, coffee and doughnuts, etc. — all free. So I ought to
save plenty of money. I want you to buy War Bonds with
every cent I send you after you put away $200.00 in a joint
bank account. Make the Bonds out jointly ...*

*Don't worry about me as I'm not in any danger. We are
miles behind the lines.*

Including his mother's name on the titles of his bank account and war bonds was a hedge against the possibility that
Bill might not survive the war. His next letter made use of
the code he had devised to let his mother know where he was:

*From Sis' letters the baby must be having an awful time.
Why hasn't she taken the baby to Dr. O'Keefe for treatment?
If I remember correctly he is in the Katz Bldg.*

*Tonite we made a stew out of our canned rations — lima
bean, pork, and tomatoes — not too bad, eh. All our food
comes in cans or waterproof packages. We hope to get our chow
hall enlarged soon. As it is now only a selected few eat in the
small chow hall.*

*A lot of our supplies are unloaded now and I hope we soon
will be able to move to our new camp — and last one for awhile.*

It is too dark to write further — will continue —

*It is now 1000 (10 A.M.) of another day. We have just fin-
ished our morning chores. This is all similar to farm life except we haven't any cows to milk. The other day some of the
boys found two wild billy goats — just kids — and brought
them to our camp. They baaaa-ed all nite and kept everyone
awake. Every morning we get up about 6 a.m. and get our
canned food opened and on the fire — also the coffee.*

Due to our crowded conditions our guests — in our tent

— have tried to get away with part of our rations. They are too helpless to look after themselves. I told a couple of 'em off. It sure burns me up to think that guys would try and steal someone else's rations when they know darn well it isn't theirs! ...

After breakfast of canned eggs, potatoes and ham, biscuits and coffee we cleaned out our tent and laid our bedding out to air. Also chopped the wood for our noon meal, brought in more water and cleaned up the surrounding area of paper, cans, boxes, etc. We still haven't gotten our mess gear so every meal we have to whittle spoons out of wood. Our "C" rations for today are of a different kind thus it helps break the monotony.

Supplies are still coming ashore and I think the Seabees are building our permanent camp. This new camp should have all the comforts of home except for streetcars! Ha!

The war news looks real good and it might be over sooner than expected — say in a year. I do hope, tho, that the Allies only take an unconditional surrender from these Japs. All of your enclosures, clippings, etc. have been received OK and well read.

Five days later he wrote again reassuring his mother that he was quite well and safe and "moderately happy." He explained more of his activities:

This evening I took my second full bath. It goes like this. First, I fill my canteen and steel helmet full of water. Then I divide the water in my helmet by putting it in some empty container. Then I find a board to stand on and, using a pair of torn shorts as a wash rag, I go to it. I rinse off in the clean water — about a quart — and use this water to wash my socks. Then with the canteen water I wash my teeth and take a drink, taking my atropine at the same time.

... Since we work most of our daylight hours it doesn't leave us much time for writing. There is always something to do like roll down our tent flaps so the sanitation squad can fumigate. This is a nightly ritual. Then we have to dust

off our sacks and then dust on the flea powder.

Today I got ahold of some scrap lumber with which I hope to build a floor for my tent when I move. One piece of it is 8 ft. by 4 ft. — just right for under my cot when we first move in as there won't be any floors then. There's one thing you have to do out here and that's look after yourself first then think about the other fellow. If you don't it would just be too bad ...

Lights and water are our main problem. What I wouldn't give for an old-fashioned kerosene lantern. My flashlite is still crated in our personal gear. It's too dark to write more.

Comments about the mail that Bill received or did not receive were a part of nearly every letter. He wrote that May 6 was a "glorious day" because his first mail in 45 days had just arrived. There were so many letters that it took him two days to find time to read them all. He continued to supply his mother with information on the nitty-gritty of his daily activities but, due to censorship, not much about the war. On May 15 he wrote:

Yesterday, three of us on the maintenance crew moved up to our new location. It was my first time to see it. It is a pretty little valley with hills sticking out here and there. There is grass and trees and bushes here — more so than at the temporary camp. We can't mention the weather on a day by day basis, but I can say that it does rain here and when it does, oh what a muddy mess it is!

At the present time only three of us are in a tent so we are quite comfortable — compared to the 15-20 that were in our old tent. On arriving at the new camp we each get a cot, mosquito bar and rifle, shells, etc. Last night I really slept well on my cot. No mosquitoes, bugs, or cold ground to put up with. They are building our galley and mess hall first so it shouldn't be long before we can eat fair meals and in comfort. When we came up last nite I brought along that lumber I mentioned before and put it in our tent as flooring. It sure is a help and it keeps our cots steady and our feet off the ground. Out here we are no longer bothered by air raids so don't worry over me ...

We are allowed to eat in the Seabee chow hall not far from here but it is quite a hike in the mud, so we are eating what canned rations we have. They brought in a big trailer tank of water last nite so we have it pretty nice considering we are camping in the rough.

Our clothes washing is a problem. Quite a few of the boys have "acquired" buckets along the way. Some have brought them all the way from Shoemaker. So we do have a way of washing when the time, place, soap and water are available.

The Red Cross ever so often gives a supply of paper, envelopes, soap, razors and stuff we need. There is one item I have wished more than once I had and that's wash rags. If you can, try and air mail me one and then send some more by regular means. I'm using a pair of shorts now as a wash rag.

There is evidence in Bill's letters of his dreams for after the war. He expected to make his home with his mother when he returned. He suggested that she sell her house, furnishings and all, so they could make a new start when he returned. In a letter written May 23 he described the dream home he would like to build for them after the war:

My idea of a home would be this: Half or all brick bungalow, all on one floor, 3 bedrooms, 2 baths, a fireplace and well arranged living room — same for kitchen. And I would like to get a 75' frontage by 120' deep at least, near a shopping district and out south and west of Paseo. I wouldn't mind saving my money for a home like that. In the living room I'd like to have twin three-quarter length divans facing one another in front of the fireplace!! The master bedroom would have its own bath and two closets and the hallways would be nothing but closets, one of them cedar. No front porch but a spacious screened side porch. Well, I can dream, anyway!

We have a likeable bunch in our tent. One of them I have mentioned before. His name is Dempsey and still another is

one of six of us who ran around together in Shoemaker. His
name is Mann. Our third member is the carpenter who is the
oldest one of us — his name is Stevens — Steve for short.
The fourth member is a guy from Arkansas, name of Carlson.
He's young and a screwball but likeable ...

Yesterday I built us a food cabinet where we have put all
our canned food. We have spaghetti and meat, ham and lima
beans, meat and beans, chicken and vegetables, meat and veg-
etables, cocoa, coffee, dried milk, cream, sugar, salt, and the
ever-present crackers. Most of these are in individual cans or
packages. When we cook we just put the can in boiling water
and warm it then dump it into a large tray. Then everyone
helps himself, using one of the empty cans as a plate. Oh yes,
we now have procured silverware. Building a fire when it is
wet is a tough job. The wood here doesn't seem to burn very
good and then everything is usually damp. One of the boys
— Carlson — got a 5 gallon bucket and put sand in the bot-
tom then we pour gasoline in it and light it. It gives off enuf
heat for emergency cooking.

Calendar dates tended to blend together as the men coped
with their primitive surroundings. Bill's next letter bore the
date "May 18 — I think." He told of putting a floor in their 16
ft. by 16 ft. pyramid tent in which he lived with four other
men. The job was complicated by rain that began after they
cleared the tent of all its contents — clothes, bedding, rifles,
canteens, etc. They had to bring it all back inside while they
were still laying the floor and mud stuck to everything.

All but one of the officers in Bill's unit were doctors so military decorum on their hospital grounds was pretty lax. He
wrote to his mother:

Speaking of procuring things is a polite way of saying
steal. Nearly everything one wants they have to steal. Of
course whether it is right or wrong depends on who you steal
it from. If you steal it from the Army or the natives, then that's
all right! If you don't procure anything from anyone you just

don't live in any comfort what-so-ever. Most of what is stolen is food, wood, scrap iron and TOOLS! Boy, do people ever like to "borrow" your tools. I'm not necessarily speaking for myself as you know I can't stand a thief.

They are beginning to install some electrical equipment, lights, etc. in our ward tents and mess hall. Our mess hall and galley is going to be quite nice. It is nearly a quarter-mile from our tent to the mess hall. This gives you an idea of how spread-out we are. We really have a system for washing clothes now. We got a big cast iron kettle and [we] fill it full of clothes, soap and water and then build a fire under it. It really does the job.

Our new galley should be in operating condition in 10 days. Golly, we won't know how to act eating out of trays and using clean silverware and eating in a comfortable, screened place. Right out in back of our tent Steve has built us a shower by putting up a frame with two barrels of water on top. We have tied a tin can over the spigot and punched holes in the can to give it a semblance of a shower.

I must close now. I received your long letter of May 7th. Your new roomers sound like nice people. Evidently you hadn't received any of my mail from here at that time. Love, Bill

When time permitted, the men walked through the native villages to look around. The residents were non-combative. Rice fields on Okinawa were in terraced squares with paths between them. One had to take care not to slip off into the flooded rice paddies. The vegetation was fertilized with human feces. The sailors were warned not to eat the native food or to drink their water. In Bill's May 30 letter:

The other day we were out of water — even drinking water and so I said, "Golly, I wish it would rain real hard for just a while so we could catch the water that runs off our tent eaves," and, by golly, sure enuf it did just that and did we ever fill up our buckets. Boy, did it ever pour. We filled up all 5 canteens, our helmets, our huge iron pot, and 2 buckets besides 4 gallon cans of water. You see we have special water purifying pills that come in our rations, altho we hardly ever use them as we are furnished most of the time with good water. Two of our boys got right out in it and took a shower then I took a bath with part of what I caught, shaved and washed my hair. Did it ever feel good. Our shower I mentioned before doesn't always have water as the barrels have to be filled by manual labor and put on the rack. As is usual, everyone likes to use our shower but no one makes any attempt to fill the barrels.

We have our own tent and surroundings about the way we want it now so until our hospital is completed we haven't much to do except go on working parties to do various jobs ... Our chow hall is very near to being in operation. It is wired for electricity and it will be my job to keep the generator going and to make repairs if necessary.

Bill was the only electrician in his unit. Until the hospital was in operation, he could not work at his own job, so he worked at other tasks such as assisting his carpenter tent mate, Steve. Glad to keep busy, he dug postholes for the power poles that were a prerequisite to getting electricity to their tents. He learned to climb poles using leg irons with spurs.

He was eligible for advancement. So in June, with nothing else to do in the evenings, he studied hard preparing to be tested for the rank of electrician's mate first class. He wrote:

Everyone has gone to bed so I'd better close and turn out the lamp. I'm ever so healthy and as happy as anyone. We get enuf to eat and plenty of sleep and our living quarters are the best on the island so I've a lot to be thankful for. Can't you write more than once a week? Love, Bill

Steve, the congenial carpenter tent mate, and Bill continued to improve their living conditions. Bill collected electrical supplies to make a hot plate so they could have coffee in the tent. They collected lumber and framed in the tent to eliminate the center pole, and they built a front "porch" on their tent. Steve built shelves to which Bill attached his "pin-up" pictures of the girls with whom he exchanged letters. When the Seabees completed the galley, mealtime chores and evening boredom were relieved. The food was better than the rations they had been eating, and the chow hall sometimes doubled as a movie theater in the evening.

On June 22, seven weeks after the arrival of Bill's unit, Okinawa was considered secured. Then full attention was given to completing the camp and preparing for the final assault on Japan. After having to look for things to fill his time and use his energy, Bill was happy to finally become very busy. Rather than filling in with various other work detail he was doing his own work — that of an electrician — and being pretty much his own boss. By the first of July, he had wired all the living tents for his hospital unit, the toilet and shower facility, the sanitation tent and his own shop. This took him three days. He was working alone — without a helper.

Bill had brought with him some switches, wall outlets, extension cord and other electrical gadgets so he was able to provide some "fancy" extras for his own tent. A drop cord with a pull chain over their writing table that Steve built was one. They also had a wall plug for their radio so they could listen to "swing music and news and rebroadcasts of popular programs in the States such as Jack Benny."

One of the extras petty officers had was an icebox made from a blood supply cold box with a hinged lid and lock. Rations of beer or pop were given to them warm. Bill's job required him to keep the coolers operating. He was able to make ice in empty cans in "his" reefer to cool beverages until they were off duty. Bartering was a way of life in the Navy. When anything was scarce, it became barter merchandise. Bill's special access to ice making in the 28-degree cooler provided him a barter medium. He traded ice for many life-on-Okinawa necessities and luxuries such as a whet stone for sharpening his knife, laundry soap, cigarettes, plywood and other lumber, carpentry, pieces of carpet, a 55-gallon drum, etc.

Construction of a "real modern laundry" was finally completed. Then native women were paid to do the laundry for the men of the hospital unit. The men's end-of-the-workday showers often coincided with the time the native laundry girls were taken home in the back of a truck. Bill said there was lots of giggling as the truck passed their open-air shower.

A boost to Bill's morale came in the form of a pay raise that he received along with confirmation that he had passed the tests for electrician's mate first class. This enabled him to save more each month. He was thinking ahead to what he would do when the war was over — like buy a house or go to college. He was looking forward to again enjoying his mother's home cooking ("What I wouldn't give for some of your iced tea or lemon meringue pie or fried chicken or peach cobbler or shrimp salad or creamed new peas and potatoes.") He thought that, once home, he would not eat out again for a long time.

Just when Bill and his tent mates had made their tent more livable and had cleared the surrounding ground of the makeshift equipment they had used before construction was completed, Bill and Steve were ordered to move to another tent. This made no sense to Bill but he complied, and he tried to put a positive spin on prospects for improving the new tent using what they learned from mistakes made on the prior one. He wrote: "The civilians don't realize how lucky they are every time they open their ice box or turn a water faucet or flip a light switch."

Bill was happy when a second chow hall was completed. He remarked about how clean it was, how well prepared the food was and how much improved was their system for serving. He said the food in the prior chow hall was getting so bad and the cooks and table service so dirty that some of the guys had opted to walk the distance to the Seabee chow. Soon ice machines were brought in and the men were looking forward to having iced beer or Cokes. While the electrical equipment was working well, Bill had time to do other things. He fashioned a ring out of metal from a Japanese propeller.

Once a month the men were given a two-day leave. Bill spent that leave time hitchhiking to the beach in search of shells or to see what was left of the towns nearby. He said that Naha, the capital city of Okinawa, was built on the side of a hill and had suffered house to house and hand to hand fighting. Nothing was left standing over waist high except one tower that he thought was a Buddhist temple. A decorated cabinet door that he picked up among the ruins was sent home as a war souvenir.

About six weeks after Okinawa was secured, an atomic bomb was dropped on each of two Japanese cities — Hiroshima was hit on August 6, Nagasaki on August 9. Half of each of those cities was completely destroyed with just one bomb, taking a toll of 70,000 killed with 110,000 terribly injured. The devastation caused by those horrific explosions has since been the topic of much discussion. Was it justifiable to unleash such powerful weapons? Those who believe the bombs were the best alternative to end the war argue that horrible as the losses were, the toll was less than a bloody invasion would have taken on both sides. Many young men in this country were being trained to take part in the invasion. They were saved from the mandate to participate. Those bombings set the stage for ending the war in the Pacific. On August 10 Japan initiated negotiations to surrender.

As soon as it appeared that Japan would capitulate, rumors began to fly among the troops on Okinawa about how soon the peace treaty would be signed and how soon and in what order servicemen would be sent home. Bill reported that the regulation crew cuts were disappearing as the guys let their hair grow in anticipation of their return to civilian life. Finally, censorship was lifted, and Bill was free to explain to his mother that his camp was about midway on the island — not far from Naha and Shuri.

Okinawa is subject to typhoons. Two "big blows" swept over the island while Bill was there. He described the one that blew in on September 16 as follows:

Wow! What a storm we did have here!! No one really knows how strong the wind was but it was strong enuf to suit me. [A later letter reported that winds were 90 miles per hour on one side of the island but estimated they were 50 to 60 mph in his area.] It began Sunday morning by raining — my day to be off work, too. Then with the rain came a gusty wind — not too bad at first — then the warning was given to all hands — first it was 'condition II' meaning the storm was 50-100 miles away and we all were to secure our tents and all loose boards, cans, etc. By Sunday evening — around 4 P.M. — the wind had grown much stronger and one tent had already been blown down. All during the storm the rain fell and the wind blew with terrific fury. Hitting tent roofs it sounded like hail. Soon it was "Condition I" and sure enuf the storm hit Sunday nite at about 8-10 p.m. It blew down a half dozen tents, plus our medical supply tent, our 16'x16' theater screen, 2 officers ward tents — sick officers quarters. A lot of the tents were somewhat sheltered but then the wind changed three times so during the whole storm, which lasted most of Sunday nite, every tent felt some damage. Our tent stood up well but our front porch screening ripped out and our protecting canvas flaps didn't have anything to hold them so wind and water blew in our front door. What a nite!

I was on a repair party until 11 p.m. then got to go to my tent as I had to get up in the morning and clear our power lines before the generators could be started. They had been shut down since 4 p.m. Sunday. I was so tired and wanted to sleep but couldn't because of the terrific noise caused by the wind blowing. A tent is far different from a house when it comes to shutting out noises. I rolled and tossed all nite then got some sleep from about 5 a.m. to 7 a.m. Monday morning. Then I went to work repairing the lines that were down. Luckily for me there wasn't any heavy wire down so I had the generators turned back on early that morning. I got most of the broken wire fixed by Monday evening although I did work until 7 p.m. — way past dark. I sure feel sorry for Steve and Mike, our carpenters! There are so many tents to be re-framed, etc. Nearly all repair work demands a carpenter for only our chow hall and surgery building are made of steel.

By the next typhoon, the tent Bill occupied had a wood floor and sides and two by four roof supports. Also, they had anchored the whole frame by stakes driven into the ground. Bill had stood in six to eight inches of water in a cave for four hours waiting out the first storm. During the second one he went to his tent, laid down on his cot, pulled his heavy canvas hammock over him and slept through the storm.

That second typhoon was a bad one for the hospital unit. Many tents were totally destroyed. Steel roofing was torn from the mess hall, the operating rooms and the main patient building. The sturdy steel flag pole was bent parallel to the ground. Bill recalled that a bully in camp had gathered other bullies around him. During that second storm, the wind blew over the latrine tent and the bullies' tent was blown into the "crap hole." The rest of the camp could hardly resist the urge to cheer. The Seabees set to work right away making repairs.

A letter to Bill from his sister Marguerite told of anxiety on the home front:

The papers reported all naval installations on Okinawa leveled, over 100,000 G.I.s [a term for servicemen] homeless, all food destroyed, as well as hospitals, medical equipment, etc., as well as saying it was the worst storm for twenty years on Okinawa and if it had happened before the end of the war, it would have been a major military disaster. So you can imagine how we felt! They reported that there were, I believe, 70 Navy dead and almost 500 injured — and here you slept right thru it! Listen, big boy, if they have another one of those storms before you leave, please stay in if you can. Both Mother and I have been almost sick with worry over you ... It just seems too good to be true that you think you'll be home for Christmas ... In fact, an article in the paper the other day said since the typhoon, supplies and living quarters were at such a premium on Okinawa that the high point G.I.s were being flown out on Super-forts making only two stops — at Guam and Honolulu. Wouldn't that be a slick way to get home in a hurry? ... We've already ordered the turkey for

Christmas — and boy oh boy, will we ever have all the trimmin's this time!

VJ Day (Victory in Japan) came with the signing of the peace treaty September 2, 1945. Release of Naval personnel was done on a point system. Points were given for length of service, overseas service, number of dependents, etc. Those with 44 points were being released in October. Bill had 42 points. In his letter of October 4 he wrote to his mother:

You are going to have to get used to the fact that I'm different — three years in the Navy has had its effect on me — You might say I'm a little bit wiser and definitely older.

He wondered if, back in civilian life, he would be tempted to queue up in every line he saw. So much of his time in the military had involved waiting in line.

The last of Bill's letters from Okinawa was written October 20. Apparently, he left Okinawa early in November. He was honorably discharged from the Navy after three years, two months and one day of service. He returned to civilian life on Christmas Eve, 1945. As he left the Navy, he was recruited to join the inactive Naval Reserve. When it was promised that the inactive reservists would be the last to be called in the event of another war, Bill signed up. The obligation incurred by that signing came back to haunt him later, causing him to alter some of his plans.

HOME FREE   24

THE HOME TO WHICH Bill returned that Christmas Eve of 1945 was the same one he had left more than three years before, yet much had changed. His father had died. His mother now owned the home they had rented at the time of Bill's induction into the Navy. Over the years of his absence Bill had become more independent. He had seen more of the world and he had witnessed war's devastation. Effie was becoming accustomed to widowhood and, though she continued to have a close supportive relationship with her stepdaughter, her son remained the center of her life. She welcomed him home with thanksgiving for his safe return and for his wholeness. She was very aware that many mothers in this nation were not so fortunate.

As Bill settled in at home, he basked in his mother's home cooking and his freedom to go when and where he pleased and to do what he chose to do. He pondered his next move as he poised on the threshold of the rest of his life. Should he look for a job? Did he really want to spend the rest of his working years as an electrician? What should he do about his obligations to his mother? She was older than the mothers of many of his peers. Would he need to provide for her? Girls were high on his list of interests. He hoped at some point to marry, but until he found someone with whom he struck the right mutual chord he enjoyed the search.

Effie was her usual chatty, outgoing self, interested in family and friends. She met monthly with the three women's groups of which she was a member — the Linwood Child Conservation Club, The Graceland Mothers' Club, and her church women's group. After Will's death, Effie had worked through the probate requirements in Missouri, Iowa and Illinois. With her usual adeptness for business management, she was beginning to realize some income from the Kirkland real estate legacies. Though problems with the Chicago properties were ongoing, the Fort Madison properties had sold, providing some capital for investment. By managing her finances carefully, Effie had made needed repairs on her home. She added to her income by continuing to rent out one or two bedrooms in her house. After Bill's discharge from the Navy, she was able to manage without her dependency allotment.

With the encouragement of his mother, sister, and brother-in-law, Bill decided to take the government up on its offer in the G.I. Bill of Rights. That legislation provided the cost of a college education, including a small living allowance, to returning veterans. Bill chose Kansas University at Lawrence, which was the nearest large university to his home. It offered a reputable business school for his major in business administration. Bill was among the thousands of veterans who matriculated into the nation's colleges and universities for the fall term in 1946. After transferring the credits he had earned at Graceland College, he was admitted as a college junior.

He pledged membership in the Phi Kappa Psi social fraternity and took up residence in the fraternity house on campus. Hunger pangs surfaced as the fraternity brothers studied during long evenings. Fast food restaurants were few or none and transportation was not as available as it is today. Bill saw in those circumstances an opportunity to make extra pocket money. He obtained permission from the fraternity's housemother to use space in the house refrigerator to store sandwich makings. His fraternity brothers were ready and willing to pay for the sandwiches he made. He also managed to negotiate for half the proceeds of the Coke machine in return for keeping it stocked with soft drinks.

Bill found life at the university a welcome change from his tour in the Navy. Though serious about his schooling, top grades were still not so essential as to block out other interests. Young women were plentiful on campus, a fact that Bill

Bill Brewster, 1947, while a student at Kansas University after World War II

enjoyed. He eventually took on a part-time job at a campus coffee spot, and he fell for the proprietor's daughter, Bonnie, who was also a college student. Bill's involvement with her took a toll on his academics. By the end of the spring semester of 1948 his engagement to Bonnie was broken.

It was time to graduate, but Bill was short some credits. Interviews with the Aetna Casualty and Surety Company (the same company for whom his brother-in-law George was the head underwriter in the Kansas City office) had netted him a job offer as a field representative. He was to begin training in August, subject to his graduation by that date. He remained in Lawrence for the summer session to obtain the needed credits.

Very much in earnest about graduating, Bill went to one of his professors and told him he needed to earn an "A" in the man's course. Bill said he would do whatever it took and he meant it. He was given instructions and he diligently went about fulfilling the requirements. To ensure his focus on his studies that summer, he moved out of the fraternity house and into an apartment with Harlan (Jim) Beatty, his friend from Graceland College who had boarded in the Brewster home in 1940-41. Harlan was also attending KU with the help of the G. I. Bill.

In the intervening war years between Graceland and KU, Harlan had continued his attendance at church. During his student years at KU, he met with the small congregation in Lawrence. Though Bill was a baptized member of the church, he had stopped attending services in his teens when his mother was occupied on Sundays as a real estate agent. Though he again had religious exposure during his two years at the church-sponsored college, he had placed his religion on hold.

In June of 1948, the Lawrence congregation was renovating an old church they had bought. The work was being done by volunteer labor. As Harlan prepared to join the work crew one evening, he invited Bill to come along. Bill needed a break from his studies, and he felt he could use some physical activity so he accepted. Surely, he had no idea how that casual decision would influence the rest of his life.

LOIS ANNE

25

As THEY MOVED TOWARD their marriage on June 2, 1929, my parents were not a typical young couple. Gilson Norris was a forty-year-old widower with six young sons and a four-year-old daughter. He earned his living by door-to-door sales work, a much more common occupation in that day than today. His work kept him away from home much of the time, and he was urgently in need of someone to share his life and the raising of his young family. Blanche Christenson was a thirty-three-year-old spinster schoolteacher. Their church, The Reorganized Church of Jesus Christ of Latter Day Saints, was important in both their lives.

Blanche first fell in love with Gilson's two youngest children and then with the rest of the family. She entered her marriage with a full commitment of all of her energies and resources. So far as she was concerned, Gilson's children became her children the day she married him. She had no use for the terms "stepchildren" or "stepmother."

Almost immediately after the wedding, the Norris family moved from northern Idaho to Blanche's home state of Missouri. Those were difficult times in the economy of this nation and of the Norris family. The stock market crash that marked the beginning of the Great Depression occurred in October of their nuptial year. Unable to find work in Missouri, Gilson peddled produce that he grew and foods that he and Blanche prepared in the kitchen at home.

I, Lois Anne Norris, entered the family on March 29, 1930, in Warrensburg, Missouri. Because times were so difficult, Mother was concerned that the older children might resent adding another mouth to feed in her first year in the family.

One-year-old Lois Anne with her parents, Blanche and Gilson Norris, 1931.

However, I was not only accepted, I lived from the beginning in the "lap of love." I was just fifteen months old when my parents were attracted to the small university town of Lawrence, Kansas, that nestled on the banks of the Kaw River. Mother had relatives there, and it was hoped that Dad might more readily find work in that city.

Lawrence, with its population at that time of perhaps 25,000, became our home for the rest of my growing-up years. Indeed, many of my siblings' descendants still live there today. Two more sisters were added to our family, one a little more than two years after my arrival and the other when I was almost ten years old. The older kids left home one by one as they grew into their upper teens. I have no memory of the time when my two oldest brothers were still living at home, but they remained close to the family. When the baby of the family arrived, only we three youngest girls remained in our parental home.

Growing up, I was not aware how difficult those times were for my family. I had no experience with which to compare them. Most of our neighbors were coping about the same as we were. I recall that Dad seemed always worried about finances, and he carefully avoided indebtedness. We children learned not to expect things that had to be bought. We became quite self-reliant and inventive, making things we wanted out of materials at hand. I don't recall ever fighting with my siblings. In fact, I avoided conflict situations unless something I considered very important was at stake.

Mother was so busy with household chores that I now wonder how she did it all. Until I was age thirteen, we had almost no modern conveniences except electric lighting. We did have an electric wringer-type washing machine, but water for it and the rinse tubs was carried from a pump over the well in our back yard. Using a Singer treadle sewing machine, Mom made over clothing for us that she acquired from the thrift store. She canned and preserved food all summer, and she baked bread so we would have plenty of nutritious food to eat.

Community activities were also wedged into Mother's busy schedule. I recall her being president of the Parent-Teachers Association of my elementary school and helping with the Community Chest fund drive. When a neighbor needed help harvesting his acre or so of strawberries, Mom donned a pair of slacks (unusual in that day) and organized the neighborhood kids to do the picking. She not only oversaw the harvest, she also marketed the berries at local grocery stores.

Before Dad finally found other jobs, he peddled produce from our garden and animals. He and Mom killed and dressed some of our chickens on Saturdays to fill orders from local householders. Among the products that Dad made and sold were butter (churned in a manual barrel churn), cottage cheese and sausage. Later he worked as a milkman, a Manor Bread home-delivery man, a *Star* mail carrier to small towns around Lawrence and eventually as an insurance salesman. Though Dad was busy making a living and being the lay pastor of our small church congregation, he found time to read to us on a regular basis.

I was especially privileged to enjoy a wonderful one-on-one companionship with Dad. When he delivered milk and then Manor Bread during the late 1930s, Dad needed a helper. With all of the older kids gone from home, I was elected. He awakened me for the milk route before dawn, and the two of us drove to the dairy to pick up the fresh bottled milk. Then we went up and down the back alleyways of Lawrence dropping off quarts and pints of milk on doorsteps and picking up the empty milk bottles. I kept the log of our deliveries while Dad drove. He praised my bookkeeping.

Schooling was important to us, and I was a fairly good stu-

dent. I related easily to my classmates. Our school often scheduled field trips to cultural events on the Kansas University
campus — such as symphony concerts and museum exhibits.
I loved to sing, and I remember the thrill of singing in a
citywide choir that the schools assembled for a special occasion. We were encouraged to read. Mother had accumulated a
small library while she was teaching, and we made frequent
use of the local Carnegie Library. During those early years,
however, I was not as avid a reader as my younger sister. I
preferred to be out and doing rather than sitting and reading.

During the teacher shortage of World War II, my mother
was one of the former teachers who returned to the classroom.
That made quite a change in our home life. I remember missing having Mom there when I came home from school, but I
liked being the recipient of a tiny but regular allowance. Money
was still in very short supply, but the family was able for the
first time to purchase a home rather than continue to rent.

My childhood was very sheltered, revolving mostly around
family, school and church. I was shy and ill at ease in social
situations, anxious when meeting new experiences. I believe
those inhibitions were related to my having been exposed to
so little of the world outside those three anchoring institu-
tions. There was no television in those days. We depended on
newspapers and an occasional newsreel at the movies for our
news. I think I was close to my teen years before we owned a
radio. My parents had neither the time nor the resources to
travel. By the time I graduated from high school, the farthest
I had ever gone from home was six hundred miles. That land-
mark trip was in 1940 when Dad, Mom, and we three youngest girls went to visit Dad's siblings in Indiana.

After graduating from Liberty Memorial High School in
Lawrence late in May of 1948, I spent my summer working as
a sales clerk in the Gambles Store in downtown Lawrence. I
was saving money and sewing my own wardrobe, preparing to
attend Graceland College in Lamoni, Iowa, in the fall. Also
that summer our small church congregation, of which my father was the pastor, was renovating the old church that we

had purchased. I was among the volunteers who met evenings to help with that renovation.

When I first walked into the church to join the work crew one evening, I wandered about looking for someone to assign me a job. As I entered the sanctuary, its lone occupant was a handsome young man on a ladder scraping paint that was peeling from the plastered walls.

I had never seen him before, but I asked, "Have you seen my dad?"

I was surprised when he replied in a teasing tone, "No, I haven't. Will I do?"

I don't recall how that exchange ended, but I remember my pleasure when that same young man came and sat beside me on the church steps during our break for refreshments. I learned that his name was Bill Brewster, that he was a student at KU and a roommate of Harlan Beatty, whom I had met.

When quitting time came that evening, Dad was detained making a call and was not available to take me home. Bill offered me a ride and I accepted. He was driving an old Model A Ford — all he could afford while going to school. He drove me directly home, but we sat in the car in front of the house a while, chatting.

I had gone on dates with high school friends, but they were kids compared to Bill. He seemed so self-confident, so mature, so open in conversation. He picked up my hand and held it gently as he talked. He seemed very interested in my plans to go to Graceland, and I learned that he had attended Graceland a decade earlier. He was impressed that I could sew, and he admired the homemade blouse I wore.

In those days there were subjects that simply were not discussed even within the family, but Bill's talk seemed very uninhibited. I don't remember all he said that night, but I recall being glad it was dark so he could not see how I blushed at some of the things he told me. Finally, he asked me a direct question that had some sexual connotation. I was flabbergasted!

I said, "Why, Bill, I don't think we ought to talk about that."

My response must have amused him. I think Bill discovered that night how easy it was and, apparently, how much fun it was to tease and to shock me. I'm sure he could also see how naïve I was, and I believe he was somewhat intrigued by that. He suggested that he pick me up for the next work night a week hence. I went into the house awed by the evening's encounter.

When Bill arrived the next week, he carried an extra pair of slacks over his arm. He explained that those were the only pair of work pants he had at school with him, and they were ripped. Since I sewed, could I fix them so he could wear them that evening? It turned out the whole crotch seam was ripped open. Mother came into the living room at that moment, saw my befuddlement at such a request, and offered to fix the trousers, mentioning that she had repaired lots of boys' pants.

After working at the church that evening, we drove up on the campus to a vantage point overlooking Lawrence. We got out of the car and were standing together enjoying the night scene below us when Bill looked down at me and asked, "May I kiss you?" When I told him he could, he gently kissed me on the lips. Then he stood back a step and said, "Hmmm, if I were going to be around long enough, I'd teach you how."

I am sure that was not intended as a putdown, and I did not take it as such. I knew I was very much a novice in that area, though his openness surprised me (as did many things about him). It was as if he was thinking out loud, considering his need to focus on his studies, to graduate so he could start insurance school in Hartford, Connecticut, about a month from then. He did not expect to return to Lawrence after school ended. Neither of us saw our acquaintance as anything but a brief interesting passage.

I saw Bill twice more before he left Lawrence at the end of July with his degree in business administration. The first was a chance meeting in the ticket line at a local movie theater. I was with a girl friend, and he was with his roommate, Harlan. They offered to sit with us in the movie and we accepted. When the show ended, they left immediately to return to their studies. The last time I saw him that summer seemed quite unusual to me. My family and I had just returned from the Sunday church services, and I had changed into a pair of shorts. I answered a knock at our door to find Bill standing there. His mother had driven to Lawrence to help him move back home at the end of the summer term. He wanted her to meet me; so I went out to the car and greeted his mother, and they went on their way.

I heard no more from Bill Brewster that year. I went off to Graceland and, after initial homesickness, began to enjoy my college experience. I occasionally thought of Bill that fall but I started dating a friend of my brother Wayne and, by spring, Bill no longer came to mind.

COURTSHIP **26**

ALMOST NO TIME ELAPSED between Bill's college graduation and his training for his role as an insurance field representative. The Aetna Casualty and Surety Company brought
their trainees to their home office in Hartford, Connecticut,
for six weeks of intensive schooling. Classes were held all day,
and study time occupied each evening.
Bill gave his full attention to learning
company procedures and the details of
the various insurance policies the company had to offer. Here, finally, was
instruction concretely connected with
the work he had chosen to do.

Once the home office training was
complete, he returned to the Kansas
City office for local orientation. His assigned field was western Kansas, west
of Highway 81. After traveling his territory three weeks out of each four-
week period, he returned to Kansas
City to file reports and attend meetings
on the fourth week. Bill entered his
new job with enthusiasm and tackled
its challenges with vigor. He enjoyed
visiting with folks in the small Kansas
towns, cultivating contacts with pro-
spective agents, making sales calls
with current agents and socializing
with them and their clients. The outgoing talents that came so naturally

**Bill Brewster, college
graduate, beginning his
business career, 1948**

Lois Anne Norris, college student, 1949

to him were put to good use.

In the summer of 1949, after he had been on the job for almost a year, Bill came through Lawrence on his way back to Kansas City. He drove to the house where my family had lived the year before, but we had moved. He was remembering me, but he could not recall my name. He looked up another of our church families and, during the course of his visit with them, he asked questions that netted the information he wanted. What is the name of the pastor? G.R. Norris. He has a couple of daughters, hasn't he? Yes. What is the name of the older one? Lois. Where are they living now? 1025 Connecticut Street.

I was back at my summer job clerking at the Gambles Store, so Bill chatted with Dad whom he found at home. Dad told him where he could find me, but thought Bill was taking too much for granted when he said, "If Lois doesn't return right after work this evening, don't worry about her. She will be going out to dinner with me."

When Bill walked into the store, I knew I had seen him before, but it took me a moment to come up with his name. In his business suit, he no longer looked exactly like the "Joe College" I had met the year before. As he approached me, I said, "Bill Brewster!" He replied, "Oh! I was hoping to have you show me some men's underwear before you recognized me!" There he went again trying to make me blush, and he succeeded.

The restaurant where we had dinner that evening was new to me. That was the beginning of Bill's untiring and delighted effort to expand my world. He took me to my first ice hockey game, my first rodeo, and my first Ice Capades extravaganza. We visited the Zoo, the Nelson Art Gallery, and Starlight Theater in Kansas City. We went tandem bicycling in Swope Park, and we picnicked at Lone Star Lake near Lawrence. (Perry Lake and Clinton Lake had not yet been formed.) We had card parties with friends and visited relatives. Bill willingly went to church with me but was honest about his thoughts that one should attend the largest and richest church in town to facilitate business contacts. Over the rest of that summer of 1949, we dated each time he returned to Kansas City.

One evening Bill took me with friends of his, a married couple, to a fancy Italian restaurant in Kansas City. I was ill at ease with the newness of the experience, but Bill and his two friends seemed to be relaxed and enjoying themselves. Bill noticed that I was cutting my spaghetti with my fork. He made a point of showing me how to twirl it on my fork while resting the tines against a spoon. Having that attention focused on me increased my unease, but I made it through the meal. Then the three of them decided that we should all go to the bar in the Muehlebach Hotel for a nightcap. I had never been in a bar, and I believed I should not go there, but I was too shy to protest or to go against the wishes of the group. Once there, Bill ordered a soft drink for me while they each had a highball. Soon the build-up of stress I was feeling churned my stomach so badly that I became sick and had to be taken home.

One might think that evening would have convinced Bill to forget me, but it did not. From Wellington, Kansas, he wrote:

Been thinking about you all day — sweet thoughts, pleasant thoughts, lonesome thoughts, mischievous thoughts and down right exciting thoughts!

We were carrying on a lively correspondence as I returned to Graceland for my sophomore year and he traveled his territory. There were no expressed commitments between us, but we got together in Lawrence or Kansas City each time we could make our busy schedules merge. He also visited me at

Graceland a couple of times that fall. He came not with flowers or chocolates but with special Hermit cookies from
Wolferman's in Kansas City. Apparently, we discussed whether
I would date other fellows. Social events at school were often
couples affairs. Bill wrote:

> *Your not having dates (at school) is swell for me but not*
> *for you. I can't honestly say I want you to date, but I think it*
> *is selfish for me to expect otherwise. I hope you will try to*
> *have a normal college year. Maybe I'm wrong but as long as*
> *you write me the kind of letters you have so far then I can't be*
> *too jealous. I just want you to do what your heart tells you to*
> *do and to be perfectly honest with me even tho I might not*
> *want to hear what you have to say. I think you know that I*
> *have been painfully honest with you.*

The second time Bill came to see me at Graceland was quite
a surprise. He dropped by with his mother and his two broth-
ers-in-law, George Wilcox and Burton Griffing. They were returning from Fort Madison where they attended the funeral
of Daisy Brewster, the widow of Bill's Uncle Jim. Daisy's death
left Jim's only surviving child, the mentally handicapped Charley, to be cared for by Angela Roxlau, the long-time maid of
the family. Jim's estate was held in trust for Charley's care.
Bill and his folks took me to the Coffee Shop in Lamoni for a
snack and a brief visit before they returned to Kansas City.

Bill demonstrated once how creative he could be in elimi-
nating his competition for my attention. One day we were
sitting in the living room of my family home when the only
telephone in the house rang. The caller was a young man I
had dated once or twice. As I talked on the phone, Bill walked
to my side, added a drunken slur to his voice and said in a
very audible tone, "Aw, come on, honey, your beer is gettin'
warm!" Of course, there was no beer and Bill was completely
sober, but the ruse worked. The caller abruptly ended our conversation and never called again. I was scandalized, but Bill
enjoyed his little joke immensely.

In all the areas that I was shy and fearful, Bill was adventuresome and confident. He seemed perfectly comfortable in any setting. Though he charmed me, my plan for my life did not include a serious relationship for at least five years. I wanted to finish my bachelor's degree before considering marriage. I knew that after my second year at Graceland, I would need to work to pay off my already-incurred college debts before self-financing my last two years — probably at K.U. My sister Donna would graduate from high school at the same time I graduated from Graceland. Family finances could not support two of us in college at the same time.

Also, I was analyzing Bill all the while and coming up with what I considered flaws. I had never lived around anyone who drank socially or smoked, and I was not sure I could tolerate that. Bill's ideas about religion worried me. However, there seemed to be no hidden agendas with this guy. I was finding him very open about everything and great fun to be with. I was becoming smitten with love, and a war between my head and my heart ensued.

After spending the 1949-50 New Year's Eve and Day in Kansas City with Bill and his mother, I went directly back to Iowa to school. Meanwhile, the sophomore (I will call him Joe) I had dated during my freshman year at Graceland stopped by Lawrence to see me. Joe was on his way to an aeronautics school in Oklahoma. I had not heard from him after he graduated from Graceland the prior June. In my absence he visited with my parents. Joe had visited in my home the year before, and my folks were favorably impressed by him. They could see that Bill and I were becoming rather serious, and they thought I might benefit from seeing Joe again. They invited him for a return visit on Easter weekend when they knew I would be home.

Mother wrote me a long letter telling me about the wonderful visit they received from Joe in my absence and cautioning me to think things through clearly. It was a good letter. I respected my parents' judgment and that letter accentuated my concerns. Bill and I were open about our doubts. His doubts

were related to my lack of readiness to make a commitment
to him. My doubts were related to my desire to complete my
education plans before marriage, my reticence to take my college indebtedness into marriage, and my reservations about
the "flaws" I thought I saw in Bill. On January 12, 1950, he
wrote:

> *I feel so sure we were meant to be mates. The only thing*
> *that has cooled me off at times have been when you indicated*
> *that you were not at all sure but what I was an alcoholic, an*
> *atheist, a nicotine fiend …*

Bill offered to stop smoking for me, but I told him not to
bother until he had a better reason. I was afraid he might
stop only temporarily unless he had a deep personal convic-
tion about it. Bill was never a heavy drinker, and he seldom
had an alcoholic beverage around me. I really did not want to
impose my values upon him. I saw no permanence in his sharing of my values unless they were something he genuinely
desired for himself.

My confusion increased during January. I not only had my
own questions, but I also honored my parents' reservations
about Bill. They were concerned about the differences in our
ages and life-styles. Though he never said so, I believe Daddy
thought that Bill was such a man of the world that he might
love me and leave me. However, I knew how strong Bill's feelings were for me, and in my heart I wanted to return them in
full measure. Bill sensed my dilemma, and he wisely, if not
confidently, gave me some space. He called early in February
to suggest that he not contact me further until school was out.
If he still wanted to see me after that, he reserved the right to
at least call. If I decided I wanted to see him before the school
year ended, the right to call would be mine. I miserably agreed
to his suggestion.

I wove an active social life into my schedule for the next
couple of months — partly to test whether I could conjure up
feelings for someone else that even approached what I felt for

Bill. When I headed home for Easter and my spring break, I felt kind of numb inside. Mother and Joe met me at the bus. I saw them standing at the door of the bus terminal while I waited by the bus for my bag to be taken from the baggage compartment. I thought, "If that were Bill, he would not be standing there with Mother. He would be here with his arms around me waiting to help with my bag." That was really not fair to Joe who had none of the "flaws" that I saw in Bill, but neither did he possess Bill's charisma.

It was a miserable weekend. I tried to be thoughtful of Joe, but it was an effort. We visited relatives of his in a nearby town, and they seemed delighted to meet me, obviously having heard that Joe was fond of me. On Sunday, we attended our church's biennial conference in Independence, Missouri. As we went up the ramp toward the balcony of the large auditorium, I looked back at the foyer. There among the throng in the crowded lobby were Bill and his mother. It took my breath away, and I quickly led Joe on up the ramp before Bill spotted us.

That afternoon, after Joe headed back to his aeronautics school, I went up to my parents' bedroom where Mom was doing some ironing. I threw myself on the bed and said, "Oh, Mama, I saw Bill this morning!"

She said, "Honey, we have eyes to see, and we don't need any more convincing that Joe is not for you. We have done our best to raise you to have good judgment, and we are prepared to support you in whatever choice you make."

I told her that I would like to call Bill, but I believed that call would mean that I would end up marrying him because he was older and more settled than the college boys I had dated. She said, "Well, isn't that what you want?" Then she suggested that we pray together about it. So the two of us knelt beside the bed. I went downstairs to call, and Bill answered the phone. I said, "Bill, this is Lois." Back in teasing mode, he replied, "Lois who?"

That was Bill's week to be in the Kansas City office so we got together, and when I returned to school we resumed our correspondence. He wrote:

I don't want to do anything that might lead you to be-
lieve that I think lightly of our relationship or of you as a
person. I sometimes really wonder if I'm worthy of you and
your goodliness, Lois. You are so near perfect in my eyes that
I feel too worldly and somewhat "tainted" along side of you.
I want very much to live the sort of life that would be said to
be respectable — one reason I've never married is that I did
not feel I could be true to my wife — Oh, I don't mean adul-
tery — but the usual flirtations that we see today. I've never
wanted that sort of marriage. When I met you and as I grew
to love you I knew that you were the sort of person I could
really trust and who would — if you wanted to — satisfy me
in such a way that I'd have no desire to want anyone else.
You stand for everything a wife and mother should stand for.
Oh, I can hardly wait for summer to get here. It means we
can be together more and being together brings me no end of
happiness.

Before I graduated from Graceland in May, 1950, I signed
a contract to teach the sixth grade in the elementary school at
Eudora, Kansas, a small town near Lawrence. To obtain more
college credits, I enrolled at the University of Kansas for the
summer session.

The closeness that developed between Bill and me that
summer was confirming, and, finally, I became convinced that
I could not be happy apart from him. I found myself loving
him as he was, and, in August, when he asked me to be his
wife, I accepted with my whole heart.

One is never completely free of outside influences. Hap-
penings in the world at large that summer and fall of 1950
caused us concern. After World War II, there was talk about
the possibility of a World War III. The United Nations was
formed to give nations a forum to work out their differences.
At the end of World War II, the Korean peninsula was liberated from almost half a century of Japanese occupation. Russia began oversight of Korea north of the thirty-eighth parallel, and the United States stationed troops in the south.

Russia vetoed a move in the United Nations to allow free elections to decide the government of Korea as a whole. Elections south of the thirty-eighth parallel determined only the government in South Korea while North Korea was ruled by a Communist regime. On June 25, 1950, less than two months before Bill and I became engaged, North Korea attacked South Korea in an effort to unify Korea under Communism. The United Nations sent in a police force and the Korean War was under way.

Bill and I were uneasy about the war situation, but we did not think that he would be called back into the Navy. We depended on the assurance he was given when he signed up in the inactive reserves, that they would be last to be called up the next time troops were needed.

As we planned for our life together, Bill did not expect me to give up my dream of finishing my college degree. We hoped to reserve our first year to adjust to married life; but we agreed that we should start our family soon after that because Bill was approaching age thirty. We thought we wanted at least two children. We believed the completion of my schooling could be worked around our family's needs.

I hoped to pay off my college debts from my first year teacher's earnings. I knew that was an ambitious objective because I also needed to take care of my personal expenses. I felt an obligation to share the expense of my room and board in my parents' home, and I needed to augment my meager wardrobe. My salary for that first year was to be $1800. My college debts were $900 — $600 owed to the college and $300 to my grandfather.

As we discussed a wedding date, Christmas vacation seemed the first logical time, but in mid-October Bill received an offer for a job transfer to Portland, Oregon. When he called me to discuss the matter, he mentioned two very positive effects of such a transfer. First, it offered advancement in his work. Second, he was feeling a need to be more independent of his mother. That independence was difficult to achieve while he continued to use her home as his home base. The distance between Kansas City and Portland would facilitate that objective. The downside was that we would not be able to see each other for seven long months while I served out my teaching contract. However, we agreed that he should accept the offer. We set our wedding date for May 27, right after my school year ended.

Parting was very difficult when Bill left for Oregon on October 27. It was even more difficult because the Korean War was heating up, and the possibility of Bill being recalled into the Navy was becoming less remote. Then came terribly lonely months for both of us. The seven months between October and May seemed an eternity. We tried to fill the void with letters and telephone calls. Sometimes it seemed the world would come to an end before we could marry.

Bill found a room to rent in a private home in Portland. He was orienting to his new job and liking it. His territory included northern Oregon and southern Washington State. He made some overnight and weeklong trips, but he did not have to stay out in his territory for three weeks at a time as he had in Western Kansas. He enjoyed exploring the beautiful landscape of the scenic Northwest.

To fill some lonely hours in Portland, Bill looked up the church because he knew I would want to attend when I joined him. He found the church people very friendly. One family invited him home to dinner, and they encouraged him to attend a series of meetings that were being offered by a minister named Peter Gibbs. The message Bill heard in those meetings spoke to his soul. He found himself wanting to be a part of that group — never mind that they were not the largest or the richest church in town. Bill was never one to be a spectator for long. He was soon studying scriptures, and he became involved in church meetings and projects in whatever way he could participate.

The Korean War escalated over the rest of 1950, and China became involved on the side of the Communists. In January of 1951, Bill was alerted to prepare his affairs and to expect orders to return to active duty in the Navy in the next four months. That would put his induction before our planned wedding. That did it for both of us! We resolved to be married before Bill again went off to war. We agreed that I should seek a release from my contract so we could set up our wedding date. My release came surprisingly easily. My principal's wife was an experienced teacher who had retired to have their family. She welcomed the opportunity to return to the classroom for the final three months of the school year. The new date that we chose was March 4. That left only six weeks to complete our wedding arrangements.

MARRIAGE   **27**

EXCITEMENT GREW BOTH IN Lawrence and in Portland as we compressed our wedding plans into those remaining six weeks. Everyone pitched in to help. Bill's "Aunt" Dodie volunteered to make my wedding gown. (She and Fred had returned to Kansas City after World War II.) I made several trips to Kansas City for fittings of my gown and to confer with Bill's mother about our guest list. Mother was teaching school at that time, and I continued to teach until the final few days before the wedding, but we managed the plethora of wedding details as well — invitations, flowers, reception arrangements, etc. We made the gowns for my two younger sisters, Donna and Janice, who were to participate in the ceremony. Dad did some redecorating of our family home. There were bridal showers given by my high school friends, by the women of the church, and by my students.

In Portland, Bill found a furnished apartment for us in a fourplex at 911 Southeast Twenty-sixth Street. We did not plan to buy furniture due to Bill's expected recall to the Navy, after which I would either follow him or return to Lawrence. The apartment had an unusual floor plan. There was a nice living room, dining room, kitchen, and bathroom, but no bedroom in sight. Both the living room and dining room converted to bedrooms with sliding double doors between them. The built-in china cupboard in the dining room had false lower doors that were actually the headboard of our bed. The bed rolled out from under the raised floor of a roomy closet/dressing room. The guest bed rolled out into the living room from under the raised floor of another closet/dressing room. Its recessed headboard was beneath a built-in desk. Bill's new church friends turned out to help him paint walls in preparation for my arrival.

Before he returned for the wedding, Bill made his weeklong business trip to eastern Oregon and Washington so he could spend most nights at home for our first few weeks. One evening during that trip he was having dinner with one of his agents and the agent's wife. During the meal, Bill mentioned his upcoming wedding. The agent winked at his wife, a former schoolteacher, and said to Bill, "Are you going to save some poor old maid schoolteacher from a lonely life?" Responding in the spirit of the question, Bill replied, "As a matter of fact, I am!"

Bill resolved to quit smoking on his thirtieth birthday, February 19, about two weeks before our wedding. He had tried unsuccessfully to quit a few times before, but this time he was determined and he prayed about it. Bill reported, "I told the Lord if He would just take away my taste for tobacco, I would stop reaching for cigarettes." Then he added, "I did and He did!" Passengers were allowed to smoke on airplanes in those days. Though Bill was smoke-free as he boarded the plane to come home for our wedding, his clothing absorbed the secondhand smoke on the airliner.

I went to Kansas City to be on hand for his homecoming, but I missed meeting him at the airport due to a mix-up in communication about his arrival time. I was at the home of his mother when Bill drew up in a taxi. He kissed me hello and then stepped back to ask if I saw anything different about him. He expected me to notice an absence of smoke odor. I looked him over carefully but I was stumped. He finally said, "Well! I've quit smoking!" We were both delighted with his success, and he remained smoke free the rest of his life.

Sunday, March 4, 1951, was a beautiful sunny day in Lawrence, Kansas. I had heard of brides having doubts as they approached the altar, but my doubts were all erased in the months preceding our wedding. I recall feeling assured of the rightness of our commitment to each other. The only snag in our festivities that afternoon was kept a secret from me until after the ceremony. The ancient pipe organ in the old

Lois Anne Norris and William D. Brewster wedding, March 4, 1951. Left to right: Everett, Janice and Donna Norris, Lois and Bill, Guiff Moore, Claude Norris, George Wilcox

church broke down shortly before our ceremony was to begin. Some resourceful soul managed to wire it back together in time for the wedding processional.

Despite some health problems, Dad escorted me down the aisle. My brother Claude was our minister. Bill and I each had only one attendant. His best man was a fraternity brother, Guiff Moore. My sister Donna was my maid of honor. My youngest sister Janice lit our candles. Our guests were ushered by my brother Everett and Bill's brother-in-law, George Wilcox.

After a reception in the church fellowship hall, we were driven to Kansas City by our best man and Georgia, the girl who later became Guiff's wife. We had dinner with them at a restaurant called the Green Parrot, near Missouri's state line. Then we were dropped off at the Meuhlebach Hotel in downtown Kansas City where we spent our wedding night.

We flew to Portland the next day and landed in a rare March snow. I was carried across the threshold of our apartment to find the lights all on, a fire blazing in the fireplace, a fresh-baked pie and homemade jelly on the kitchen table, and a bowl of fragrant flowers on the dresser in my dressing room. Bill had left the key with one of the church families. They came in shortly before our scheduled arrival, made those preparations for our homecoming and discretely left the scene. Bill had planned for us to spend our honeymoon in Timberline Lodge on Mt. Hood, but the snow over the weekend closed the roads on the mountain so we stayed in our own apartment.

Bill had a natural talent for cooking. He had stocked the kitchen with a few staple food items before he returned to the Midwest for the wedding. When we awoke that first morning in the apartment, he suggested that we have pancakes for breakfast. He said there was pancake mix in the cupboard. I had never made pancakes. My father was the official pancake maker in the Norris household. However, I figured I could manage by following the recipe on the package.

I ventured into the kitchen to take up my wifely duties, and I thought things were going just fine as I began to beat the pancake batter. About that time Bill walked up behind me, looked over my shoulder to see what I was doing and said in a teasing voice, "My little wife can't cook worth a darn!" He believed pancake batter should be folded rather than beaten. I simply handed him the spoon so he could finish making the pancakes. There were no hurt feelings over that incident. I was happy to have him assume the role of pancake cook then and forever after.

The newness of our married life was exciting. It seemed a real lark to go out shopping together after breakfast that morning. We purchased a number of kitchen items, and we bought some groceries. Bill added a six-pack of beer to the items in our grocery cart, and those beers were placed in our refrigerator when we got home. Over the next three or four weeks, Bill drank most of that six-pack, but the last can or two remained untouched. Finally, I asked him what should be done with the remaining supply. He told me to throw them away, and that was the last of any alcoholic beverage in our household. Bill's dropping of his smoking and drinking habits seemed to make him as happy as it did me.

On our first Sunday in Portland, Bill introduced me to the

church congregation that had made him feel so welcome. They welcomed me into their midst, also. We continued to attend services regularly. In May, two months after our wedding, Bill accepted ordination to the lay priesthood. This meant that he was authorized to perform certain ministerial functions on a volunteer basis.

Bill's impending recall to the Navy changed more than our wedding date. Because I abbreviated my first year of teaching in Kansas, I was able to repay only my college debt to Graceland. My debt to Grandfather Christenson remained. Because we expected to leave Portland in a few months, my tentative plans to go to school and/or to teach were abandoned.

A letter from the Navy, dated ten days after our wedding, ordered Bill to report to Seattle, Washington, on May 20 for "outfitting and assignment to general detail." He had applied for a deferment but it was denied. Then a letter from the Navy dated April 10 stated, "The amount of obligated service remaining in your current naval reserve enlistment ... has been determined to be insufficient for your return to active duty at the present time. Therefore, your active duty orders will be cancelled unless you desire to volunteer for active duty." Bill quickly replied that he did not wish to volunteer, and the official cancellation of his orders arrived in a letter dated May 25, 1951.

Settling into my role as housewife was wonderful when Bill was in town, but I was lonely and fearful when he had to be away overnight. As a member of a large family, I had never before spent a night alone. On those lonely nights, I placed "booby traps" by the doors so I could sleep. Together we looked for ways to alleviate my loneliness. Our first major purchase was a new electric Singer sewing machine, and our second was a reconditioned Electrolux vacuum cleaner. I enjoyed the sewing lessons that came with the purchase of the sewing machine. I filled a lot of lonely hours sewing and cleaning the apartment.

Our neighbors across the hall were friendly. Karl was an attorney and his wife, Mary, worked in the office of a medical supply company. Upon returning from her work one day, Mary knocked on our door and asked me if I would like a job. The wife of a doctor had come into Mary's office that day and mentioned that the receptionist in her husband's office was leaving and they were looking for a replacement. I went for an interview at Dr. Smith's office, which was on Belmont Street about eight blocks from our apartment. After the questions about my educational background and experience, they inquired about my plans to have children. I told them honestly that we expected to wait a year before starting our family. That seemed satisfactory to them, and I was hired immediately.

That job proved both interesting and educational for me. Dr. Smith was a fatherly figure about 65 years old. His nurse, Frankie, was a kindred spirit. The office atmosphere was happy and friendly, and it solved my problem of loneliness. Along with greeting patients, answering the phone and typing letters and statements, I learned to do urinalysis and electrocardiograms, to develop x-rays and give basal metabolism tests. When I could not read his terrible handwriting, Dr. Smith willingly deciphered it for me, and he explained the meaning of the medical terms involved. Though patient records were confidential, my job required an awareness of their content, and I found them interesting.

Bill and I did not want to become dependent on two incomes. When I began earning a salary, we made two financial decisions that served us well all of our lives together. Rather than adding my income to the family cash-flow account, we resolved to deposit it in a savings account to be used only for special projects, the first of which was to repay my college debt to Grandpa Christenson. We accomplished that by the end of 1951. Grandpa died the following year. I was glad to have met that obligation while he was living.

The second vow that we made regarding our finances was to try to avoid installment purchases for anything except for our car and home. We had no credit cards in those days, but when we acquired credit cards, we tried to pay each monthly billing in full. We wanted to avoid accumulating interest due to smaller monthly payments.

Learning to cook for Bill was a challenge. The diet in the

Norris household was somewhat bland compared to that of
the Brewsters. On my visits to the Brewster household during our courtship, I used every opportunity to observe his
mother doing her cooking. After our marriage, I was alert to
any hints of Bill's wishes. When he mentioned a dish he would
like, I searched my cookbook or I used a common sense approach to try to provide it for him. Bill was patient and helpful as I learned to satisfy his tastes. He was a master at positive reinforcement. When I prepared a dish that he knew could
be improved, he ate it with apparent appreciation. Then he
said, "That was good, honey, but next time why don't you try
adding (this or that)."

One day he said, "Let's have some ham hock and beans." I
had never cooked a ham hock. When I asked for one at the
meat counter, the butcher sold me an old dried-up looking
thing. I took it home and boiled it twenty minutes or so and I
added a can of butter beans. At dinner that evening I thought
our main dish definitely lacked appeal, but Bill ate it without
comment. After we went to bed that night, I was about to drop
off to sleep when Bill began to laugh a deep belly laugh. Coming in the dead of night it startled me, and I asked, "What in
the world are you laughing about?" When his laughter slowed
enough that he could speak, he said, "That was the darndest
mess you fed me for dinner tonight!" I joined in his laughter
because I agreed with him.

From the beginning, laughter was often shared in our
household. Bill had a wonderful sense of humor. He loved to
tell stories, and we developed lots of inside jokes that required
only a hint to start us laughing together. The great differences
in our backgrounds and personalities seemed to complement
each other. It was a joyous adventure doing things together,
learning our roles and discovering how to please each other.
Bill seemed to place me on a figurative pedestal during our
courtship, and he continued that attitude toward me with patience and tenderness after we married. We learned very early
that the happiness of each of us depended upon the happiness
of the other.

FAMILY   28

WE WERE PLANNERS AND goal setters. In the beginning, Bill was usually the leader in our planning, but I was always granted veto and amendment powers. As time went on, I began to initiate some of our plans, but the process and the goal setting were mostly mutual. Our plans were not considered absolute. They were subject to adjustment in response to new insights and changing conditions.

In May of 1952, we were ready to start our family. We moved into an unfurnished apartment in an apartment court that housed mostly young married couples. Its address was 52 Southeast Fifty-seventh Avenue. We painted the walls to suit ourselves and bought the few items of furniture that we could afford. Inexpensive twin dressers and bed had to suffice in our bedroom. We were determined to wait until we could pay cash for a nicer suite. We had a sofa for the living room, but a canvas lawn chair served until we could afford an easy chair of our choice. A card table and folding chairs stood in for the dining room furniture we would buy later.

I gave notice at work, and I quit as soon as a replacement was in place. However, in fairly short order my replacement proved unsatisfactory, and I was asked to return to work until pregnancy made my retirement needful. In those days, women usually did not work in public close to their delivery time. I returned to work for the next five months, and I had morning sickness most of that time. Most mornings I went into the rest room and lost my breakfast shortly before setting out to have lunch. Dr. Smith gave me frequent injections of Vitamin B to keep up my energy.

Our little one was scheduled for arrival on April 9 and, sure

Pamela Jean Brewster, six months old. October 1953.

enough, my labor began late that afternoon. Sonograms were not in use at that time, so we did not know the sex of our unborn child. I was instructed to come to the hospital when my contractions were five minutes apart, so we checked in at about 9 P.M. We did not expect delivery to be long or difficult. Bill reminded me that Indians had been known to stop behind a clump of sagebrush to give birth and then to catch up with the tribe. But my labor dragged on all that night and into the next day. Finally, the contractions stopped, and the nurses had me up walking the halls of the hospital.

Having sat up all night with me, Bill was very tired. He said his stomach, too, was hurting, and he decided to go home for a little rest. He had been gone only a couple of hours when my labor began again with a vengeance. Finally, I was told that I was ready for the delivery room. I overheard someone say, "Where is her husband? He was here a while ago." I said, "Oh! Never mind him! Let's go!" Husbands were not allowed in the delivery room in those days anyway. However, Bill returned in time for the birth.

Pamela Jean was born about 8:30 p.m., April 10, 1953, weighing in close to seven and a half pounds. Dr. Smith remarked, "Isn't that just like Lois, giving me time to enjoy dinner before I had to arrive at the hospital?" Of course, if I had been able to choose, I'd have interrupted his dinner the night before with my delivery! As we looked together at our precious, perfect little daughter, Bill gave a sigh of relief and declared, "When I get so I can stand it again, we'll have another one!" As was standard practice at that time, I remained in the hospital five days. It was wonderful to be pampered with special care, including back rubs every night.

Pam revolutionized our lives. We had prepared as much as we could, but we still had so much to learn. Thank goodness for my former employer and good friend, Dr. Smith, and for church friends who came to our aid more than once. When Pam was five months old, we proudly brought her to Lawrence and Kansas City to show her off to grandparents and other relatives.

Our well-laid plans were to give Pam a sibling near her second birthday, but six months ahead of schedule we were expecting again. (Bill recovered from Pam's birth rather quickly.) Prescribed constraints during a normal pregnancy were more stringent in those days than they are today. Immediately, I was advised to stop the swim classes I was enjoying at the YMCA. I also was told I should not drive the car during the last six weeks before my expected delivery date of October 5, 1954.

In anticipation of the expansion of our family, we decided to buy a house. We contracted to have a small three-bedroom house built for us at 1215 Southeast Eighty-eighth Street. We came to call it our "learning house." It cured us of wanting to build in the future. All of our subsequent homes were existing structures when we bought them.

Our bare-bones financing for that beginning house left us little room to alter the prescribed plans, but we were allowed to make one change. Because our lot was rather narrow, we opted to have the house placed with its narrow end facing the street. We did not accurately visualize the effect of that change. Once built in that configuration, with the picture window in the living room and the large dining room window on the narrow end of the house with the front door between them, the house took on somewhat the appearance of a storefront. When the front door was open, one could look straight down the hall into the bathroom. Despite its idiosyncrasies, many things about that house fit our needs better than had the apartment. In June, my youngest sister, fourteen-year-old Janice, came for a six-week visit. She helped with Pam while we moved and settled in.

Our telephone rang on August 30 with the sad news that my father had died of a heart attack. Bill was unable to get away from his work, and he was apprehensive about having his very pregnant wife travel at that time. However, the doctor gave me clearance to go, and I returned to Kansas for the funeral. The flight was tiring with my energetic sixteen-month-old daughter perched on what was left of my lap, but I was glad to be with Mother at that difficult time. For the first time in many years, all of my siblings were together. The return flight to Portland was easier because Ruth, the wife of my eldest brother, accompanied me, holding Pam all the way.

October 5 came and went, but my labor did not begin. Bill's mother arrived to take care of Pam while I was confined. As the days dragged on, we became concerned that Mom Brewster would need to return home before the baby arrived. Finally, on October 23, I began to have twinges that we recognized as the beginning of my labor. We did not become excited. We were experienced, and we did not want to go to the hospital early, so we went shopping for the new clothes dryer we needed. My labor was progressing rapidly when we checked into the hospital about eight or nine o'clock that evening. The doctor arrived and estimated that delivery would be about midnight, so he decided to stay on at the hospital.

I went into hard labor that continued on and on without progressing toward delivery all the rest of the night. The baby was not in breach position, but he was turned so he could not help with the birth. About eight o'clock the next morning the doctor used forceps to intervene. Though terribly bruised about the head and face, our son heralded his arrival with lusty cries. We were all worn and weary from our overnight ordeal, and Bill reserved any teasing comments about having more children. We just felt blessed that both mother and baby survived, and our wounds were such that we would both recover.

Mark William weighed in at eight pounds and three ounces on October 24, 1954. After all of his struggle to enter this world, he was a very placid baby and easy to care for. Before many months passed, he and his sister were playing, eating, bathing and sleeping on the same schedule.

In June of 1955, we traveled to the Midwest to introduce our new arrival to our extended families. We had just returned to Portland

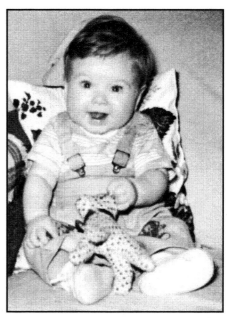

Mark William Brewster, six months old. April 1955.

when Bill was offered another job transfer, this time based in Omaha and traveling western Iowa and eastern Nebraska. It was tough deciding whether or not to accept the offer. Bill loved Portland and the Northwest, but after we weighed the pros and cons, he decided it was wise to accept the transfer. We believed that we would eventually need to be closer to the Kansas City area because of the advancing age of both of our mothers, and Omaha was a giant step in that direction.

We were able to sell our home quickly by allowing the buyer to assume our mortgage. Bill's company sent in movers to pack and transport our household goods. By August, the children and I were again visiting Mother in Lawrence while Bill located an apartment for us in Omaha.

The winter of 1955-1956 that we spent in Omaha was not an easy time for us. The manager of the Des Moines office, Bill's boss, made things difficult in several ways. Though a small subsidiary office was located in Omaha, Bill was allowed little or no office time for planning and filing his reports. He was required to stay out in his territory all week, every week.

Coming home late Friday nights, he had to leave town again early on Monday mornings. The manager imbibed regularly, and he chided Bill for abstaining from alcohol. Our toddlers and I were marooned at home without transportation. We did not get well acquainted with the city, and we had very little outside contact except the weekly ones at church.

After almost eight years with the Aetna, most of them good years, Bill decided to leave the company. He began surveying job possibilities in Lawrence and Kansas City. He finally accepted a position as an account executive with Thomas McGee and Sons, a large general insurance agency in Kansas City. In late April, we moved into an apartment at 8145 Virginia Street in south Kansas City so Bill could begin work on May 1, 1956. It was a good change for us. Bill enjoyed his work with clients who remained with him over time, and it was wonderful to have him no longer traveling but able to come home every night. I was still pretty much homebound with our two toddlers, but I was more acquainted with the city and its public transit system, and we had extended family members within visiting distance.

A DREAM REALIZED   **29**

As SOON AS WE were settled in Kansas City, we began attending church in Prairie Village, a suburban community on the Kansas side of the city. That congregation included many young married couples with young families, and we felt right at home. We had attended there a year or so when Bill was asked to serve a term as presiding elder for the congregation of our church at Grandview, Missouri, a suburb south of Kansas City.

Bill tackled those new volunteer responsibilities as energetically as he did his insurance work. He was kept so busy, leaving home early and coming home late, that we saw less and less of him. We had just one car in those days. There were many times that he needed to go straight from work to church, and it was just not feasible for the family to join him. So I stayed home nursing the children through childhood diseases or just staying out of the way so Bill could get done all the things he needed to do. As the months went by, I became more than just lonely; I became depressed.

Bill recognized that I was having a problem, and he sat me down to discuss what we could do about it. As we talked, we decided it was about time to revive the dream that I had put aside when we married — that of finishing my college degree. We had planned from the beginning for me to return to school after we had our family. Pam was already attending a nearby kindergarten. If we were to remain in the apartment for the coming school year, she would have to ride a school bus to attend the first grade. We wanted to avoid that bus ride. We decided to buy a home near an elementary school on the Kansas side of the Kansas City metropolitan area. Then I would commute to Kansas University at Lawrence on a part-time basis.

The Brewster family in 1958: Lois; Mark, age 3¹/₂; Pam, age 5, and Bill.

After Bill served his year at the Grandview church we began shopping for just the right house. In January of 1959 we stopped in front of a house for sale at 2909 West Seventy-second Street in Prairie Village. Bill and I looked at the house, then at each other, and we said in unison, "This is the one." It was directly behind an elementary school. It had a floor plan that we had been admiring and a fenced-in backyard. We moved into that house on our eighth wedding anniversary, March 4 — a great way to celebrate.

A second car was next on the list of acquisitions necessary to implement our plan to send me back to school. A former neighbor was selling his old brown Pontiac, dubbed Henrietta, for $100. Henrietta's trunk had been smashed in a wreck, but she ran all right and that was all we required. We also made good a promise to the children that we would get them a dog after we moved. Scooter, a female beagle, became a member of our family for the next twelve years. Guinea pigs, a hamster, and gold fish eventually joined Scooter to form our household menagerie.

With the purchases of a home and a second car accomplished, I enrolled in Kansas University for the eight-week summer session of 1959. I remember a young college student, who was helping with the enrollment process, expressing surprise that someone would start back to college at the ripe old age of 29. He should have met my mother who was a role model for me. She returned to teaching in 1943 with her 60-hour teaching certificate. She also returned to college each summer until she received her bachelor's degree in 1952 when she was 56 years old.

During the three summer sessions that I attended KU, the children and I drove to Lawrence each Monday morning, and we returned to Prairie Village each Friday afternoon. Bill drove Henrietta to his work while I commuted so I could drive our newer, more dependable car. Mother had great empathy for my cause. The children and I were able to stay with her while we were in Lawrence. She cared for our little ones while I attended morning classes. Mom was recovering from a broken hip that first summer. When pain caused her to remain in bed, our little ones climbed into bed with her. She read to them and taught them card games and seemed to relish their company.

At home during the winter, I worked on some of the requirements for my graduation by taking a correspondence course or two and by completing required reading. Tests relating to that work were administered on campus the following summer. Some of my required courses were not offered in the summer sessions; so, during the fall semester of my final year at KU, I commuted alone to the campus three days a week. Bill continued his unflagging support. On the mornings I had to leave early, he got the children up, served their breakfast and got them off to school before he headed for work.

Though Mother required crutches to move about, she insisted that I bring my ironing to her, including Bill's starched white business shirts. Permanent press had not yet come into its own. Parking was a problem on campus. When the distance between classes was greater than I could walk in the allotted ten minutes, Mom met me in her car and drove me from one class to the next. During the spring semester, I fulfilled a student teaching requirement in an elementary school near our home.

It was a proud day in May of 1963 when I walked down the hill in cap and gown to receive my Bachelor of Science in Education degree. I broke the dress code by wearing red shoes so my family could pick me out of the crowd of graduates marching into the stadium. I was so grateful for the sacrifices of my husband and my mother. I was very aware that they had made my success possible.

Finding a teaching position proved fairly easy once I was able to obtain a letter from my former principal — the one whose wife served out my first year teaching contract. From Denver, where he had moved with his family, he supplied the needed document in which he praised my work. I taught sixth grade and then fourth grade, for a total of three years, in the Porter School in Prairie Village where I had done my student teaching. Then I retired to give more time to my family and to work on a master's degree. Porter School is gone now. A city park occupies the site. The Prairie Village School District was unified with the Shawnee Mission School District after my tenure.

The location of our home on Seventy-second Street proved ideal for our young family. Both of our children had many friends living nearby. They went to school without even having to cross a street. When school was cancelled on winter snow days, our street was blocked off so the children could enjoy sledding on the curve of its hill. Mark especially enjoyed spending the entire day out there with the neighborhood kids, sailing down the hill on their sleds and trudging back up to repeat the process. I could watch them from the front kitchen window as I went about my household chores. On Halloween, we felt safe allowing our youngsters to join neighborhood kids who were out trick-or-treating. The children were growing and becoming increasingly involved with school and church activities as well as attending Boy Scouts and Girl Scouts and, at various times, taking piano, swimming, tennis, and dance lessons.

Bill was involved in all sorts of activities outside his insurance work at Thomas McGee and Sons. He served a three-year term as presiding elder of the Prairie Village congregation of our church. He was president of the Kansas City alumni chapter of his college fraternity for a year. He served on a fund-raising committee for improvements to our church campground. He was an assistant scoutmaster for Mark's Boy Scout troop. After Mark became an Eagle Scout and graduated out of scouting, Bill became institutional representative for our church to the Heart of America Council of the Boy Scouts. He served for a year or two as a captain in the United Fund charity drive. He was a member of the Lions Club.

Bill's culinary prowess was often on display. He enjoyed cooking outside on charcoal grills. One of his specialties was barbecued chicken. Several times over the years we had parties of up to fifty friends in our backyard for a barbecue feast. One year, he suggested that his Lion's Club serve beef stew in place of their usual Pancake Day fundraiser. Of course, they made him chairman of that effort. Advance ticket sales numbered about 450. Bill spent the night before the fundraiser doing the cooking. He called me at 1:00 am with a worried voice saying, "Lois, this stew meat has been cooking quite a while, and it's still tough." I replied, "Just keep cooking it, Bill." He did and he served up a tasty stew.

While the children were still small, we took family jaunts to the Ozarks, had a week-long stay at the YMCA camp near Estes Park in Colorado and a family fishing trip in Minnesota. Summer times we went as a family to church camps, called reunions, and the kids attended church youth camps.

Pam turned twelve years old in April of 1965 and Mark would be eleven that October. We decided to take the family on an eastern trip to attend the New York World's Fair, to tour the nation's capital and visit many other sites along the way. Bill planned ahead, packing more than I thought possible into our sixteen days. We stopped in Fort Madison for a brief visit with Charley Brewster, son of Bill's Uncle Jim. We visited friends in Chicago and toured the Museum of Science and Industry with them. We toured three sites of historic significance to our church on our way to Springfield, Massachusetts. Cousins there took us to Mystic Seaport in Connecticut.

During our three days in New York City, we left our car in the hotel garage and rode the subway. Besides spending a couple of days at the Fair, we took the ferry to the Statue of Liberty and were treated to a private tour of the city by a cousin who lives there. We headed down the coast to Jamestown and Williamsburg by way of the Chesapeake Bay bridge/tunnel, then on to Washington, D.C. where the Capitol, the Archives, the Smithsonian, Mt. Vernon, and the monuments were the focus of our visit. After leaving Washington, we toured the Gettysburg battlefield. At our final stop with relatives in Lexington, Kentucky, we were favored with a viewing of Uncle Reynold's impressive collection of Springfield rifles, all of which he had restored to mint condition. We returned home on schedule to take up our busy schedules again.

INHERITANCE 30

B ILL AND I WERE awakened on our sixteenth wedding anniversary, March 4, 1967, by the ringing of our telephone. That call brought news of the passing of Charley Brewster, the mentally handicapped son of Bill's Uncle Jim. Charley was 82 years old. Though he had grown to adulthood and old age, Charley had remained a perpetual child. He had survived the deaths of his entire family — mother, father, sister, and stepmother. Angela Roxlau, Charley's nurse and housekeeper, had never married but devoted all of her adult years to serving the family and Charley. Having begun work for the family while still in her teens, Angela was in her sixties when Charley died. Charley's closest surviving relative was Betty Garrott Handel, the adopted daughter of his sister Starr. At that time, Betty lived with her husband and children in Atlanta. She came alone to Charley's funeral.

Bill and I were the only representatives of the Will Brewster wing of the family able to attend the funeral. We drove to Fort Madison the day before that memorial. We checked into an old, but recently redecorated, hotel where reservations had been made for us. It was located on one of Fort Madison's main streets. Railroad tracks ran parallel between that street and the Mississippi River.

The refurbishing of the hotel did not include updating the beds. When we retired for the night, we rolled involuntarily into a smothering oneness in the middle of the mattress. Staying on one's own side of the bed required holding on to the edge for dear life. As we struggled to defy gravity and get some sleep, we were jarred by the sound of air brakes as eighteen-wheeler trucks stopped for the stoplight below our window.

That sound had not yet dissipated when a train whistle sounded on the nearby tracks. Soon barges passing on the river added their horns to the chorus. Our shattered efforts to sleep made the night seem very long. When we arose in the morning, Bill packed his bag and declared, "We're not spending another night in this hotel! If we need to stay over another day, we'll find a room elsewhere."

The funeral was scheduled for 11 a.m. We had breakfast before dropping by the Brewster home at 722 Avenue F where a solemn, but welcoming, Angela greeted us. In the living room a chair was placed before the television set, its back to the rest of the seating in the room. That chair was where Charley had spent much of his time. As folks arrived to accompany Angela in the funeral coach, I turned Charley's chair around to help accommodate the new arrivals. When the coach arrived, Angela returned that chair to its original position before the television set. Obviously, she wanted things in the house to remain, as long as possible, as they had been when Charley was alive.

That morning Bill and I were the last to leave the house that Uncle Jim had shared with his family and that Charley had been the last family member to occupy. How we would have loved to explore that house — to note its contents, to find old pictures, anything revealing more of the history of the family that lived there! But there was no time. Angela told us that Daisy, Jim's second wife and stepmother to Charley, had destroyed everything pertaining to her brother-in-law, Will Brewster, and his family. It was known in the family that Daisy was not fond of Will. Years before, Angela had saved the large leather-bound Brewster Bible, dated 1844, from the auction block and had given it to Will's family.

At the funeral home, the proprietor, a little old lady the age of Charley, stepped out spryly to open the doors of the funeral coach. I had to squelch my urge to run to help her as I would have my own grandmother. The service was not long. A Presbyterian minister officiated. After the burial in the city cemetery, Bill and I had a brief time to view the gravestones on the other Brewster graves located there.

We were invited to lunch at the home of the widow of Frank McClurg. Frank, who died in 1965, was a nephew of Daisy. He was also associated with Uncle Jim, either at the bank or at the Scheaffer Pen Company, or perhaps both. He and Craig Scheaffer were trustees of the estate of Uncle Jim's daughter Starr after her death in 1943. Frank's widow was a gracious hostess. She presided over a lovely luncheon served by a maid in a white uniform.

We had an afternoon appointment with A. Anthes Smith, president of the Fort Madison Savings Bank. The purpose of our meeting was to hear the provisions of Uncle Jim's will. Betty Handel was also at the bank that afternoon, but bank officials met separately with her. We heard that Betty had exhausted the sums she had already received from her mother Starr's estate and had come back too often for more. She was to inherit the Brewster home and its furnishings but none of the other assets. After any debts were paid, and I suppose some provision for Angela, the corpus of Jim's estate was to be divided three ways among the children of Jim's brother Will — Bill and his half-sisters, Marguerite and Barbara. Bill, the only adult survivor bearing the Brewster surname, was also to receive the large gilt-framed portrait of his grandfather, Charles Brewster.

I saw irony in the disposition of the estate of Jim Brewster. I thought back over the lives of the three children — Martha, Jim, and Will — of the immigrant Charles Brewster. Martha had a sad, dependent life. Deserted by her husband and supported by her father's legacy, her life ended in a mental institution. Her only child, another Charley, became an invalid at an early age and he survived his mother by less than a year. Jim's life was settled and focused. He built on the fortune his father left to him. His estate was held in a trust that took care of his widow and his handicapped son for the rest of their lives. Will used his share of his father's fortune to finance his many adventurous exploits and lost it all. However, Will's children now stood to inherit the fruits of Jim's stewardship. That is

not to say that Will's children were ungrateful or unworthy
recipients.

At the end of our interview with the kindly Mr. Smith, I
asked if he could point us toward a local source of family history. He was able only to give us a hand-written chronology of
the bank and its officers, two of whom were Bill's Grandfather Charles and his Uncle Jim. Sometime later, Mr. Smith
sent us a copy of the item from the Fort Madison newspaper
about Bill's grandfather that appears in the first chapter of
this book.

Over the next several years, we received voluminous correspondence from Mr. Pollard, the bank's aging attorney. Bill
remembered his father's dislike of Mr. Pollard. As the many
lengthy haranguing letters filled with legalese about the estate continued to come in, Bill sympathized with his dad. In
addition to the letters, however, came checks and stock certificates. They did not come in large amounts. They just filtered
in now and then.

I wanted to keep a record of those incoming assets, but Bill
was not so inclined. I did not press the issue because it was
his inheritance, not mine, and I was busy with other things. I
do not know the total amount that Bill received, and I doubt
that he had more than a generalized notion of it. The legacy
did not make us independently wealthy. Bill did not give up
his insurance work or I my desire to continue my education
and my career in teaching. It did add an element of ease to
our lives, but it also added a new financial concern to what we
already had in place. To the question, "How shall we best budget to meet our goals?" was added, "How can we maintain what
we have inherited."

Bill invested the funds as they came. He studied, joined
an investment club for a time, and visited frequently with a
stockbroker and knowledgeable friends. Until then, I knew
nothing of investing beyond bank savings accounts. To begin
my education about stocks, Bill gave me $5,000 to invest. That
capital was to be mine alone. He would have no say in how it
was invested, but he would share information with me if I

were to ask. I enrolled in a seminar offered by an investment firm. After those meetings, I invested in three stocks. That provided an incentive to follow the course of the market. A year or so later I joined an investment club that met monthly. At those meetings, I heard investment jargon, I took my turn preparing reports on individual stocks, and I began to understand some of the investment literature and charts. The club did not make its members rich. In fact, we did little more than break even, but the exposure was helpful.

Bill and I soon learned that investing can be an up-and-down road. When we made mistakes, or unpredictable factors caused losses, we tried to learn from them. As a result of both good and bad experiences, we adopted our own set of helpful guidelines such as the following:

1. Diversifying among various forms of investments can help minimize the risk that is present in all investment.
2. Spend only the interest (income) from investments, not the principal.
3. Leveraging (borrowing to buy stocks) is a poor practice.
4. Selling short is not for amateurs.
5. Acquiring high quality stocks and bonds and holding them for the long term is usually the best policy.
6. Mutual funds, chosen carefully, allow one to benefit from professional expertise and are often safer than choosing individual stocks.

We made a concerted effort to teach our children how to handle finances. We sat down with them one evening in their early teens and listed the annual expenses that were exclusive to each of them. We removed from the listing their winter coats and their Sunday dress-up clothes. We felt the need for parental supervision of those items. Then we opened a bank checking account for each child. We deposited one-twelfth of each one's annual budget amount into their account.

Our agreement was that each was to keep an accounting of his/her expenditures. When their accounts were found to be reasonably accurate at the end of the month, we deposited another twelfth of their annual budget into their bank accounts for the following month. That approach seemed to work fairly well for both of them. Toward the end of their high school years they both worked at part-time jobs. Pam worked as an assistant in the office of an orthodontist, and Mark became a "car jockey" in the repair shop of a large automobile distributorship.

Financial assets were not the only Brewster family legacy that Bill inherited, nor were they probably the most important. He inherited personality traits from both of his parents — his very practical, talkative mother and his adventurous father who was not given to concern for detail. Like his mother, he wanted his job and his home life to remain stable and secure. His father's love of adventure surfaced as Bill was drawn to streams and woodlands to fish and hunt. Catching very few fish and bagging little or no game did not seem to dampen his spirits. He enjoyed the challenges of camping and being out in the wild. I recall his saying that he would love to explore places where man has never been.

Bill indulged his wilderness leanings only three or four times annually during those busiest of our years. Usually a long weekend had to suffice for such trips, but once a year he enjoyed a weeklong fly-in fishing trip in Canadian waters. He never seemed to lack buddies for his wilderness trips, and he took our son Mark along whenever he could. As an Assistant Scoutmaster in Mark's Boy Scout troop, Bill especially enjoyed helping lead the troop's high adventure expeditions in the mountains of Colorado and the Canadian boundary waters.

Bill always came home from his outings with stories to tell. On one of the Canadian trips, two of the men lost an indispensable cotter key miles from camp on a rock ledge ten or twelve feet below the cold clear surface of a lake. Somehow they managed to retrieve the key, secure the propeller on the boat motor with it, and make it back to camp. Another time the guys returned to camp to find evidence of a bear's visit. Once Bill and two buddies were canoeing a river in Washington State. An unexpected six-foot waterfall suddenly loomed ahead. Unable to avoid it, they shot the falls. The canoe remained upright but they all got soaking wet and could not remember ever being so cold before.

Bill usually cooked for the guys on his outdoor adventures. He sometimes joked that he would not go if he couldn't do the cooking. I don't recall his ever being challenged by someone wanting to take over that job. For months in advance of each trip, he pored over camping catalogs and recipe books, adding to his survival equipment and preparing to surprise the guys with a new recipe. Some of Bill's stories reported how his culinary efforts were received. A buddy once had the audacity to scrape the cheese sauce off his Welsh Rarebit. Another time, far from civilization, Bill surprised a worn and weary hiker with a dessert having whipped topping chilled in a mountain stream.

Bill enjoyed variety. In many ways, he liked to avoid patterns and repetition. As much as possible, Bill chose a different route to work each day. Fortunately, his work schedule did not require that he arrive at the office at eight and leave at four or five, though he usually worked a full day, often putting in ten or eleven hours. Dinner times at our house were flexible, depending upon his work schedule. He preferred not to eat the same food twice in one week, but he was not demanding about his preferences. I developed a repertoire of dishes that could be kept warm in the oven until he arrived for dinner, and I became creative in the preparation of leftovers. He made me feel cherished, and I found pleasure in catering to his preferences.

Surprising us with unanticipated gifts was more fun for Bill than observing traditional gift-giving times — such as birthdays. Because of my background, I was not a practiced shopper, and I was reticent to spend money on myself. Bill liked to shop. He sometimes shopped for clothes for me and called me downtown for fittings. His ever-innovative ways of recording, or not recording, the checks he wrote sometimes taxed my ability to keep straight our family accounts.

We often enjoyed times of comfortable silence at home, but in social situations, Bill seemed an inexhaustible fount of thoughts and words. There were times when I was completely lost for words, but Bill knew just the right things to say. When we were in the company of other people and I wanted to say something, I might have to wait quite a while to find enough of a lull in the conversation to speak. I recall one time, when I interjected, that Bill said, "Lois, you interrupted me in the middle of a sentence!" I replied, "Oh Bill, you've been in the middle of a sentence ever since I've known you." He laughed and I was able to add my "two cents worth" to the conversation.

Living with Bill was never dull and uneventful, but it could occasionally get a little frustrating. I never knew which of his inherited traits would surface at any given time — the staid, practical ones of his mother or the carefree, adventurous ones of his father. I recall complaining once to my mother about something Bill did. Mother gave me no sympathy. She said, "You knew he was that way when you married him." Mostly, I loved Bill just the way he was, and I learned to partner with his unique personality. His overriding sense of humor was a great blessing to both of us. He was not just my husband; he was my faithful companion and my best friend.

EXPANDING HORIZONS $\quad$ **31**

IN THE SUMMER OF 1967, we were ready for another major vacation trip. Our ultimate goal was to show the children their birthplace in Portland, Oregon, but there were many places to visit along the way. We planned to drive to Portland, sell our Oldsmobile there and fly home. We mailed an auto-for-sale advertisement to our friends, the Lapworths, with whom we would stay in Portland, with a request that the ad be submitted to the newspaper just before our arrival.

We headed for Los Angeles by a southern route. Our first stop provided a brief visit with Oklahoma City relatives on Effie's side of the family. Continuing west on I 40, we stopped in Amarillo, Texas, for a picnic, but had to retreat with our food to our air-conditioned car when a huge swarm of flies tried to commandeer our lunches. There were no video games to help kids pass the hours on the long drive across New Mexico and into Arizona in those days, so I read to the family a children's novel about the early Spanish settlement of California. We stopped briefly in Albuquerque and in the Petrified Forest.

As we neared Flagstaff, the weather changed drastically. The heat suddenly abated and the air became chilly. We connected with Guiff and Georgia Moore in Flagstaff. We had not seen them since Guiff was best man in our wedding. Georgia prepared a picnic, and we enjoyed it with them on the rim of the awe-inspiring Grand Canyon.

When we arrived in Anaheim, we found a sad message awaiting us at our hotel. Ona Lapworth called to report that her husband Wayne had died of cancer a couple days before. It was not possible for us to get to Portland in time for the funeral. We returned Ona's call to give her our heartfelt condolences and to tell her we would arrange to stay in a hotel in Portland rather than to intrude in her home at such a sad time. She insisted, however, that she wanted us to come as planned, so we maintained our original schedule.

Visiting California was a first-time experience for the children and me. Disneyland was full of wonders for both adults and children. While in Los Angeles, we drove across the city during rush hour to have dinner in the home of Grandmother Christenson's sister in Sherman Oaks. Aunt Florence gathered all of her family to share that meal with us.

As we headed north along the coast, we visited an old Spanish mission like one in the children's novel that I read to the family along the way. We stopped to have a picnic on the beach, and we suggested that the kids put on swimsuits if they were going to play in the surf. Expecting to stay out of the water, they did not suit up, but Mark was soon soaked to the skin in his street clothes and loving it. As we walked along the beach, a diver came up out of the water with a harvest of abalone. He offered us an abalone steak, which we declined since we had no way to cook it. When I told him I would love to have an abalone shell, he gave us one. It was heavily encrusted with seaweed, so we put it in a grocery sack and tucked it among our luggage in the trunk of the car.

Bill had made reservations months before for us to tour the castles at San Simeon, the former home of publishing magnate, William Randolph Hearst. We were properly impressed by the opulence of the elaborate European furnishings, the statuary that appeared to rest on the surface of the water in the outdoor swimming pool and the gold tiles of the indoor pool.

Leaving San Simeon, Bill believed the coastal highway would be a slow route northward. He checked the road map and noted that the super highway was only a few miles inland, so he plotted a shortcut to reach it. His shortcut proved a winding hilly road that made very slow going. Both Pam and Mark became carsick in the back seat, and we had to stop now and then for them to recover. It took us longer to reach highway 101 than we would have spent on the scenic coastal route. Bill thought he would never hear the end of comments about his shortcut.

The weather was warm as we skirted San Francisco and spent the night in a motel in Petaluma. When we entered the car the following morning, we noticed a rather bad odor. It worsened as we continued northward during the heat of the day. At a rest stop, we traced the smell to the abalone shell the diver had given us. Bill threatened to throw it out, but I prevailed on him not to do so. We rolled down the windows to help us live with our smelly cargo.

Kid-like, Pam and Mark had become restless when we stopped among the giant trees in Redwood National Park. Releasing pent-up energy took the form of teasing and taunting as they climbed and ran along some of the fallen logs. Mark managed to push his sister off a log, causing her to sprain an ankle. Pam nursed a limp throughout the rest of our trip.

Though we missed Wayne Lapworth in Portland, Ona and their son and daughter welcomed us and seemed to take comfort in our visit. We were relieved to plunge that smelly abalone shell into a bucket of Clorox water and let it soak in the back yard while we visited with the Lapworths and introduced our children to their birthplace. After several days, we removed our seashell from its bath and cleaned away the seaweed. We discovered an oyster attached to the shell of the abalone. The decaying oyster was the source of the odor that had caused us so much discomfort. Once the oyster shell was broken off, the abalone shell was no longer offensive.

The beautiful scenery of the Northwest brought back many happy memories to Bill and me. We tried to show Pam and Mark many of the scenes we had enjoyed in the first years of our marriage — the beach at Seaside, the mountains, the Columbia River gorge, the deep forests. Those scenes prompted the kids to ask why we had moved away from it all.

We visited our church's Lewis River Campground in Washington state. While swimming in the Lewis River, Mark discovered a large steelhead salmon lethargically moving through the water. It had evidently spent itself swimming upstream to spawn. Mark was able to catch it in his hands and, with help, pull it from the water.

On a trip with the Harold and Donna Hager family to their cabin on the slopes of Mt. Hood, we recalled a similar visit there when Pam was just three months old. On that prior visit, we arrived at the cabin with a carload of equipment and supplies for the baby and discovered that we parents had forgotten our own pajamas and tooth brushes.

About midway through our visit with the Lapworths, we received a response to our advertisement, enabling us to sell the car. That paved the way for our airline flight home at the end of our visit. The abalone shell returned with us, and it resides on my fireplace mantle today.

By 1968 we were outgrowing the little house that had served us so well during the children's elementary school years. We moved to 8145 Rosewood Drive in Prairie Village, a mile or so from our former home. We moved in July so we would be settled before school started. Pam entered the same high school that she would have attended from the old address but Mark had to change junior high schools. Troubled with dyslexia, Mark had finally begun to conquer the perceptual problems that had made his learning to read so difficult. He had done very well in seventh grade, but changing schools for his eighth grade year was tough for him. Fortunately, his math, listening, and social skills soon helped him adjust.

Florida was another destination that attracted us beginning in the late 1960s. We had relatives there on both sides of the family. Bill's sister and brother-in-law, Marguerite and George Wilcox, moved to Naples, Florida, in about 1967 after he retired. Julie, the younger of their two adopted daughters, moved with them while Sarah remained in Kansas City. Their son, George, who is mentally handicapped, remained in an institution in Missouri. George Sr. was an avid golfer and fisherman, and Marguerite (Sissy) found an outlet volunteering for a mental health agency in Naples.

When we first saw Naples, it seemed a sleepy small town compared to the spreading municipality that it is today. The Wilcox's yard held a huge banyan tree, a grapefruit tree, a towering banana "tree" and many other tropical plants that were new to us. They lived within walking distance of a white-sand beach on the Gulf of Mexico. George always had his boat ready to take us shelling on one of the nearby mangrove islands or to indulge

Pam and Mark with Pam's big catch on little Marco Island in south Florida, June 1968

Bill's and Mark's enjoyment of fishing. Pam surprised everyone by catching the biggest snook of all on her one fishing foray with them. Sissy and George were wonderful hosts during our visits.

Bill's sister Barbara also lived in Naples. Bill had seen Barbara only two or three times because she grew up in the care of her maternal grandparents in Ohio and Florida. Our Florida visits supplied opportunities for brother and sister to become better acquainted.

On the other side of the Florida peninsula, in a suburb of Miami, lived my sister Donna with her husband, Ed Sintz, and their three daughters, Ann Kristin, Lesley, and Julie. For many years Ed was the head librarian, supervising the large and developing library system for the city of Miami and Dade County. Donna earned a master's degree in library science and worked as a school librarian. Our visits with the Sintzes were full of happy times and new experiences, such as visiting an art fair at the Viscaya estate, and attending a "meet the authors" gathering. Bill impressed the Sintz girls by making smores for them on a picnic at the beach. The beach scene above my mantel was purchased in Miami.

One year we went to Florida for Christmas. We had Christmas breakfast with the Wilcoxes in Naples and headed for Miami about noon to have Christmas dinner with the Sintzes. About ten miles out of Naples on the Tamiami Trail, our car blew a radiator hose. We were sure no car repair shop would be open on Christmas Day. We believed our only option was to call the Wilcoxes to come get us. We thought we would have to leave the car beside the road until the next day when it could be towed for repair.

There were no cell phones in those days. We spotted a house a hundred yards or so up a gravel side road into the swamplands. Bill walked to that house and knocked on the door, hoping to use their telephone. In the house were two couples preparing their holiday meal. When Bill told them his errand, one of the men said he was an auto mechanic. He took a look at our disabled vehicle and knew immediately what to do. From an old derelict auto in his yard, he salvaged a radiator hose and installed it in our car. Using a plastic milk bottle, he brought swamp water from the roadside ditch and filled our radiator. Our benefactor refused any payment. He simply wished us a Merry Christmas and waved us on our way. We arrived in Miami only a little late for dinner.

Along with other families in our church group, we participated several times in a People-to-People program that placed foreign visitors in American homes for brief visits. Our first guests were Antonios Papadapoulos and George Papaleontiou, both from Cyprus. Then came Toyokazu Sato from Osaka, Japan. I recall driving Toyo and some of his fellow student-visitors to Lawrence to see Kansas University. Along the way the Japanese visitors marveled at the open spaces in our countryside. We were impressed by the politeness of our Japanese guest. Toyo and our son Mark became good friends. The two hated to say good-bye when Toyo had to return to his homeland. As he prepared to depart, Toyo gave Mark his kimono. In contrast to his traveling companions, Toyo did not expect ever to be able to return to the United States. An arranged marriage awaited him and he did not appear happy at that prospect.

In December of 1968, we had two very different guests — Professor Bhide from India and Herman Herrewegan from Belgium. Both were teachers but the similarity ended there. Professor Bhide told us he was chairman of the psychology department at Bombay University. He informed us that we did not speak English; we spoke American. He said that *he* spoke English. Herman taught electronics in a secondary school. He appeared quite amused by the actions and speech of his fellow guest.

Mario Maida, a humble little man from Cochabamba, Bolivia, came the following year. He was a teacher of linguistics. He wanted to improve the lot of peasants in his country who lived in windowless huts and often became blind from living in darkness. He also wanted to bring them Christianity. He went to Indiana University to further his studies before returning to Bolivia.

In January of 1970, Cristina Rabino came with a group of students from Argentina. She was seventeen years old — a year older than our Pam. Cristina was a sprightly, pretty girl with olive skin and raven-black hair. She was to stay with us for six weeks and to attend high school with Pam. Though the Argentine students came to attend classes, they were also very interested in getting together with their fellow visitors for a good time.

Diego, a cousin of Cristina's, was married and attending law school at Tulane University in New Orleans. Diego and his wife invited Cristina and Pam to attend the Marde Gras celebrations in New Orleans. People-to-People administrators ruled that Cristina could go only if accompanied by an adult chaperone, so I went along. It was pleasant to enjoy the warmth of the south, escaping the February cold of Kansas City. The two girls were housed with Diego and his wife in their small apartment. I slept in the apartment of one of their friends. The Marde Gras festivities lasted several days and offered some of the most surprising people-watching sights my eyes had ever witnessed.

There were numerous parades with colorful floats and marching bands. Pam and Cristina caught armloads of the strings of beads that were thrown from the floats into the crowds of spectators. Various friends of our hosts who lived near the parade routes entertained with hors d'oeuvres after each of the parades. The home of a vice consul of the Union of South Africa was the site of one of those parties. Apartheid was practiced in South Africa at that time. I had read the book *Cry the Beloved Country,* and I asked the vice consul if that book presented an accurate depiction of life in his country at that time. He was not ready to concede that point.

While Pam and Cristina went with escorts to an evening rock concert, we adults toured the French Quarter, viewing the historic sites and the architecture. We stopped to sample chicory coffee and doughnuts sprinkled with powdered sugar. As we strolled among the crowds on Bourbon Street, we saw more than a few parading transvestites. Open doors of the saloons revealed nearly naked young women swinging the tassels on their brief costumes while dancing on the bars inside.

One afternoon we wandered through antique shops on Magazine Street where I found some brass and blue enamel candle sconces that I have often wished I had bought. That evening we took our hosts and the vice consul as our guests to a shrimp dinner in a restaurant on Lake Pontchartrain. Later, we were spectators at a street dance. A dead-end street lined with lovely old homes was blocked off for the event. Dancers of all ages responded to the music of a black jazz ensemble. Later in the evening, mellowed by liquor, many dancers seemed to be leaning on each other for support.

We spent the final night of Mardi Gras on a hotel room balcony overlooking Bourbon Street. Friends of our hosts had rented the room. That balcony offered a safe and comfortable site for viewing the throngs below. At one point an inebriated passerby looked up and saw a man drinking a mug of beer on the balcony next to ours. The pedestrian yelled, "Hey! How about a drink?" He stood under the balcony with open mouth. The man on the balcony responded by pouring some of the beer from his mug onto the man on the street. While some of the beer did reach the man, I could not tell if any actually went into his mouth.

After leaving the hotel, we stopped for a snack. It was about 2 a.m. when I asked our Latin host, Diego, what time we would start for the airport to make our 8 o'clock flight that same morning. He responded with 7 a.m. I asked if it might not be prudent to allow a cushion of time in case of traffic problems. "No, no!" blustered Diego. "If we miss the flight, I will buy you new tickets."

The next morning on our way to the airport, with no time to spare we came upon a huge traffic backup. An eighteen-wheeler had overturned and completely blocked all the lanes. Diego was not sure of an alternate route, but he drove on the shoulder and turned onto a side road breaking all speed limits. Arriving at the airport at 7:55, we rushed in and asked the attendant at the ticket counter to have our flight held until we reached the gate. As we ran down the corridor of the airport, I looked back and discovered Cristina was missing. We quickly located her in a gift shop looking for a hostess gift for the hosts who had just dropped us off! We boarded the plane an instant before takeoff.

The afternoon after our return, Cristina was invited to a tea for her group of Argentine visitors and their host students. Pam was unable to go with Cristina because she had to make up schoolwork that accumulated while we were in New Orleans. Cristina was to call for us to pick her up when the party ended, but she did not call. Instead, she went joy riding with a group of eight young folks in a Cadillac driven by one of the host teenagers. In speeding down a stretch of road the kids had dubbed "thrill hill," the driver lost control and slammed into a tree. Cristina was seated at the point of impact and was the worst injured of the group.

A policeman called our home to notify us of the accident. Bill and I rushed to the hospital where we found Cristina unconscious in the emergency room. Her lip was sliced completely through into her cheek and her pelvic bone was fractured in four places. As her surrogate mother, I went to the hospital each day to be with her. She was in shock for the first week. She did not remember the accident, and she asked me the same questions about it each day.

Plastic surgeons did wonders repairing Cristina's face. Her bones required longer to heal. She was hospitalized for several weeks and was not able to return home when her group left for Argentina. When she was finally dismissed from the hospital, she was on crutches but was expected to be able to walk on her own in time. She remained with us several days before the People-to-People organization arranged for her trip home. We heard from Cristina à few times after she returned home. She went back to school and later she married and had a child. Eventually, we lost contact, but we have often wondered how, or if, that accident changed her life and how she fared in the political purges that took place in her native land.

I did not teach school during the late 1960s because we believed it was important for me to be at home during our children's teen years. I took one course each semester at the University of Missouri in Kansas City (UMKC), slowly working toward the master's degree that I completed in 1970. Then I found a part-time position as a reading specialist at the Barstow School, an independent (private) school that has been a part of the Kansas City scene for more than a hundred years.

FLEDGLINGS FLY   **32**

PAM ENROLLED IN GRACELAND College in the fall of 1971. I suffered separation pangs when we moved her into the dormitory. I wept on our way home and off-and-on for three days. I avoided disturbing her room at home, even enough to empty her wastebasket. I felt at odds with myself — disgusted that I should react in that way — and I was glad to return to my time and thought-consuming duties at school. The three of us remaining at home adapted slowly to the void left by Pam's departure. Mark had his schoolwork, his participation on the gymnastics team, and many friends to connect with. Mark and Bill purchased an old car at a police auction for Mark to work on in his auto mechanics class. Bill and I stayed occupied with our jobs and duties at home and at church.

Pam became engaged to a young man who graduated from Graceland and went on to pursue a graduate degree at Kansas State University at Manhattan. After her sophomore year, Pam followed him to K-State. In the new environment at Manhattan, they saw their relationship differently, and the engagement was soon broken. As Pam left Graceland and enrolled for her junior year at K-State, her brother graduated from high school and became a freshman at Graceland. With both of our children off to college, our home *really* seemed empty. We felt blessed that they were doing well, and we looked forward to holidays and school vacations when they returned home briefly.

Graceland's annual homecoming weekends were special to us while our children were on campus. They were times for the family to be together and for us parents to renew acquaintances with former school friends and to meet the kids' roommates. Richard Mark, one of Mark's roommates, became im-

portant in our lives thereafter. During her two years at
Graceland, Pam was on the drill team that performed preci-
sion drills at halftimes of the football games. Mark became
captain of the cheerleading troop. He was also on the volley-
ball team and later joined the tennis and synchronized swim
teams. Homecoming schedules featured performances of each
of those activities.

The television series "Leave it to Beaver" featured the
Cleaver family consisting of June and Ward, the parents, and
two sons, Wally and Beaver. Mark's Graceland roommate one
year resembled Wally Cleaver, so Mark and his roommate were
sometimes called Wally and Beaver. At a homecoming dance
that year a student photographer snapped a picture of Bill
and me trying to do a then-popular dance step called "The
Twist." Characteristically, Bill was really getting into those
moves, and I was more inhibited. Someone mounted that picture on the door of Mark's dorm room with the caption "Ward
and June Cleaver." The picture was published in the campus
newspaper and later in the yearbook.

Pam needed transportation to her student teaching assignment during her last year at K-State, so she and her brother
pooled their resources to buy a bright orange Volkswagen

**Lois and Bill trying the Twist during a homecoming dance at
Graceland College in 1975.**

Pam and Mark Brewster with their twin cars, 1976

Beetle. The main attraction of that small car was its low-cost maintenance and exceptionally good gas mileage. The agreement was that Mark would drive the car to Graceland until Pam's student teaching assignment began. Pam would keep it the rest of the school year. That seemed a satisfactory arrangement for a time. Eventually, however, Pam bought out Mark's half, and Mark purchased another Volkswagen Beetle, a twin to the one he had owned with his sister.

Both children returned home for the summer of 1975, Pam as a graduate of K-State with a bachelor's degree in education and Mark as an aspiring junior at Graceland College. When we suggested that Mark might benefit from attending a large university, he declined; but he agreed to attend the summer session at Kansas University to sample university life. He stayed with his Grandmother Norris while attending classes, but he returned home on weekends. The greatest benefits of his weeks in Lawrence, according to Mark, were the visits he enjoyed with his grandmother over her dinner table. His experience at KU did not change his resolve to return to Graceland.

When Pam began looking for a teaching position, she found a shortage of available positions and an over-abundance of teachers seeking jobs. She decided to live at home and work toward a master's degree in learning disabilities at the K-State extension campus nearby. Pam's job as an assistant in the orthodontist's office where she had worked during her high

school days continued to provide employment for her whenever she was at home during her college years. That same job
provided her spending money while she lived at home and attended graduate school.

Another dimension to Pam's life was developing as she
worked toward her master's degree. Remember that Graceland
roommate of her brother Mark whose name was Richard Mark?
Richard left Graceland after his sophomore year to enter the
University of Missouri at Columbia as a pre-dental student.
Pam and Richard began wearing out the highway between
Columbia and Prairie Village. By the summer of 1976, a seri-
ous romance was brewing.

Between Mark's junior and senior years at Graceland, he
decided to spend the summer with some of his classmates seeking construction jobs in Houston. He was not feeling well before they left. A doctor diagnosed his symptoms as influenza,
gave him a prescription and did not discourage him from travel.
Mark had been in Houston a week or so when he called to say
that he was still ill, had been diagnosed with mononucleosis
and was coming home. He went to bed as soon as he arrived,
and he did little other than sleep for a couple of weeks.

With less than two months of the summer remaining, we
thought he would abandon his Texas plans, but we were mistaken. The minute Mark began to feel normal again, he hopped
a plane and went right back to Houston. He quickly landed a
job. Mark enjoyed observing life from a variety of windows.
He found his brief "window on life" as a member of a construction crew enlightening and interesting. Only after he was
safely home at the end of the summer did he tell us about
walking I-beams four stories above a concrete floor.

Mark received his bachelor's degree in business from
Graceland in the spring of 1977. We assumed that he would
return to live at home while he settled into the work force.
Again we were mistaken. After brief trips to Canada and
Florida, he moved into an apartment in Independence, Missouri, with three of his college buddies. Over the rest of that
summer, while contemplating his next move, he supported him-

**Wedding party of Pamela Jean Brewster and Richard George Mark
December 27, 1977**

self by doing some house painting and redecorating with a friend. Then in September he took a position in the Neighborhood Councils organization in Independence. His roommates moved on with their lives, and Mark rented an apartment alone.

By the fall of 1979, Mark was considering a new job with CDA, an agency that managed properties belonging to our church. For a couple of months while he thought about that, he went to help with the harvest on an Iowa farm that belonged to the family of one of his school friends. Part of his work there involved time in the farrowing barn. His "windows on life" were increasing. He returned to Independence and worked for CDA for the next several years.

The Kansas City School District hired Pam after she earned her master's degree and interned for a year as a learning disabilities specialist. Richard finished his undergraduate work at Columbia and enrolled in the Dental School at the University of Missouri in Kansas City. They were married December 27, 1977, among a "grove" of six Scotch pine Christmas trees and groupings of Christmas candles in our home church in Prairie Village. For their reception, the nutrition-conscious Pam chose to replace the traditional heavily frosted white wedding cake with a pyramid of spiced whole-wheat applesauce bundt cakes — surprisingly delicious!

Pam and Richard moved into a small apartment in Independence while she continued to teach, and he worked toward his doctorate in dentistry. The following year Pam obtained a teaching position in the Independence School District.

A confusion of names began for us when Pam married Richard, making her surname exactly the same as her brother's given name. If we could have looked down the years when our son was born we might have named him differently. As it is, when someone speaks of Mark, we need clarification as to who is being referenced.

Social activities in Independence among young single folks included student nurses in the Graceland Nursing Program. One of those student nurses was Tacey Hampton, a native of California. Once Tacey graduated, she worked as an intensive care nurse in the neo-natal department of Children's Mercy Hospital in Kansas City. Mark courted Tacey as she completed her degree and began her career.

They were married July 26, 1980, in our Prairie Village church. Tacey is the eldest of seven sisters, all of whom were included in the wedding party along with four of Tacey's friends. Mark's friends, who were to escort Tacey's attendants, arrived at the church for the ceremony ahead of Mark. Each of the escorts wore the wildest necktie he could find to greet Mark at the door of the church. Once they had enjoyed their joke, they switched to conservative identical ties, and the happy occasion went as planned. Mark and Tacey drove off in their convertible "Brewmobile," and then flew to Cancun to honeymoon. They took up residence in a small house on Kansas Street in Independence.

Tacey Jane Hampton and Mark William Brewster were married July 26, 1980.

EMPTY NEST 33

WITH BOTH OF OUR children married and establishing homes of their own, our thoughts turned to travel, to retirement and to the needs of our aging mothers. Back in 1958, Mother Brewster, Effie Lanore, sold her home at 1314 East Twenty-ninth Street and bought the one at 7701 Main Street in Kansas City with her cousin, Glayd Timanus. That house served them well for 20 years. They nursed Glayd's mother, Addie Randal whom Effie always called "Aunt," until her death. Then George Saunders, Glayd's bachelor brother, came from Denver to live with them. Glayd's final illness lasted several months. She died in about 1979. Glayd's daughter, Barbara, came from Washington state for her mother's funeral. Because her Uncle George was in ill health, Barbara placed him in an assisted-living apartment. He slowly declined and died about a year later.

When Glayd passed away, Effie was 95 years old and had late onset diabetes. She was losing her eyesight and could not manage their house alone, so she came to live with us. It was Bill's responsibility to dispose of most of her belongings and arrange the sale of the house that Effie and Glayd had owned jointly. When we took Effie to the eye doctor to document her blindness, he said, "I think these cataracts can come off now." We were astounded! We had assumed her blindness was due to her diabetes. Effie said, "Oh, doctor, do you think I should have that surgery at my age?" He replied, "Well, if you were *my* mother you should." The cataract removal restored Mom's eyesight and allowed her many enjoyable hours of reading during the remaining two years of her life.

Effie had another health problem that soon became very

serious. A wound on her foot would not heal, and her toes began to turn black. Surgery provided an arterial bypass in her groin improving the circulation in that leg and allowing her foot to heal.

Effie needed more care than I could provide while teaching, so I retired after the 1979-80 school year. She stayed with us about six months before moving into a nursing home in Olathe. Always frugal, she chose that site because it was less expensive than those nearby, but it was out of the way for family visits. With her improving health, Effie became unhappy there. My mother, Blanche, had moved to a town house in In-

Effie Lanore James Brewster, pictured here in 1974. Born January 20, 1884; died March 9, 1981.

dependence, and she invited Effie to come live with her. That amicable arrangement lasted several months until Effie's heart problems required more care than Blanche could provide. Then Bill moved his mother into Resthaven, our church's rest home in Independence.

Effie's breathing difficulties increased. We were called to her bedside on March 7, and we spent most of the weekend with her while she received oxygen to ease her breathing. On Monday morning, March 9, 1981, Mark went to his grandmother's bedside. She seemed to know he was there though she was unable to speak. She passed away peacefully as he sat holding her hand. She was 97 years old.

Bill was experiencing burnout on his job. The insurance industry was undergoing changes. Competition and price wars made for uncertainties in providing for and maintaining clients. The old traditions of reciprocal loyalty between insurance companies and their clients were eroding. A proliferation of lawsuits and abuses of insurance were taking a toll. To maintain profitability, companies were becoming very selective as to the risks they would agree to insure. Bill sometimes felt his own integrity was compromised when the companies he represented reversed a commitment he had made to a client or when he was unable to place insurance for customers he had served for many years.

Counting the eight years Bill worked for the Aetna, he had been in the insurance business 35 years. After his sixty-second birthday, he decided to retire, but he was very concerned about what to do with his time in retirement. Our church solved that problem by asking him to go to financial planner's school to qualify to do financial counseling for members seeking it. He was also asked to work with needy people who came to the church for assistance. So, at the end of March, 1983, he retired and took a new lease on life.

I had returned to teaching at the Barstow School for the 1982-83 school year, again in the third grade. I joined Bill in retirement after the 1983-84 school year. Even before I retired, I was thinking of all the things I still wanted to learn. As always, Bill encouraged me. He arranged for me to audit his first financial planner's course, which was an overview of the more detailed courses to come. We enjoyed going to school together.

More flights of educational fancy were in store for me. I joined adult education upholstering classes and reupholstered several of our worn chairs and a sofa. I enrolled in computer courses at the local community college, and by 1986, I was brave enough to invest in a computer of my own. It bothered me that I did not understand our income tax returns, so I attended an H & R Block tax course. Upon completion of that course I was offered a job during tax season — January 1 to April 15. I accepted their offer, and I continued to work for them during tax seasons for the next fourteen years. Of course, I needed to attend tax school every fall. That was fine with me.

Bill found a nice niche in his work for the Church. He enjoyed the camaraderie in the Kansas City Stake office and being able to help folks in need. He loved talking to those who came for advice and help with their financial planning. He was free to take time off for activities like golfing and long weekend camping trips for canoeing and fishing.

Though I am not a camping or fishing enthusiast, I joined Bill on some of those trips. After I learned some campers' strategies for keeping warm — like pulling one's clothes into the sleeping bag to warm them before getting up and dressing on a cold morning — I found I could tolerate it fairly well. I relished the companionship of my husband, and I found the Ozark scenery especially soothing, pleasant, and sometimes even awe-inspiring when viewed from a canoe leisurely floating down a clear-water stream.

We traveled to the Pacific Northwest several times for Bill's fishing expeditions with Bob Mason, a friend who lived there. While the men were away, I stayed in Seattle being entertained by Bob's wife Joan, or I went to Fox Island across Puget Sound from Tacoma to visit my Uncle Everett and Aunt Clara in their summer home. After Bill returned to Seattle, the two of us took trips on our own. Once we took a bus tour across southwestern Canada from Vancouver to Calgary. In 1986, we attended Expo '86 in Vancouver. We also took a sentimental journey southward to revisit Portland, Oregon, and the scenes of the early years of our marriage.

Our children put off starting their families for a time. Pam and Richard waited for Richard to finish dental school and start his dental practice. Mark and Tacey waited to take a sabbatical from their jobs for an extended trip before starting their family. We began to think we would never have grandchildren. We, of course, had no idea that the future held a veritable wealth of grandchildren for us. Pam and Richard began their family in 1982 with the birth of James. Then, over the next thirteen years, Christopher, Jeffrey, Sean and Lesley joined them. Haley arrived to start Mark and Tacey's family in 1984. Then came Kelsey, Brinks, Molly, Trevor, Adam, Abby, and Travis (who died at birth).

During Bill's semi-retirement, we discovered the fun of Elderhostels. In 1985, we flew to Boston and rented a car to drive up the coast to the University of New England at Biddeford, Maine. The three classes offered were: (1) Natural History of the Coast of Maine, (2) Let's Go to the Opera, and (3) The French Experience in North America. We chose that Elderhostel because of its location and class numbers 1 and 3 above. I thought Bill might not enjoy class number 2, but I was mistaken. The teacher was animated and made his class so interesting that neither of us would have missed a single session.

After that first experience, we were hooked on Elderhostels. In 1987, we traveled to Americus, Georgia, for the Elderhostel at Georgia Southwestern College — Jimmy Carter territory. We met interesting fellow hostelers including a woman who had done stunt flying and had flown to provide target practice for anti-aircraft trainees in World War II. On a field trip to the site of the Andersonville Civil War Prison, we found the name of my great-great grandfather, William Ray Toney, in the listing of prisoners' names in the card catalog at the visitors' center.

Succeeding Elderhostels we attended were as follows:

1988 — Lake Superior State University at Sault St. Marie, Michigan, which we attended with Howard and Frances Vaughan.

1991 — University of South Alabama at Gulf Shores, Alabama, as part of our fortieth wedding anniversary celebration.

1992 — Camp LaForet, Colorado Springs, Colorado.

1993 — Bonclarken Conference Center, Hendersonville, North Carolina.

1994 — Big Mountain Ski and Summer Resort at Whitefish, Montana, sponsored by Flathead Valley Community College and featuring day-hikes in Glacier National Park.

1996 — Hawaii's Lyman Museum and Mission House with one week in Hilo and a second week in Kailua-Kona.

In about 1985, Mother Norris (Blanche) moved to Raytown, Missouri, with my sister Janice and her family. Mother was no longer driving her car, and her health was declining. I needed to be on call to help Mom when she required assistance while Jan was at work. Raytown and Independence are suburbs on the eastern side of Kansas City. Our residence in a western suburb necessitated frequent trips

Bill and Lois Brewster, 1987

across Kansas City to meet Mother's needs and to visit our children and grandchildren in Independence. In 1989, we decided to move to Independence to shorten our travel time.

In preparation for that move, Bill resigned his position in the church office, but he still felt the need for some sort of work to fill his time. Our son Mark had worked several years in real estate in Independence and had recently changed to marketing for a utility company. Mark's involvement in real estate inspired his dad to try his hand in that industry. Bill and I enrolled together in real estate school. I had no ambition to sell real estate, but I welcomed the opportunity to be Bill's study-buddy and to learn about the real estate market. After passing the necessary tests, Bill began work in the same office Mark had vacated in Independence.

Bill located a house for us at 17912 East Twenty-fifth Street Court in Independence. It was smaller than the home we were vacating, and it needed some alteration to accommodate our furnishings. We had lived in the same house in Prairie Village for twenty-one years, so there was a lot of sorting and disposing to be done. We were quite comfortable in our new surroundings once the carpentry and redecoration were finished. Though there were many things we missed about our former home and neighborhood, we found it good to be close to Mother and our children. Bill's work helped acquaint him with the nooks and crannies of Independence. My seasonal work transferred easily to an H and R Block office in Independence. Our work and our affiliation with the nearby congregation of our church provided us a new circle of friends.

END AND BEGINNING 34

WE WERE STARTLED AND concerned in 1991 when a cancerous polyp was discovered in Bill's colon. Surgery to remove an eight-inch section of the colon left doctors optimistic that they had also removed the cancer threat. In 1993, Bill underwent radiation treatments for prostate cancer after which tests indicated that threat was at least minimized, but Bill decided it was finally time to retire completely. Though he was not enjoying his usual robust health, he was able to spend more time golfing and camping and life was still good. We limited some of our travel because Mom Norris was so frail we expected to lose her at any time.

Then in the summer of 1995, tests revealed that the cancer in Bill's colon had not been eradicated. It had metastasized. Beginning in September, he received chemotherapy treatments. Successive tests indicated progress in keeping the cancer at bay until early in 1996 when the readings changed direction. Bill was faced with a decision to have a chemo port surgically inserted to deliver a constant dosage of chemotherapy or to stop treatment completely and let the disease take its course. We were told the difference between the two approaches could be a little extra time with the chemo, but Bill's quality of life would probably be less than if the chemotherapy were simply stopped. Bill was advised to take a month or two to decide which course he preferred.

We decided to attend an Elderhostel in Hawaii in March while Bill thought through his options. Despite the pending weighty decision, we were able to enjoy the trip, which was spent mostly on the "Big Island." Classes on the history and the flora and fauna of Hawaii held our interest. Field trips took us to historic sites and scenes of natural beauty. We visited the caldera atop the Kilauea volcano, and we walked through the huge Thurston Lava Tube. During the second week, we were equipped with snorkeling gear and were taken to a sheltered inlet. Once we were all in the water, our guide threw out some fish food. A multitude of small fishes of many colors and descriptions immediately gathered within our view. Bill said he counted fifteen varieties before he lost track of which ones he had already counted. There were only two brief occasions during those two weeks in which Bill simply needed to rest rather than to participate.

When we returned to the oncologist, Bill shared his decision not to have a chemo port inserted but to let nature take its course. Many interested friends and family members suggested natural remedies, several of which we pursued. We were not able to detect benefit from those. As his condition slowly worsened, Bill did everything he could to prepare the way for me in widowhood.

By July, he was spending most of his time in bed. He was very patient and cooperative, making it possible for me to care for him at home during the rest of his illness. Finally, the Kansas City Hospice nurses came to provide help with equipment and medications. A hospital-type bed was installed for Bill in our bedroom next to our bed. The Hospice nurse taught me ways to move him and to change the sheets on his bed while he remained in it. After we learned that morphine caused Bill to hallucinate, he was given alternative medications that seemed to control pain, but none of the many remedies we tried were effective in relieving his nausea. Bill stopped eating about the first of October.

When I retired on the night of November 14, Bill seemed comatose, and he remained unresponsive in the morning. He had not been able to tolerate being shaved for two or three days, but he offered no resistance to my shaving him that morning. After I bathed him and dressed him in clean pajamas, I went to the kitchen to call our children to report on our night. When I returned to the bedroom a few minutes later,

Bill had stopped breathing. I immediately went back to the telephone to call the Hospice nurse and our children. The nurse arrived first and confirmed that Bill was gone.

Both families of our children soon arrived, and we sat in the living room to talk together and to try to help our little ones understand what had happened. Mark used the illustration of what happens to a glove when the hand is removed from it. He reminded the children that as long as a hand is in a glove, it can move and do all sorts of things, but when the hand is removed the glove is just a shell that cannot do anything. He said the part of Papa that enabled him to move and hug and talk had gone. What was left was just a shell like a glove without a hand in it.

I told them that Papa's body was still in his bed, and I would go with anyone who wanted to see him but no one needed to go if he or she didn't want to. When I asked if anyone wanted to go to see Papa, nine-year-old Kelsey raised her hand. As I took Kelsey by the hand and started down the hall, all the others followed. We stood around the bed, and I bent over Bill and kissed him. I did that for two reasons: 1) I wanted to do so, and 2) I wanted the children to feel that there was nothing scary about their grandfather's death.

Once we had looked and talked quietly at Bill's bedside, we returned to the living room to share happy memories of him. Richard left to get James who was already at school when I reported Bill's passing. James arrived to spend a little time at his grandfather's bedside before the undertakers came to remove the body.

The support I received on every side during the whirl of activity over the next few days was such a blessing. While Mark and Richard had to return to their work, Pam and Tacey stayed to help. Tacey telephoned a long list of family and friends while Pam and I went to the funeral home to make the final arrangements. When we considered what clothes to send for Bill for the visitation at the funeral home, Pam and Mark protested against the idea of choosing a business suit. They believed their Dad would have preferred a golf shirt and sweater, so that is what we arranged. Mark and Richard hauled Bill's solo canoe to the vestibule of the funeral home for the visitation, and they surrounded it with Bill's camping and fishing equipment. We also made a display of awards Bill had received for his work in the Boy Scouts and in the church.

Because the church in Prairie Village was our home congregation for so many years, we had the memorial service there. I chose a collage of pictures of Bill and of our family. My niece, Sona, formatted them in a folder and had copies reproduced for those who came to the service. We included an insert with Bill's obituary on one side and, on the other, a series entitled "Letters to Bill." Over the years, Pam's and Mark's Christmas and birthday gifts for Bill and me often included brief personal notes that we treasured and saved. Two of those treasures were the first "Letters to Bill," as follows:

> *Teacher, provider, fishing buddy, traveling partner, camping buddy, scouting backer, canoeing buddy, discipliner, golf partner, helper, advisor. You have been all these things to me, Dad. Thank-you for your unconditional acceptance that allowed me to be me. With love, respect, and a debt of gratitude. Your son Mark*

> *Dear Dad, Thank-you for all the things you taught me. Whenever I run across someone who doesn't know how to do something, I'll remember you and wonder why their dad didn't teach them. Thanks for questioning every boy I went out with — especially the one with the Corvette — remember? Thanks for the big hugs. I Love You! Pam*

Then I added a note from me and one on behalf of our grandchildren:

> *Dear Bill, How does one, who has been paired so long in such a happy team, go on alone? I'll treasure all the precious memories in my heart and I'll join you one day. I love you! Lois*

*Thanks for playing with us, delivering groceries with us,
letting us help you get out mailings for your club, and taking
us out to lunches and treats. We love you, Papa*

After the memorial service the church ladies provided a reception for us. Among those who stayed to greet us were two Laotian couples who waited quietly for an opportunity to speak to me. They had tears in their eyes as they recited to me the many ways Bill had spent his energy and opened his heart and his wallet to help them.

All three of my sisters came in shifts to be with me. Jan, my youngest sister, stayed with me the first night I was alone. Lorraine, my older sister, stayed the next night and returned to Tulsa after the memorial service. Donna, who is nearest my age, and her husband Ed arrived from North Carolina in time for the memorial service and they spent a week with me. Two or three days after the memorial service our children and grandchildren and my two younger sisters and their husbands went with me to the cemetery to deliver Bill's ashes to their final resting place in the memorial wall at the Mound Grove Cemetery in Independence.

My first feeling at Bill's death was that of relief that he was no longer suffering. Then adrenaline took over as I worked through all of the events immediately following his death. It was almost a week later when all the urgent requirements had been met that I relaxed and ran into what seemed a wall of grief. I began to think of all that I had lost and the loneliness seemed more than I could summon the courage to face. Fortunately, Donna and Ed were still with me and they seemed to understand that I needed to retreat to my bedroom and weep. The sadness and the loneliness were not dissolved by that one night of weeping, but it seemed to relieve tensions and I was able to go on.

One of the sympathy cards I received carried a message that best expresses my journey over the years since I lost Bill:

Grief, like the ocean comes in waves only to recede and

come yet again. But with it comes healing. Memories wash ashore and are bathed by the Golden Sun. Grab hold of those memories and let them fill the emptiness.

William DeForest (Bill) Brewster — Born February 19, 1921; died November 15, 1996.

A month or so after Bill died, I was organizing and putting away a group of cassette tapes. I had to look twice at one of the tapes to decipher the scribbled label that read, "In the event of my death. B. Brewster." I was not aware of that tape prior to that time. I took it to the tape player. The header on the tape was so long that I began to think Bill had tried to record something and failed, but the message finally began. Bill's voice noted the date, August 3, 1995, which was about the time he learned that his colon cancer had metastasized. He said it was early morning, he couldn't sleep, and he wanted to leave some thoughts for his loved ones. He continued by addressing each of us individually, beginning with me, our son, our daughter, our son-in-law and our daughter-in-law, before leaving a message to each of our grandchildren, including Lesley who was then only fourteen months old. (This was before we had Adam and Abby.)

He told of the faith that had sustained him since the spiritual awakening he experienced in Portland, Oregon, just before our marriage. He expressed his love for each of us, his pride both in our accomplishments and in the kind of persons we had become and were becoming. He admonished our grandchildren to pursue education and to seek those occupations

Lois with her support group of children and grandchildren, 2001

that would make the world a better place. He encouraged them to be kind and to cultivate a variety of interests and friendships. He suggested that they become involved in their home communities and in organizations that help the poor and needy. He reminded them to pray about the directions their lives should take. He counseled them against fanaticism but encouraged them to develop a quiet, sustaining spiritual relationship with their Creator.

It is our belief and our firm hope that, even as Bill's life here has ended, his soul, his essence, has begun life anew in another realm. With Bill's death and the ending of our companionship here, I, too, have begun a new journey, one that has required me to seek answers to the question, "Who am I now that so large a part of me is gone?" Though it is often a lonely path, it is not always sad. I am finding new interests, new paths of service, personal strengths of which I was unaware and lots of loving support from family and friends.

The title of this book, *Brewster Gold*, was chosen for both literal and figurative reasons. The literal one has to do with the gold that Charles Brewster brought west in the false bottom of a horse-drawn wagon and with the pursuit of gold that occupied most of the adult life of Will Brewster. The figurative reason involves my opinion that the most golden of Will Brewster's discoveries was his son, Bill.